I
Hear a
Symphony

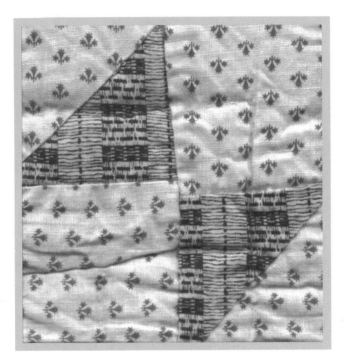

anchor books

D O U B L E D A Y

N E W   Y O R K   L O N D O N   T O R O N T O   S Y D N E Y   A U C K L A N D

I Hear a Symphony

AFRICAN AMERICANS

CELEBRATE LOVE

edited by

PAULA L. WOODS AND FELIX H. LIDDELL

An Anchor Book
PUBLISHED BY DOUBLEDAY
a division of Bantam Doubleday Dell Publishing Group, Inc.
1540 Broadway, New York, New York 10036

ANCHOR BOOKS, DOUBLEDAY, and the portrayal of an anchor
are trademarks of Doubleday,
a division of Bantam Doubleday Dell Publishing Group, Inc.

Book design by Terry Karydes

Pages 326–34 constitute a continuation of this copyright page.

Library of Congress Cataloging-in-Publication Data
I hear a symphony : African Americans celebrate love / [compiled] by
Paula L. Woods and Felix H. Liddell. — 1st Anchor Books ed.
p.   cm.
1. American literature—Afro-American authors.   2. Afro-Americans—
Literary collections.   3. Love—Literary collections.   I. Woods,
Paula L.   II. Liddell, Felix H.
PS508.N314   1994
810.8′0354—dc20
94-6742
CIP

ISBN 0-385-47502-0
Copyright © 1994 by Paula L. Woods and Felix H. Liddell

1   3   5   7   9   10   8   6   4   2

For our mothers,
Addie and Florence,
who carried the melody . . .
For Irene,
who helped sort out the words and emotions . . .
For Maureen,
who inspired . . .
For Faith,
who believed . . .

ACKNOWLEDGMENTS

From the minute we began to collect material for *I Hear a Symphony*, friends, colleagues, acquaintances, even total strangers began to send us their favorite stories, letters, years-old scraps of paper carried in wallets, all expressing loving sentiments by African Americans. We believe this spirit of sharing and expressing of loving emotion have enriched not only this book but our lives as well. We cherish and thank you all for helping to make this book become a reality.

Special thanks go to Esme Bhan of Moorland–Spingarn Research Center for clueing us in early to another "forgotten history" and cheering us on; to Diana Lachtanere, Mary Yearwood, and Andre Elizée at the Schomburg Center for Research in Black Culture for tremendous support and encouragement in researching materials in the Manuscript Division; to Andrew Simon for opening wide the doors of Amistad Research Center; and to Ann Allen Shockley of Fisk University for her graciousness and expertise.

To artists, art historians, private collectors, gallery owners, and museum officials—Rae Alexander-Minter, Kimberly Cody, Courtney DeAngelis, Judge Norma Y. Dotson, David Driskell, Laurel Duplessis, Dr. Walter O. Evans, Suzanne Jackson, Eileen Johnston, Alitash Kebede, June Kelly, Jerald Melberg, Jennifer Persti, Stephanie Pogue, Lieschen Potuznik, Betye Saar, Sherry Washington, and Deborah Willis—we deeply appreciate your input, insight, and generosity.

Thanks also to Mary Bart for her researching skills and tenacity; to Ivan Cury and Sylvia Whitlock for reaching back into memory to provide worthy contributions to the manuscript; and to Sophronia Ann Collins for a piece of detective work beyond measure in finding the heirs to the Loney Butler correspondence.

To Blanche Richardson of Marcus Books in Oakland; James Fugate and Tom Hamilton of Eso Won Books in Inglewood, California; Desirée Sanders of Afrocentric Books in Chicago; and Clara Villarosa of Hue-Man Experience in Denver—thank you for confirming how much this book is needed in our communities and for your steady support and enthusiasm.

To Tina, Marita, Jill, Saundra, Terry, and Nikky—thank you for your talent, generosity, and friendship. And to our brothers, Essex, Peter, and Lenard, who gave so freely of their time and attention—we are grateful.

To Faith Childs, who has had plenty of it, thanks for believing in us and for being an agent extraordinaire and trusted advisor. And, finally, thanks to Martha Levin and Delia Kurland of Anchor/Doubleday for your belief in our vision, respect for the work, and willingness to work with us through personal tragedy, illness, and acts of God. We're so glad to find a home in that rock!

CONTENTS

I. *Black Must Be Beautiful Again*

II. *Families of the Heart*

III. *A Jewel for a Friend*

IV. *For Better, For Worse*

V. *See the Heart*

VI.   *A Home in That Rock*

VII.   *I Leave You Love*

PART I

Black Must
Be Beautiful
Again

e talk about it, cry about it, write songs about it, "mph, mph, mph" about it in church or at the hairdresser's, but what do we *do* about the love in our lives? How do we begin to understand, to grasp and hold on to the love we feel for ourselves, our families and friends, our communities?

Love does not spring up, fully formed, out of a vacuum. It does not exist in isolation. We cannot love other human beings without first loving and accepting ourselves. And until we remember, cherish, and celebrate the miracles we truly are in this universe, in our Blackness and our position as children of God, no other love is possible.

So says Bebe Moore Campbell as she reminds us of the beauty we must tap in our own Black selves, the truths we must tell to regain the meaning behind the rhetoric of self-love and well-being. So say James A. Emanuel and Mari Evans, important voices who tell truths as relevant today as they were over twenty years ago. So say Howard Thurman and Brenda Tapia, who remind us of the spiritual foundations of love and our connection to Spirit so essential to our ability to love and achieve in life. And so say Haki Madhubuti, W. E. B. Du Bois, Naomi Long Madgett, and Ruth Forman, who remind us of the majesty we bring to the table of loving as African-American men and women.

One of the fallacies in our quest for the knowledge of who and whose we are is to believe that another person, place, or thing can substitute for the work we must do with ourselves, the inner realization of our role in the world. Both Terry McMillan and Langston Hughes give us stirring examples of how we make, and can unmake, that mistake.

And, finally, when we look into the cosmos, through Charles Chesnutt's words, we see the dark and shining light of our being. In this first movement toward a renewal of African-American love let us recognize, celebrate, and protect the wonder and glory that shine within our eyes at all costs. The price for not doing so is way too high.

BLACK MUST BE BEAUTIFUL AGAIN
Bebe Moore Campbell

Elijah Pierce, *Burying the Hatchet*, 1973. Painted wood, glitter, 11⅜ × 18 × 1¼ in.
National Museum of American Art, Smithsonian Institution,
Washington, D.C. Gift of David L. Davies.

What shook Los Angeles on April 29 was not the earthquake I was expecting. I'm an East Coast woman, Philly born and bred. I was raised in a town where the ground, at least, stayed put, and in the eight years that I've spent in my adopted West Coast home, my constant fear has been that the place would be shaken apart by 10 seconds of cataclysmic natural forces while I screamed from inside a stalled elevator. And so I stocked up on bottled water and canned goods and memorized emergency measures: stay calm; check for injuries; clean up dangerous spills—all the while praying that the much-feared disaster would leave L.A. in peace for another millennium.

But that city's peace has been irrevocably shattered. In the aftermath of the Rodney King brutality verdict, the trembler that ripped L.A. into screaming fragments was measured, not by a Richter scale, but in blood and flames; the upheaval came, not from the bowels of the earth but from the depths of human anguish and rage. The pain rumbled through hearts as well as the streets.

The Los Angeles rebellion of 1992 is still for now, but the tally of human and material annihilation has broken all previous records for American civil unrest: 51 dead; 2,383 injured; more than 600 fires; nearly 15,000 arrests; and at least $785 million in property damage. Watts, Newark, and Detroit pale in comparison. The largest urban disturbance in United States history left a landscape strewn with rubble, devastation, and trampled dreams. Days, even weeks after the urban unrest that turned neighborhood blocks into smoky ashes, the news shows are still replaying their tapes, as if there is some lesson for us all hidden in the images of ruin. There is a cacophony of cries to rebuild Los Angeles, and surely that must be done. There are neighborhoods with no grocery stores, where women now must board city buses to buy bread, eggs, and milk for their families; 4,000 people mourn their lost jobs, and many uninsured merchants are bankrupt, with little hope of ever resurrecting their razed shops without financial intervention. Certainly, there are pressing economic woes that must be addressed.

But if burned and looted businesses demand presidential and national attention, the reconstruction that African Americans must immediately concern ourselves with and ultimately give our full regard to isn't one that will be composed of bricks and mortar, but of hearts and souls. For African Americans, there is an essential truth hidden amidst the ruins: we must love ourselves back to emotional health first, and then economic well-being.

As I look at communities that have been scorched by the wrath of an enraged and oppressed people, I am reminded of earthquake emergency measures: there is a dangerous spill seeping across the land; most of us are injured, and calm can no longer be guaranteed. And yet, we are looking for a way to make sense of the devastation, and none of us wants to be

visited again by either angry hordes bent on destruction or trucks full of
armed federal troops. We are seeking hope. But many of us are looking in
the wrong direction.

Hope for African Americans is not in government loans or enterprise
zones. We cannot put our faith in Peter Ueberroth or President Bush or the
Supreme Courts, nor can we hold our breath waiting for justice. Ultimately,
we cannot afford to look for either vindication or validation that comes from
outside us. We must rebuild our communities, but first we must rebuild our
minds. In 1992, as the embers of Los Angeles still smolder, the challenge
that African Americans face is the same one we have always faced, only now
there is an urgency that we can no longer ignore—we must finally negotiate
and translate our slave heritage and the single, cruelest legacy of that 246-
year odyssey: the unconscious belief in our inferiority, a mindset that leads
to a lack of self-love. We must seek absolute healing not because we are sick,
but because we have been wounded by centuries of oppression and denigra-
tion, because we are bleeding internally and the injuries we have sustained
sap our strength and rob us of our greatness. And yet, the balm that we need
isn't mysterious or rare; indeed, it's one we've used before.

Black must become beautiful again, and this time we must mean it.

The slogan has an eerie, nostalgic ring and evokes the ghost of platform
shoes, mile-high 'fros, bright-colored dashikis, raised fists, and As Salaam
Alaikum. I say those words, and I am young again, swaying to the strains of
Marvin Gaye. For those of us who lived through that time, the era is memo-
rable not because of its style, but because of the sweet promises it rendered.
Arguably, no period has ever been as empowering, as self-affirming for
African Americans. The '60s was when, collectively, we began to move
toward loving ourselves. We began to embrace our hair, our color, our
features, and doing so made us stronger. The trouble is, that brief shining
moment of self-love didn't last long enough. Didn't go deep enough. The
'60s gave us the prescription for healing, but we failed to take the strong
medicine necessary for the cure.

We had things to do other than attend to the pain deep inside of us. We were marching, sitting in, lying in, trying to integrate. And the fact that we succeeded in sitting next to white people, in going to their schools, eating at their restaurants, and working next to them convinced some of us that we were as good as they were. That being with white people was all the healing that was needed. We didn't have to attend to the feelings inside of us, the ones that quietly and persistently said that no, we weren't good at all. We said Black is beautiful, but we didn't believe it.

The fires of 1992 call for a new movement, a revolution of the spirit. The demonstrations we hold now must be personal and emotional. The marches we attend must be in our minds. We must campaign for self-love and healing as though our very lives are at stake. They are.

African Americans should address the challenge of loving ourselves with the courage of Rosa, Martin, Malcolm, and Fannie Lou, rolling up our sleeves to do the hard emotional work within our families, with our neighbors and friends, in our churches and while we're waiting in barbershops and at the beauty parlor. This is the time to challenge the taboos and start talking out our ancient pain. We have to tell each other our stories, the ones that make us scream: the stories about being the darkest or the lightest in the family; the tales about being passed over for promotions; the ones about growing up on welfare and still feeling ashamed because some in our family remain financially dependent on the government. The stories about hating the width of our noses, the darkness of our eyes, the kink of our hair. About being scared of white folks. Still. Of feeling *less than.* Even now. Let's talk about the pain that imprisons us, and then let's read the books, say the affirmations and prayers, do the mental exercises, form the support groups, and yes, communicate with the therapists who will help us break out of our emotional jails. We can learn to love and value ourselves. The '90s is a good time to take up the journey where we left off. We are immersed in a decade where self-awareness and self-help have become the mantras of the masses, where 12-step programs have freed people of addictions. African Americans can benefit from the new knowledge, and we can mine our own psychological experts for specific techniques to address our emotional distress. By any means necessary. We must do whatever must be done to heal ourselves. Black must become beautiful again, and this time we must mean it.

Self-love and prosperity are inextricably linked. When we love ourselves, we'll buy what we can afford instead of what we think we need to affirm us, and we'll save the difference for a business in our own neighborhood. When we love ourselves fully, recycling Black dollars won't be an option; it will be an obsession. Loving ourselves means we won't go to Beverly Hills or Fifth Avenue to shop until we have exhausted all the Black-owned possibilities in our own communities. At last we will recognize that the white man's ice isn't colder, just more expensive.

Self-love and motivated children are inextricably linked. When we love ourselves, we can find the time to help those who look like us, whether this means adopting a class as a group, becoming a big sister or brother, tutoring, or encouraging Black children whenever we can. When we love ourselves, we get involved with Black children who are at risk, not because it's our duty, but because they are our children, and not helping them is not only unimaginable, it is obscene.

Racism will never disappear. America will never be fair to all of its people. African Americans can learn to respond to racial discrimination in a self-affirming and not a self-defeating way. The healing of Los Angeles begins with each one of us. And no, this revolution isn't going to be televised; it's going to be internalized. When we finally stop asking America to love us and begin to love ourselves, we will prosper as a people. Our giant step forward will cause the ground beneath our feet to tremble as no earthquake ever has; we will believe in our dreams, and that alone will make them come true.

Up, ye mighty race, you can accomplish what you will. Say it loud: I'm Black, and I'm proud. Salaam Alaikum, sisters and brothers. Black must be beautiful again. And this time we must mean it.

NEGRITUDE

James A. Emanuel

Black is the first nail I ever stepped on;
Black the hand that dried my tears.
Black is the first old man I ever noticed;
Black the burden of his years.

Black is waiting in the darkness;
Black the ground where hoods have lain.
Black is the sorrow-misted story;
Black the brotherhood of pain.

Black is a quiet iron door;
Black the path that leads behind.
Black is a detour through the years;
Black the diary of the mind.

Black is Gabriel Prosser's knuckles;
Black Sojourner's naked breast.
Black is a schoolgirl's breathless mother;
Black her child who led the rest.

Black is the purring of a motor;
Black the foot when the light turns green.
Black is last year's dusty paper;
Black the headlines yet unseen.

Black is a burden bravely chanted;
Black cross of sweat for a nation's rise.
Black is a boy who knows his heroes;
Black the way a hero dies.

Henry Bozeman Jones, *Dance—Sixth Day of Creation*,
n.d. Lithograph, 9⅝ × 7½ in. The Howard University
Gallery of Art, Permanent Collection, Washington, D.C.

FROM DREAMING OURSELVES DARK AND DEEP

BLACK BEAUTY

bell hooks

Where there is a woman there is a magic. If there is a moon falling from her mouth, she is a woman who knows her magic, who can share or not share her powers. A woman with a moon falling from her mouth, roses between her legs and tiaras of Spanish moss, this woman is a consort of the spirits.

—Ntozake Shange
Sassafrass, Cypress and Indigo

In a space before time and words, the world was covered in a thick blanket of darkness. It was a warm and loving covering. Since it was hard for the spirits who inhabited this space to see one another they learned to live by and through touch. So if you were running around lost you knew you were found when arms reached out in that loving darkness to hold you. And those arms that held the spirits in that beautiful dark space before time are holding us still.

This is a little origin story I made up. I thought of it one day when I was trying to explain to a little brown girl where the babies lived before they were born—so I told her they lived in this world of loving darkness. I made up this story because I wanted this little brown girl to grow up dreaming the dark and its powerful blackness as a magic space she need never fear or dread. I made it up because I thought one day this little brown girl will hear all sorts of bad things about the darkness, about the powerful blackness, and I wanted to give her another way to look at it. I held her hand, just like my father's father, Daddy Jerry, a man who worked the land, who knew the earth was his witness, had once held my hand in the darkest of summer nights and taught me that the blanket of night I was scared of was really longing to be my friend, to tell me all its secrets. And I reminded her, as he reminded me way back then, that those arms that first held us in that dark space before words and time hold us still.

*T*o love means to have an intrinsic interest in another person. It is not of necessity contingent upon any kind of group or family closeness. True, such closeness may provide a normal setting for the achievement of intrinsic interest, but the fact that two men are brothers having the same parents provides no mandatory love relationship between them. In his letter to the Philippians, the Apostle Paul writes, "My prayer to God is that your love may grow more and more rich in knowledge and in all manner of insight that you may have a sense of what is vital, that you may be transparent and of no harm to anyone, your life covered with that harvest of righteousness that Jesus Christ produces to the praise and glory of God." Men do not love in general, but they do love in particular. To love means dealing with persons in the concrete rather than in the abstract. In the presence of love, there are no types or stereotypes, no classes and no masses. . . .

One day a woman was brought to Jesus because she had been taken in adultery and her accusers wanted Jesus to pass judgment upon her. It was his claim that he was not opposed to the law and it was the insistence of the law, said her accusers, that a person caught in adultery should be stoned to death. Did Jesus agree with the law and thus condone the stoning of the woman or did he not? His reply to the question seemed at once to be an evasion. He said, "Let the man among you who is without sin cast the first stone." The implication being that after that any man may throw. Then he did a curious thing. He was such a gentleman that he did not look at the woman in the face and add his gaze to the stares of the hostile accusers. No, he looked on the ground. After a time, he lifted his face, looked the woman in the eyes and said, "Woman, where are your accusers? Does no man condemn you? Neither do I. Go into peace and don't do it anymore." He met her where she was, admittedly an adultress, but he dealt with her at that point of fact as if she were where, at her best, she saw herself as being. Thus he took her total fact into account and enlivened her at a point in herself that was beyond all her faults. A person's *fact* includes more than his plight, predicament, or need at a particular moment in time. It is something total which must include awareness of the person's potential. This, too, is a part of the person's fact. This is why love always sees more than is in evidence at any moment of viewing.

Who and Whose You Are:
An Interview with Brenda Tapia
Felix H. Liddell and Paula L. Woods

Brenda Tapia is the creator and director of the critically acclaimed Love of Learning Program at Davidson College outside of Charlotte, North Carolina. Love of Learning, which began in 1987, is an innovative program designed to increase the number of African American students who are well prepared for the academic rigors of selective colleges and universities. The program, which accepts thirty students per year, works with children from the ninth grade through high school on mastery of oral and written English, mathematics, science, test-taking, preparation for the Scholastic Achievement Test (SAT), and personal development. Tapia, an ordained minister, has been director of the program since its inception.

Q: The Love of Learning program is based on family. What do you try to instill in these young people about family?

A: Basically, I'm trying to help them understand that we live in community, that no man or woman is an island unto themselves. I think the Creator did something very interesting because He did not give everything to any one individual. We need each other. I don't think that it's possible for us to exist completely by ourselves. So what I'm trying to do with the kids in the Love of Learning program is to help them, first of all, know who they are, their relationship with God, so that they *can* be in community with one another because I realize that things are set up such that for any of us to succeed, regardless of race, color, creed, we've got to do it together. In fact, I thought that was what Spike Lee was saying in his film *Jungle Fever,* that either we work together or we die together. You could see it in that scene in the

Taj Mahal. One of the things that I noticed was the people who were in that crack house were white, black, old, young, rich, poor. They were a microcosm of the world and they were dying. Unless we, as a society and a people, including my Love of Learning children, learn how to live together, then we can assuredly know we're going to die together.

Q: You often discuss teaching children about not only who they are but *whose* they are. What does that mean?

A: When a child first comes to Love of Learning and I ask them who they are, I always hear, "Well, I am Brenda Howard Tapia." Okay, I'll say, that's a good place to start, but you are more than that. They'll look at me with these quizzical eyes and they'll say, "Well, what do you mean?" and I'll say, "What is the sum of your character? Who are you?" Questions like that help people turn within and begin to acknowledge themselves. It's very easy in this physical and material society to be totally out of touch with yourself. If you were to really talk to most doctors and psychologists, you would find that many of the illnesses that people have stem from the fact that people are totally ignoring themselves. They're caught up in other things. So in terms of helping a child to know who they are, I'm talking about taking time to listen to yourself, to spend time with yourself, to get out of the bathtub and admire every inch of your body and to be familiar with it. That's very important and it's not narcissistic; before you can be in love and enjoy someone else, you have to love you. And the first step is knowing who you are. Every aspect, inside and out, of who you are is important: what makes you happy; what makes you sad; what turns you on; what turns you off; what you're good at doing; what you need to work on; where are your shortcomings; what your strengths are. The next step, or what this exploration leads you to discover, is to know *whose* you are.

In the church we have heard for so long that we are created in the image and the likeness of God, but we never really stop and read that particular line of Scripture, to understand what it means. I mean, you're saying that you are made in the image and likeness of that Being who has created everything that we can see, touch, and feel. Well, what does that say about you? What does that say about your capabilities? That's what I mean when I say to my kids that I want them to know *whose* they are. I want them to understand the nature of God, and by understanding the nature of God and who God is, they begin to realize that there is nothing that they cannot do in partnership with God. It's a very powerful realization.

Q: What happens when your young people understand this fact?

A: When they finally understand it, I get telephone calls from principals and guidance counselors at their schools who say, "What did you do to this child?" And my first response: "Well, did they say something they shouldn't have said?" because I've found that a lot of kids start speaking up and saying what they believe, and although adults *say* they want to hear that they really don't want the truth. And when my kids start telling the truth, there's an air of confidence about them. One principal called and said, "You know, three Love of Learning students were walking down the hall with about fifty to one hundred other kids and they stood out! It was like their feet didn't touch the ground. Their heads were high, their shoulders were pulled back, and they were straight, and they were completely oblivious to the name-calling the other students were doing." Several Love of Learning students had come to his office the day before complaining about the math class they had been assigned. They had Prealgebra at Davidson College, the site of our program. The student made it clear they were *not* going to take Prealgebra. They knew they needed to be in Algebra I. They were not going back. "Miss Tapia says we keep going forward, and that's where we're going. So you need to put us into Algebra I class. And if you have a problem with that, then maybe you need to talk to our parents, and if that's not enough you need to talk to Miss Tapia at Davidson, but we're taking Algebra I." And the principal said,

"Now, Miss Tapia, you and I know they don't get credit for what they do at Davidson. But those boys were so convincing I'm going to put them in an Algebra I class." He did and they did well. So, it's an air, it's an attitude our students develop. Because if we really understand the message that Jesus brought to us, we would change. The kingdom He was talking about came as a result of not a physical change per se, but a change in attitude.

I guess you could say I teach my children in Love of Learning to look at the glass as half full as opposed to half empty. Because if you're thirsty, a glass half full of water means a lot more to you than one that's half empty. And the thirst that I'm talking about is a thirst for knowledge and life and the desire to be all that you can possibly be. So many of our young people, as well as older adults, are not even glimpsing their capabilities. And I feel that a part of our staff's job is to help people to wake up and to realize all that they can do, that the sky is the limit.

Q: We've talked about gangs and what gangs give children. What role do you think gangs play in our young people's lives?

A: Well, one of the first things that I see that gangs give a young person is an acknowledgment of their existence. Too many of our young people are walking around with parents who are so busy working to give them the material things they want that many times they do not give them what they need. We're not talking about the basics; I mean designer clothes and all of those things that we really don't need. But what parents don't acknowledge is the child's presence. A child will come home from school and say, "Hi, Mom," and Mom will mumble something. "Mom, guess what happened?" And Mom says, "Mmm-hmm," but she isn't listening. So the child says, "I stole a school book," and Mom says, "Uh-huh" and then the child really knows that Mom is not listening. But a gang acknowledges the person. Gangs listen to them and they talk to them. So one of the things that we do in Love of Learning is that we give kids positive attention. And that is a need that adolescents have.

Adolescents in some ways remind me of schizophrenics. In clinical psychology, when we were taught about dealing with schizophrenics, one of the things that you do is to give them boundaries. Because a schizophrenic doesn't have any boundaries you put your arms around them, if you can, so that they can feel their limits. That's what adolescents are searching for. Adolescence is probably one of the most difficult stages of development in our existence as human beings. As adolescents, we're no longer children yet we're not adults. Our bodies are going through all of these changes. Your chest starts expanding, your voice starts changing, all this is going on, and it's a very frightening time. So what we give in Love of Learning is the very same thing that kids derive from gangs. It's a sense of stability, it's an acknowledgment of who you are. It's also task-oriented— many of us have too much free time on our hands. I think that there was a reason when the Creator made us not to have given us microwaves and all of this instant stuff. Because when we are busy—old people used

Aaron Douglas, *The Creation*, 1935.
Oil on masonite, 48 × 36 in. The Howard University
Gallery of Art, Permanent Collection, Washington, D.C.
Photo: Jarvis Grant.

to talk about it in terms of "an idle mind is the devil's workshop"—we don't have time for trouble.

So, in the Love of Learning Program, we keep the students very busy. People wonder, "How do you get these kids to go to class from 7:45 A.M. until 8:30 P.M.?" You would be surprised; most young people want something to do. One of the things you have to realize with young people is, many times, you can't pay any attention to what they say. How many times have I said to a child, "Let's do something," and heard "Nah, I don't want to do that." And many parents give in to that rather than say "Well, we're going to try, and after you have tried it, if you don't want to do it again, fine." And then after they've tried it, you try to stop them and they say, "No, no, no, let's do it some more." "Well, wait a minute, I thought you didn't want to do this."

Love of Learning provides structure. We acknowledge the children as individuals. We involve them in things that are healthy for them. We also respect them. I realize one of the gifts that God has given me is that I rarely see people where they are. I see them where they *can* be. And I try to encourage my staff at Love of Learning to realize that we don't know who these people might become. One of these kids that's getting on your last nerve may be the doctor who has the cure for AIDS. You know, that child that can't seem to be still may be a future Supreme Court justice. There are some people who probably met Bill Clinton as a child or when he was just the governor of Arkansas and thought, "No big deal." Now he's the President of the United States. And I'm sure there are people that regret that they didn't give him more time or that they weren't nice to him so that now they could be the President's friend. Well, I'm just trying to help people early in the game recognize the potential of students. Be nice to them now so that you have a front-row seat at their Inauguration or at the Oscar ceremonies when they pick up their Academy Award. We don't know who they are so we need to treat them as if they can be anything, because they *can.* I strongly believe that.

All of us know of people who were told repeatedly "You ain't nothing.

Your daddy wasn't nothing. Your mama wasn't nothing. And you ain't going to be nothing." And that's exactly what they became—nothing. Just think about the impact of saying the opposite. "You can do this. You're brilliant. You're going to be a great success." I constantly remind my kids they are the best and the brightest in the Charlotte-Mecklenburg school system. And so I expect the best and they come forth with it. Because most of them are just looking for somebody to give them some recognition, to give them some attention, to acknowledge them. All of us need that.

We also touch them a lot. That's something else that a lot of people are afraid to do. They may have problems with touching, but I know the people that I hire and so that I don't worry about sexual molestation. It amazes me in this society how much we handle babies. Go to anybody's house who's just had a baby and watch all the neighbors and all the relatives, everybody's just touching them all over. But then as that child grows up, we stop touching them, especially when they reach puberty. And that's when they really need to be touched. So we do a lot of hugging here. When I greet kids, it's with a hug. Doesn't matter that I've never seen the child before because their spirit I *have* seen before. And that's what you have to acknowledge. So you need to touch them. When kids come into my office and they're upset, the first thing I say to them is "Well, we'd better deal with your problem but I need my hug." And I have those kids thinking that I just can't live without hugs. And so they get into the spirit of it. Watch gangs. They do a lot of touching. It may be done in a rough way, whatever, but they do a lot of touching.

Q: How does the Love of Learning program change the parents' relationship with their children?

A: Parents with kids in the program begin to stop and think. And as a consequence, they change. I've had a lot of parents who have gone back to school themselves. I've had a lot of parents who are taking risks in terms of career, asking for job promotions that they should have had before but didn't feel like they were worthy of getting. One of the first things we do with parents is a workshop on communication and building positive self-esteem. We require that parents feel good about themselves because we expect them to be full partners in their children's education. They have to feel comfortable in talking with principals, teachers, and guidance counselors. And when you realize the average educational level of most of our parents is about tenth or eleventh grade, you understand how a parent could feel very intimidated about confronting teachers and principals. Also, many members of the black community have put teachers and principals on pedestals—along with ministers, they were the closest thing to God. And so a lot of people still feel awed by teachers and school personnel. And so we do a lot of self-esteem work with parents in the beginning of the Love of Learning program so they can feel comfortable in working with school personnel. Because we have found that the students who get the best of what our school systems have to offer are those who know parents are going to be checking up on them.

Our own parents are some of our best teachers and those seem to be the most popular workshops we offer, where we give them a chance to talk with each other. Parents many times work in isolation. It takes all of their time to get to work and keep the house running and get kids where they need to be. And sometimes they end up talking *at* their children rather than *with* them. Hearing other parents talking about this helps them change.

Q: Who or what inspired you to dedicate your life to Love of Learning?

A: I was fortunate enough to have grown up in an extended family. My parents and I, for the first nine years of my life, lived in a house with my maternal grandmother, grandfather, six uncles, and two aunts. Our household was one where the attitude of the adults was that I was just a miniature adult. There was no such thing as "children should be seen and not heard" or people spelling around me.

My aunt and grandfather were particular inspirations. My mother's sister, my aunt, was a schoolteacher who was bedridden when I was four and five. She loved to read and so she taught me to read and to love learning. My grandfather was also always pushing education. Although he had to drop out of school when he was in the fifth grade to support his family, his education did not stop because he could not go to formal school. We used to have twelve o'clock and six o'clock meals as a family. You had to be there. And when you came to the table, everybody had to bring something that they had learned that day. And just because I had not started school I was not exempted. Somebody in the family had to get with me so I would have something prepared to discuss. Because that was how my grandfather learned, from our conversations. And so at an early age I learned that the two keys to freedom, to life, to success and happiness, was knowing and serving God and an education. And that education is about more than school. Even when you have completed as much school as you can, you don't stop learning. You keep learning, keep asking questions. That's one thing I have to thank my family for.

So that's where the seed was planted, but what happened to make me pull all of that together was my own experience growing up. My mother, once we moved away from the extended family, sheltered me from racism to such an extent that when I went to an all-white high school for the first time in the eleventh grade, kids running from me was a shock. And there's a memory that's very vivid in my mind. In my chemistry class this girl had come in and put her books down and gone to bathroom. I walked into the classroom and took the seat behind her. When she came back and saw me sitting behind her, she stopped dead in the doorway, looked at me, let out this blood-curdling scream, and ran. And I thought she did it because I was ugly. I had no idea that it was not that I was ugly but that it was just because I was black. So, all the ways that I was being treated because I was black, because I had been protected from the whole white/black thing, I took personally. My ego was constantly being chipped away. Then when I went to Howard, I experienced the same thing because I was the wrong shade of black. So, in other words, I suffered from low self-esteem myself, and I

realized the problems that it caused me in life. And I have always wanted
to make it better for somebody else. I wish that someone had been there
for me at various times to make some of the hurdles that I had to jump
over easier. But because no one was there for me means I want to be there
for somebody else. I don't like pain, and I don't like to see other people
in pain. And so Love of Learning for me comes out of my desire to keep
people from hurting, to give people the tools that they need to be all that
they were created to be.

See, we've been sold a bill of goods in this country and many of us have
bought it hook, line, and sinker without even realizing it. Our life many
times is a reflection of that. We wouldn't be killing each other if we knew
who we were, if we had not been blocked in terms of love, if we had not
somehow been made to feel that we were unlovable. Because that's a lot of
what it is. Most children don't realize that when they walk down a street or
are into a school and a child is being nasty to them, that's because they're in
pain. And if we could just remember that and not react to the words, but
to deal with the people. That's what I try to do with the kids in Love of
Learning, to get them in touch with that. You know, don't just like me because of what's coming out of my mouth. Look beyond that and look beyond
that in yourself. And we're teaching kids to love. It's funny, but Davidson
College thinks I'm running an academic program, a precollege program.
I'm actually building the kingdom. A lot of what I'm doing can be found
in Jesus' Sermon on the Mount where he teaches us how we should relate
to one another. And that's how we work with the kids. I tell them, if you
can do it here, you can do it anywhere else you go. You can create it—the
kingdom of heaven—within.

SPEAK THE TRUTH TO THE PEOPLE

Mari Evans

Speak the truth to the people
Talk sense to the people
Free them with reason
Free them with honesty
Free the people with Love and Courage and Care for their Being
Spare them the fantasy
Fantasy enslaves
A slave is enslaved
Can be enslaved by unwisdom
Can be enslaved by black unwisdom
Can be re-enslaved while in flight from the enemy
Can be enslaved by his brother whom he loves
His brother whom he trusts
His brother with the loud voice
And the unwisdom
Speak the truth to the people
It is not necessary to green the heart
Only to identify the enemy
It is not necessary to blow the mind
Only to free the mind
To identify the enemy is to free the mind
A free mind has no need to scream
A free mind is ready for other things

To BUILD black schools
To BUILD black children
To BUILD black minds
To BUILD black love
To BUILD black impregnability
To BUILD a strong black nation
To BUILD.

Speak the truth to the people.
Spare them the opium of devil-hate.
They need no trips on honky-chants.
Move them instead to a BLACK ONENESS.
A black strength which will defend its own
Needing no cacophony of screams for activation
A black strength which attacks the laws
exposes the lies disassembles the structure
and ravages the very foundation of evil.

Speak the truth to the people
To identify the enemy is to free the mind
Free the mind of the people
Speak to the mind of the people
Speak Truth.

FIRST MAN
Naomi Long Madgett

Sculpted from the clay of Africa,
first man in all the universe,
you were created in the image of a tree.
Transplanted now to foreign soil,
you are still wondrous in your towering vigor
and amplitude, and in the shade you give.

Tender birch or seasoned oak, mahogany or cedar,
baobab or ebony, you are the joy of a new Eden,
crested with leaves as varied
as fades and dreadlocks.

Your countenance, like rings of a stalwart trunk,
tells the unmatched story
of how you persevered and flourished
in spite of bitter storms.

Majestic man, enduring man of myriad visages,
continue to grow strong and tall
within the circle of my love.

Henry Bozeman Jones, *Peckin*, n.d. Linocut, 8⅞ × 6⅞ in.
The Howard University Gallery of Art, Permanent Collection, Washington, D.C.

QUESTION:

WHAT IS THE GREATEST CHALLENGE
YOU FACE AS A BLACK MAN?

Haki R. Madhubuti

ANSWER: My continued quest is to be a responsible, loving, and effective Black man, husband, father, writer, educator, and publisher in this ocean of *white world supremacy* (racism) and not to allow *white supremacy* to alter or destroy my memory, spirit, drive, integrity, worldview, convictions, and values that are the results of twenty-five years of work, excruciating pain, serious study, critical thinking—actions and organized struggle.

Also, with my wife, my challenge is to pass on to our children positive Afrikan (Black) values: which demand the maintenance and development of our family, extended family, community, and people, by highlighting and pushing progressive ideas as well as historical examples of Harriet Tubman, Nat Turner, Martin R. Delaney, Marcus Garvey, Mary McLeod Bethune, Fannie Lou Hamer, Martin Luther King, Malcolm X, and others.

My fight is to be an inspired example of a caring, healthy, intelligent, and hardworking brother who understands this *war* and works daily for the development of our brothers into multitalented, family-based, conscientious Black men who will not settle for anything less than self-determination and beauty for all people.

FROM THE DAMNATION

OF WOMEN

W. E. B. Du Bois

"Wait till the lady passes," said a Nashville white boy.

"She's no lady; she's a nigger," answered another.

So some few women are born free, and some amid insult and scarlet letters achieve freedom; but our women in black had freedom thrust contemptuously upon them. With that freedom they are buying an untrammeled independence and dear as is the price they pay for it, it will in the end be worth every taunt and groan. Today the dreams of the mothers are coming true. We have still our poverty and degradation, our lewdness and our cruel toil; but we have, too, a vast group of women of Negro blood who for strength of character, cleanness of soul, and unselfish devotion of purpose, is today easily the peer of any group of women in the civilized world. And more than that, in the great rank and file of our five million women we have the up-working of new revolutionary ideals, which must in time have vast influence on the thought and action of this land.

For this, their promise, and for their hard past, I honor the women of my race. Their beauty, —their dark and mysterious beauty of midnight eyes, crumpled hair, and soft, full-featured faces—is perhaps more to me than to you, because I was born to its warm and subtle spell; but their worth is yours as well as mine. No other women on earth could have emerged from the hell of force and temptation which once engulfed and still surrounds black women in America with half the modesty and womanliness that they retain. I have always felt like bowing myself before them in all abasement, searching to bring some tribute to these long-suffering victims, these burdened sisters of mine, whom the world, the wise, white world, loves to affront and ridicule and wantonly to insult. I have known the women of many lands and nations, —I have known and seen and lived beside them, but none have I known more sweetly feminine, more unswervingly loyal, more desperately earnest, and more instinctively pure in body and in soul than the daughters of my black mothers. This, then, —a little thing—to their memory and inspiration.

UP SISTER
Ruth Forman

Jus get your beautiful black behind up
off that cold Armstrong tile

Don't you give up
jus cuz you don't see nowhere to go
We have faith in you

You are brilliant and bold
like nobody I have ever seen before
How the hell you think you got this far anyway?

Can't do it no more huh
too tired . . . too achin
to arch to the ceilin one more time
Jus to find you back on the floor tomorrow

Girl don't you know that floor got
the change that fell out my pocket
when I was huggin my knees by the corner last night?
And Bessie's birth control
and Billie's Marlboros
and mascara and matches and mace
and everything else you could find
in a woman's pockets that fall out

when she collapses with a hundred-pound sigh
But you know how we leave that floor?
Some hand reaches in that darkness
and pulls you up by the waist
even when you don't want to go
cuz it has faith in you
See you got to get up cuz you're Us
and when you fall We get bruised

Sometimes you can't do it by yourself
but you got a hand reachin out right now
Don't you know
you got a hundred hands
from every single Black woman who claims that floor

Yes you'll find yourself here again
But for now
jus worry about getting your beautiful black behind up
off that cold Armstrong tile
And don't worry about that lipstick sittin by your corner
I'll get it next time I'm here.

Emilio Cruz, *Gold Necklace*, 1990. Pastel on paper, 50 × 30 in.
Courtesy of Alitash Kebede Fine Arts, Los Angeles, CA.

QUILTING ON THE REBOUND
Terry McMillan

ive years ago, I did something I swore I'd never do—went
out with someone I worked with. We worked for a large insurance company
in L.A. Richard was a senior examiner and I was a chief underwriter.
The first year, we kept it a secret, and not because we were afraid of jeopar-
dizing our jobs. Richard was twenty-six and I was thirty-four. By the second
year, everybody knew it anyway and nobody seemed to care. We'd been
going out for three years when I realized that this relationship was going
nowhere. I probably could've dated him for the rest of my life and he'd
have been satisfied. Richard had had a long reputation for being a Don Juan
of sorts, until he met me. I cooled his heels. His name was also rather
ironic, because he looked like a black Richard Gere. The fact that I was
older than he was made him feel powerful in a sense, and he believed
that he could do for me what men my own age apparently couldn't.
But that wasn't true. He was a challenge. I wanted to see if I could
make his head and heart turn 360 degrees, and I did. I blew his young
mind in bed, but he also charmed me into loving him until I didn't care
how old he was.

Richard thought I was exotic because I have slanted eyes, high cheek-
bones, and full lips. Even though my mother is Japanese and my dad is
black, I inherited most of his traits. My complexion is dark, my hair is nappy,
and I'm five-six. I explained to Richard that I was proud of both of my
heritages, but he has insisted on thinking of me as being mostly Japanese.
Why, I don't know. I grew up in a black neighborhood in L.A., went
to Dorsey High School—which was predominantly black, Asian, and
Hispanic—and most of my friends are black. I've never even considered
going out with anyone other than black men.

My mother, I'm glad to say, is not the stereotypical passive Japanese wife either. She's been the head nurse in Kaiser's cardiovascular unit for over twenty years, and my dad has his own landscaping business, even though he should've retired years ago. My mother liked Richard and his age didn't bother her, but she believed that if a man loved you he should marry you. Simple as that. On the other hand, my dad didn't care who I married just as long as it was soon. I'll be the first to admit that I was a spoiled-rotten brat because my mother had had three miscarriages before she finally had me and I was used to getting everything I wanted. Richard was no exception. "Give him the ultimatum," my mother had said, if he didn't propose by my thirty-eighth birthday.

But I didn't have to. I got pregnant.

We were having dinner at an Italian restaurant when I told him. "You want to get married, don't you?" he'd said.

"Do you?" I asked.

He was picking through his salad and then he jabbed his fork into a tomato. "Why not, we were headed in that direction anyway, weren't we?" He did not eat his tomato but laid his fork down on the side of the plate.

I swallowed a spoonful of my clam chowder, then asked, "Were we?"

"You know the answer to that. But hell, now's as good a time as any. We're both making good money, and sometimes all a man needs is a little incentive." He didn't look at me when he said this, and his voice was strained. "Look," he said, "I've had a pretty shitty day, haggling with one of the adjusters, so forgive me if I don't appear to be boiling over with excitement. I am happy about this. Believe me, I am," he said, and picked up a single piece of lettuce with a different fork and put it into his mouth.

My parents were thrilled when I told them, but my mother was nevertheless suspicious. "Funny how this baby pop up, isn't it?" she'd said.

"What do you mean?"

"You know exactly what I mean. I hope baby doesn't backfire."

I ignored what she'd just said. "Will you help me make my dress?" I asked.

"Yes," she said. "But we must hurry."

My parents—who are far from well off—went all out for this wedding. My mother didn't want anyone to know I was pregnant, and to be honest, I didn't either. The age difference was enough to handle as it was. Close to three hundred people had been invited, and my parents had spent an astronomical amount of money to rent a country club in Marina del Rey. "At your age," my dad had said, "I hope you'll only be doing this once." Richard's parents insisted on taking care of the caterer and the liquor, and my parents didn't object. I paid for the cake.

About a month before the Big Day, I was meeting Richard at the jeweler because he'd picked out my ring and wanted to make sure I liked it. He was so excited, he sounded like a little boy. It was beautiful, but I told him he didn't have to spend four thousand dollars on my wedding ring. "You're worth it," he'd said and kissed me on the cheek. When we got to the parking lot, he opened my door and stood there staring at me. "Four more weeks," he said, "and you'll be my wife." He didn't smile when he said it, but closed the door and walked around to the driver's side and got in. He'd driven four whole blocks without saying a word and his knuckles were almost white because of how tight he was holding the steering wheel.

"Is something wrong, Richard?" I asked him.

"What would make you think that?" he said. Then he laid on the horn because someone in front of us hadn't moved and the light had just barely turned green.

"Richard, we don't have to go through with this, you know."

"I know we don't *have* to, but it's the right thing to do, and I'm going to do it. So don't worry, we'll be happy."

But I *was* worried.

I'd been doing some shopping at the Beverly Center when I started getting these stomach cramps while I was going up the escalator, so I decided to sit down. I walked over to one of the little outside cafés and I felt something lock inside my stomach, so I pulled out a chair. Moments later my skirt felt like it was wet. I got up and looked at the chair and saw a small red puddle. I sat back down and started crying. I didn't know what to do. Then a punkish-looking girl came over and asked if I was okay. "I'm pregnant, and I've just bled all over this chair," I said.

"Can I do something for you? Do you want me to call an ambulance?" She was popping chewing gum and I wanted to snatch it out of her mouth.

By this time at least four other women had gathered around me. The punkish-looking girl told them about my condition. One of the women said, "Look, let's get her to the rest room. She's probably having a miscarriage."

Two of the women helped me up and all four of them formed a circle around me, then slowly led me to the ladies' room. I told them that I wasn't in any pain, but they were still worried. I closed the stall door, pulled down two toilet seat covers, and sat down. I felt as if I had to go, so I pushed. Something plopped out of me and it made a splash. I was afraid to get up but I got up and looked at this large dark mass that looked like liver. I put my hand over my mouth because I knew that was my baby.

"Are you okay in there?"

I went to open my mouth, but the joint in my jawbone clicked and my mouth wouldn't move.

"Are you okay in there, miss?"

I wanted to answer, but I couldn't.

"Miss." I heard her banging on the door.

I felt my mouth loosen. "It's gone," I said. "It's gone."

"Honey, open the door," someone said, but I couldn't move. Then I heard myself say, "I think I need a sanitary pad." I was staring into the toilet bowl when I felt a hand hit my leg. "Here, are you sure you're okay in there?"

"Yes," I said. Then I flushed the toilet with my foot and watched my future disappear. I put the pad on and reached inside my shopping bag, pulled out a Raiders sweatshirt I'd bought for Richard, and tied it around my waist. When I came out, all of the women were waiting for me. "Would you like us to call your husband? Where are you parked? Do you feel light-headed, dizzy?"

"No, I'm fine, really, and thank you so much for your concern. I appreciate it, but I feel okay."

I drove home in a daze and when I opened the door to my condo, I was glad I lived alone. I sat on the couch from one o'clock to four o'clock without moving. When I finally got up, it felt as if I'd only been there for five minutes.

I didn't tell Richard. I didn't tell anybody. I bled for three days before I went to see my doctor. He scolded me because I'd gotten some kind of an infection and had to be prescribed antibiotics, then he sent me to the outpatient clinic, where I had to have a D & C.

Two weeks later, I had a surprise shower and got enough gifts to fill the housewares department at Bullock's. One of my old girlfriends, Gloria, came all the way from Phoenix, and I hadn't seen her in three years. I hardly recognized her, she was as big as a house. "You don't know how lucky you are, girl," she'd said to me. "I wish I could be here for the wedding but Tarik is having his sixteenth birthday party and I am not leaving a bunch of teenagers alone in my house. Besides, I'd probably have a heart attack watching you or anybody else walk down an aisle in white. Come to think of it, I can't even remember the last time I went to a wedding."

"Me either," I said.

"I know you're gonna try to get pregnant in a hurry, right?" she asked, holding out her wrist with the watch on it.

I tried to smile. "I'm going to work on it," I said.

"Well, who knows?" Gloria said, laughing. "Maybe one day you'll be coming to my wedding. We may both be in wheelchairs, but you never know."

"I'll be there," I said.

All Richard said when he saw the gifts was "What are we going to do with all this stuff? Where are we going to put it?"

"It depends on where we're going to live," I said, which we hadn't even talked about. My condo was big enough and so was his apartment.

"It doesn't matter to me, but I think we should wait awhile before buying a house. A house is a big investment, you know. Thirty years." He gave me a quick look.

"Are you getting cold feet?" I blurted out.

"No, I'm not getting cold feet. It's just that in two weeks we're going to be man and wife, and it takes a little getting used to the idea, that's all."

"Are you having doubts about the idea of it?"

"No."

"Are you sure?"

"I'm sure," he said.

I didn't stop bleeding, so I took some vacation time to relax and finish my dress. I worked on it day and night and was doing all the beadwork by hand. My mother was spending all her free time at my place trying to make sure everything was happening on schedule. A week before the Big Day I was trying on my gown for the hundredth time when the phone rang. I thought it might be Richard, since he hadn't called me in almost forty-eight hours, and when I finally called him and left a message, he still hadn't returned my call. My father said this was normal.

"Hello," I said.

"I think you should talk to Richard." It was his mother.

"About what?" I asked.

"He's not feeling very well," was all she said.

"What's wrong with him?"

"I don't know for sure. I think it's his stomach."

"Is he sick?"

"I don't know. Call him."

"I did call him but he hasn't returned my call."

"Keep trying," she said.

So I called him at work, but his secretary said he wasn't there. I called him at home and he wasn't there either, so I left another message and for the next three hours I was a wreck, waiting to hear from him. I knew something was wrong.

I gave myself a facial, a manicure, and a pedicure and watched Oprah Winfrey while I waited by the phone. It didn't ring. My mother was downstairs hemming one of the bridesmaid's dresses. I went down to get myself a glass of wine. "How you feeling, Marilyn Monroe?" she asked.

"What do you mean, how am I feeling? I'm feeling fine."

"All I meant was you awful lucky with no morning sickness or anything, but I must say, hormones changing because you getting awfully irritating."

"I'm sorry, Ma."

"It's okay. I had jitters too."

I went back upstairs and closed my bedroom door, then went into my bathroom. I put the wineglass on the side of the bathtub and decided to take a bubble bath in spite of the bleeding. I must have poured half a bottle of Secreti in. The water was too hot but I got in anyway. Call, dammit, call. Just then the phone rang and scared me half to death. I was hyperventilating and couldn't say much except "Hold on a minute," while I caught my breath.

"Marilyn?" Richard was saying. "Marilyn?" But before I had a chance to answer he blurted out what must have been on his mind all along. "Please don't be mad at me, but I can't do this. I'm not ready. I wanted to do the right thing, but I'm only twenty-nine years old. I've got my whole life ahead of me. I'm not ready to be a father yet. I'm not ready to be anybody's husband either, and I'm scared. Everything is happening too fast. I know you think I'm being a coward, and you're probably right. But I've been having nightmares, Marilyn. Do you hear me, nightmares about being imprisoned. I haven't been able to sleep through the night. I doze off and wake up dripping wet. And my stomach. It's in knots. Believe me, Marilyn, it's not that I don't love you because I do. It's not that I don't care about the baby, because I do. I just can't do this right now. I can't make this kind of commitment right now. I'm sorry. Marilyn? Marilyn, are you still there?"

I dropped the portable phone in the bathtub and got out.

My mother heard me screaming and came tearing into the room. "What happened?"

I was dripping wet and ripping the pearls off my dress but somehow I managed to tell her.

"He come to his senses," she said. "This happen a lot. He just got cold feet, but give him day or two. He not mean it."

Three days went by and he didn't call. My mother stayed with me and did everything she could to console me, but by that time I'd already flushed the ring down the toilet.

"I hope you don't lose baby behind this," she said.

"I've already lost the baby," I said.

"What?"

"A month ago."

Her mouth was wide open. She found the sofa with her hand and sat down. "Marilyn," she said and let out an exasperated sigh.

"I couldn't tell anybody."

"Why not tell somebody? Why not me, your mother?"

"Because I was too scared."

"Scared of what?"

"That Richard might change his mind."

"Man love you, dead baby not change his mind."

"I was going to tell him after we got married."

Deborah Willis, *No Man of Her Own*, 1992.
Photography, quilt pillow, 24 × 22 in. Courtesy of the artist.

"I not raise you to be dishonest."

"I know."

"No man in world worth lying about something like this. How could you?"

"I don't know."

"I told you it backfire, didn't I?"

For weeks I couldn't eat or sleep. At first, all I did was think about what was wrong with me. I was too old. For him. No. He didn't care about my age. It was the gap in my teeth, or my slight overbite, from all those years I used to suck my thumb. But he never mentioned anything about it and I was really the only one who seemed to notice. I was flat-chested. I had cellulite. My ass was square instead of round. I wasn't exciting as I used to be in bed. No. I was still good in bed, that much I did know. I couldn't cook. I was a terrible housekeeper. That was it. If you couldn't cook and keep a clean house, what kind of wife would you make?

I had to make myself stop thinking about my infinite flaws, so I started quilting again. I was astonished at how radiant the colors were that I was choosing, how unconventional and wild the patterns were. Without even realizing it, I was fusing Japanese and African motifs and was quite excited by the results. My mother was worried about me, even though I had actually stopped bleeding for two whole weeks. Under the circumstances, she thought that my obsession with quilting was not normal, so she forced me to go to the doctor. He gave me some kind of an antidepressant, which I refused to take. I told him I was not depressed, I was simply hurt. Besides, a pill wasn't any antidote or consolation for heartache.

I began to patronize just about every fabric store in downtown Los Angeles, and while I listened to the humming of my machine, and concentrated on designs that I couldn't believe I was creating, it occurred to me that I wasn't suffering from heartache at all. I actually felt this incredible sense of relief. As if I didn't have to anticipate anything else happening that was outside of my control. And when I did grieve, it was always because I had lost a child, not a future husband.

I also heard my mother all day long on my phone, lying about some tragedy that had happened and apologizing for any inconvenience it may have caused. And I watched her, bent over at the dining room table, writing hundreds of thank-you notes to the people she was returning gifts to. She even signed my name. My father wanted to kill Richard. "He was too young, and he wasn't good enough for you anyway," he said. "This is really a blessing in disguise."

I took a leave of absence from my job because there was no way in hell I could face those people, and the thought of looking at Richard infuriated me. I was not angry at him for not marrying me, I was angry at him for not being honest, for the way he handled it all. He even had the nerve to come over without calling. I had opened the door but wouldn't let him inside. He was nothing but a little pipsqueak. A handsome, five-foot-seven-inch pipsqueak.

"Marilyn, look, we need to talk."

"About what?"

"Us. The baby."

"There is no baby."

"What do you mean, there's no baby?"

"It died."

"You mean you got rid of it?"

"No, I lost it."

"I'm sorry, Marilyn," he said and put his head down. How touching, I thought. "This is all my fault."

"It's not your fault, Richard."

"Look. Can I come in?"

"For what?"

"I want to talk. I need to talk to you."

"About what?"

"About us."

"Us?"

"Yes, us. I don't want it to be over between us. I just need more time, that's all."

"Time for what?"

"To make sure this is what I want to do."

"Take all the time you need," I said and slammed the door in his face. He rang the buzzer again, but I just told him to get lost and leave me alone.

I went upstairs and sat at my sewing machine. I turned the light on, then picked up a piece of purple and terra-cotta cloth. I slid it under the pressure foot and dropped it. I pressed down on the pedal and watched the needle zigzag. The stitches were too loose so I tightened the tension. Richard is going to be the last in a series of mistakes I've made when it comes to picking a man. I've picked the wrong one too many times, like a bad habit that's too hard to break. I haven't had the best of luck when it comes to keeping them either, and to be honest, Richard was the one who lasted the longest.

When I got to the end of the fabric, I pulled the top and bobbin threads together and cut them on the thread cutter. Then I bent down and picked up two different pieces. They were black and purple. I always want what I can't

have or what I'm not supposed to have. So what did I do? Created a pattern
of choosing men that I knew would be a challenge. Richard's was his age.
But the others—all of them from Alex to William—were all afraid of
something: namely, committing to one woman. All I wanted to do was se-
duce them hard enough—emotionally, mentally, and physically—so they
wouldn't even be aware that they were committing to anything. I just wanted
them to crave me, and no one else but me. I wanted to be their healthiest
addiction. But it was a lot harder to do than I thought. What I found out was
that men are a hard nut to crack.

But some of them weren't. When I was in my late twenties, early thir-
ties—before I got serious and realized I wanted a long-term relationship—I'd
had at least twenty different men fall in love with me, but of course these
were the ones I didn't want. They were the ones who after a few dates or one
rousing night in bed ordained themselves my "man" or were too quick to
want to marry me, and even some considered me their "property." When it
was clear that I was dealing with a different species of man, a hungry ele-
ment, before I got in too deep, I'd tell them almost immediately that I hope
they wouldn't mind my being bisexual or my being unfaithful because I was in
no hurry to settle down with one man, or that I had a tendency of always
falling for my man's friends. Could they tolerate that? I even went so far as to
tell them that I hoped having herpes wouldn't cause a problem, that I wasn't
really all that trustworthy because I was a habitual liar, and that if they wanted
the whole truth they should find themselves another woman. I told them that
I didn't even think I was good enough for them, and they should do themselves a favor, find a woman who's truly worthy of having such a terrific man.

I had it down to a science, but by the time I met Richard, I was tired of
lying and conniving. I was sick of the games. I was whipped, really, and allowed myself to relax and be vulnerable because I knew I was getting old.

When Gloria called to see how my honeymoon went, I told her the truth
about everything. She couldn't believe it. "Well, I thought I'd heard 'em all,
but this one takes the cake. How you holding up?"

"I'm hanging in there."

"This is what makes you want to castrate a man."

"Not really, Gloria."

"I know. But you know what I mean. Some of them have a lot of nerve, I swear they do. But really, Marilyn, how are you feeling for real, baby?"

"I'm getting my period every other week, but I'm quilting again, which is a good sign."

"First of all, take your behind back to that doctor and find out why you're still bleeding like this. And, honey, making quilts is no consolation for a broken heart. It sounds like you could use some R and R. Why don't you come visit me for a few days?"

I looked around my room, which had piles and piles of cloth and half-sewn quilts, from where I'd changed my mind. Hundreds of different-colored threads were all over the carpet, and the satin stitch I was trying out wasn't giving me the effect I thought it would. I could use a break, I thought. I could. "You know what?" I said. "I think I will."

"Good, and bring me one of those tacky quilts. I don't have anything to snuggle up with in the winter, and contrary to popular belief, it does get cold here come December."

I liked Phoenix and Tempe, but I fell in love with Scottsdale. Not only was it beautiful but I couldn't believe how inexpensive it was to live in the entire area, which was all referred to as the Valley. I have to thank Gloria for being such a lifesaver. She took me to her beauty salon and gave me a whole new look. She chopped off my hair, and one of the guys in her shop showed me how to put on my makeup in a way that would further enhance what assets he insisted I had.

We drove to Tucson, to Canyon Ranch for what started out as a simple Spa Renewal Day. But we ended up spending three glorious days and had the works. I had an herbal wrap, where they wrapped my entire body in hot thin linen that had been steamed. Then they rolled me up in flannel blankets and put a cold washcloth on my forehead. I sweated in the dark for a half hour. Gloria didn't do this because she said she was claustrophobic and didn't want to be wrapped up in anything where she couldn't move. I had a deep-muscle and shiatsu massage on two different days. We steamed. We Jacuzzied. We both had a mud facial, and then this thing called aroma-therapy—where they put distilled essences from flowers and herbs on your face and you look like a different person when they finish. On the last day, we got this Persian Body Polish where they actually buffed our skin with crushed pearl creams, sprayed us with some kind of herbal spray, then used an electric brush to make us tingle. We had our hands and feet moisturized and put in heated gloves and booties, and by the time we left, we couldn't believe we were the same women.

In Phoenix, Gloria took me to yet another resort where we listened to live music. We went to see a stupid movie and I actually laughed. Then we went on a two-day shopping spree and I charged whatever I felt like. I even bought her son a pair of eighty-dollar sneakers, and I'd only seen him twice in my life.

I felt like I'd gotten my spirit back, so when I got home, I told my parents I'd had it with the smog, the traffic, the gangs, and L.A. in general. My mother said, "You cannot run from heartache," but I told her I wasn't running from anything. I put my condo on the market, and in less than a month it sold for four times what I paid for it. I moved in with my mother and father, asked for a job transfer for health reasons, and when it came through, three months later, I moved to Scottsdale.

The town house I bought feels like a house. It's twice the size of the one I had and cost less than half of what I originally spent. My complex is pretty standard for Scottsdale. It has two pools and four tennis courts. It also has vaulted ceilings, wall-to-wall carpet, two fireplaces, and a garden bathtub with a Jacuzzi in it. The kitchen has an island in the center and I've got a 180-degree view of Phoenix and mountains. It also has three bedrooms. One I sleep in, one I use for sewing, and the other is for guests.

I made close to forty thousand dollars after I sold my condo, so I sent four to my parents because the money they'd put down for the wedding was nonrefundable. They really couldn't afford that kind of loss. The rest I put in an IRA and CDs until I could figure out something better to do with it.

I hated my new job. I had to accept a lower-level position and less money, which didn't bother me all that much at first. The office, however, was much smaller and full of rednecks who couldn't stand the thought of a black woman working over them. I was combing the classifieds, looking for a comparable job, but the job market in Phoenix is nothing close to what it is in L.A.

But thank God Gloria's got a big mouth. She'd been boasting to all of her clients about my quilts, had even hung the one I'd given her on the wall at the shop, and the next thing I know I'm getting so many orders I couldn't keep up with them. That's when she asked me why didn't I consider opening my own shop? That never would've occurred to me, but what did I have to lose?

She introduced me to Bernadine, a friend of hers who was an accountant. Bernadine in turn introduced me to a good lawyer, and he helped me draw up all the papers. Over the next four months, she helped me devise what turned out to be a strong marketing and advertising plan. I rented an 800-square-foot space in the same shopping center where Gloria's shop is, and opened Quiltworks, Etc.

It wasn't long before I realized I needed to get some help, so I hired two seamstresses. They took a lot of the strain off of me, and I was able to take some jewelry-making classes and even started selling small pieces in the shop. Gloria gave me this tacky T-shirt for my thirty-ninth birthday, which gave me the idea to experiment with making them. Because I go overboard in everything I do, I went out and spent a fortune on every color of metallic and acrylic fabric paint they made. I bought one hundred 100-percent cotton heavy-duty men's T-shirts and discovered other uses for sponges, plastic, spray bottles, rolling pins, lace, and even old envelopes. I was having a great time because I'd never felt this kind of excitement and gratification doing anything until now.

I'd been living here a year when I found out that Richard had married another woman who worked in our office. I wanted to hate him, but I didn't. I wanted to be angry, but I wasn't. I didn't feel anything toward him, but I sent him a quilt and a wedding card to congratulate him, just because.

To be honest, I've been so busy with my shop, I haven't even thought about men. I don't even miss having sex unless I really just *think* about it. My libido must be evaporating, because when I *do* think about it, I just make quilts or jewelry or paint T-shirts and the feeling goes away. Some of my best ideas come at these moments.

Basically, I'm doing everything I can to make Marilyn feel good. And at thirty-nine years old my body needs tightening, so I joined a health club and started working out three to four times a week. Once in a while, I babysit for Bernadine, and it breaks my heart when I think about the fact that I don't have a child of my own. Sometimes, Gloria and I go out to hear some music. I frequent most of the major art galleries, go to just about every football and basketball game at Arizona State, and see at *least* one movie a week.

I am rarely bored. Which is why I've decided that at this point in my life, I really don't care if I ever get married. I've learned that I don't need a man in order to survive, that a man is nothing but an intrusion, and they require too much energy. I don't think they're worth it. Besides, they have too much power, and from what I've seen, they always seem to abuse it. The one thing I *do* have is power over my own life. I like it this way, and I'm not about to give it up for something that may not last.

The one thing I do want is to have a baby. Someone I could love who would love me back with no strings attached. But at thirty-nine, I know my days are numbered. I'd be willing to do it alone, if that's the only way I can have one. But right now, my life is almost full. It's fun, it's secure, and it's safe. About the only thing I'm concerned about these days is whether or not it's time to branch out into leather.

I Thought It Was Tangiers I Wanted

Langston Hughes

I know now
That Notre Dame is in Paris,
And the Seine is more to me now
Than a wriggling line on a map
Or a name in travel stores.

I know now
There is a Crystal Palace in Antwerp
Where a hundred women sell their naked bodies,
And the night-lovers of sailors
Wait for men on docks in Genoa.
I know now
That a great golden moon
Like a picture-book moon
Really rises behind palm groves
In Africa,
And tom-toms do beat
In village squares under the mango trees.

I know now
That Venice is a church dome
And a net-work of canals,
Tangier a whiteness under sun.

I thought
It was Tangiers I wanted,
Or the gargoyles of Notre Dame,

Or the Crystal Palace in Antwerp,
Or the golden palm-grove moon in Africa,
Or a church dome and a net-work of canals.

Happiness lives nowhere,
Some old fool said,
If not within oneself.

It's a sure thing
Notre Dame is in Paris,
But I thought it was Tangiers I wanted.

Henry Ossawa Tanner, *Tangier Mosque/Street in Tangier*, ca. 1912–14. Etching on paper,
7 × 9¼ in. National Museum of American Art, Smithsonian Institution,
Washington, D.C. Gift of Mr. and Mrs. Norman B. Robbins. Photo: M. Baldwin.

WHY DO WE LIVE?
Charles W. Chesnutt

*T*his is an old question—the unsolved problem of the ages; a large question, which involves the whole human race for all time. We find ourselves here; we accept the situation. That we should live is part of the universal plan, with which few of us have either the temerity or the desire to interfere. The more intimate, personal inquiry, which each individual can answer for himself, would be, "Is life worth living?"

I should answer unhesitatingly, "Yes." The pleasures of sense, the physical and social activities of life, are worth the having. The obstacles we encounter in their pursuit give us the joy of the conflict and oftentimes the glory of the victory. To the cultivated mind the study of nature in its manifold forms, including man, its flower and crown, is a source of never-ending wonder and delight. I think life would be well worth living if it lasted but ten or twenty or fifty or seventy years, and that were all. But when one reflects that through the medium of recorded thought one can live back, in mental retrospect, over six thousand years of history, and in imagination can project himself indefinitely into the future; and when to this is added the blessed hope of immortality, he would be ungrateful indeed who did not accept the boon of conscious existence and be thankful to the Creator who has taken him from the cold and senseless earth and made of him living spirit, able to perceive, however vaguely, something of the wonder and the glory of the universe.

PART II

Families of the

Heart

That African-American families survive at all is a miracle we should all celebrate, for we continue to build, nurture, struggle with them in the face of centuries of contempt, misunderstanding, neglect, and prejudice from without and, sadly sometimes, from within. But no day is set aside, as it is for mothers, fathers, even grandparents, to remember what the African-American family has endured, how we've loved and won.

Pauli Murray, in her book *Songs in a Weary Throat,* quotes a learned "scholar" of a hundred years ago who made this assertion about Black people and their families: "The Negro has little home conscience or love of home, no local attachment of the better sort. . . ." Were we to truly believe this, we could not have prevailed as we have. Could not have nurtured the familial love that has withstood the destruction of our homeplaces unprecedented in world history. We must acknowledge our survival first, as does Elizabeth Keckley, seamstress and confidante to First Lady Mary Todd Lincoln, who in her memoirs honors the love within her family that transcended their enslavement on different plantations and a separation that lasted most of her childhood.

Despite, or maybe because of, centuries of scorn and her early institutionalized rape in the name of "stocking" plantations, the Black woman as mother has held a special place in our hearts and minds. One may remember, as Nikki Giovanni writes, a mother's or grandmother's hands. Or perhaps it's the soft regrowth of her hair, as John Edgar Wideman so powerfully evokes, that stirs us. It may be the way she listened to our triumphs or worries, focusing for that moment totally on us to the exclusion of other people, our siblings, or the world. Or how she pumped us up with chicken soup, ginger ale, stories, and wisdom when we were too sick or weary to deal with the world.

While the love of our mothers is accepted and legendary, the love of our fathers can be a much murkier affair. Their love, like in Lenard Moore's poem "Pathway: From Son to Father," is often taught by deeds rather than words, measured by the quality of their silences. And yet our fathers, too, speak to us of love. Witness the vibrant love of the Watsons, father and son, who give words to a special bond that transcends position, duty, or the possibility of death on a foreign shore.

We are all blessed with children in our families, whether they were our siblings or the children who may grace our own unions. Howard Thurman speaks to us about the responsibilities we have to our children in word, action, and deed while other contributors, like Ira B. Jones and Audre Lorde, rejoice in the special blessing of children in our lives. Sometimes the message is one of welcome, like Claude A. and Etta Moten Barnett's letter to their new grandchild, or a fierce declaration of protection of young life from the evils of our society; all our sons and daughters should be blessed with Opal Palmer Adisa's determination—she's not *having* it!

However our families are constituted, by the accident of birth or the careful assembly of othermothers, uncles and aunties, or "play" brothers and sisters, let us pause to honor their presence in our hearts and the richly complex rhythm they add to our lives and loves.

Photograph on page 53: Hilton Braithwaite, *Foxglove, Oakland, California*, 1980. Silver gelatin print, 16 × 20 in. Courtesy of the photographer.

From Behind the Scenes

or,

Thirty Years a Slave,

and Four Years in the White House

Elizabeth Keckley

I was my mother's only child, which made her love for me all the stronger. I did not know much of my father, for he was the slave of another man, and when Mr. Burwell moved from Dinwiddie he was separated from us, and only allowed to visit my mother twice a year—during the Easter holidays and Christmas. At last Mr. Burwell determined to reward my mother, by making an arrangement with the owner of my father, by which the separation of my parents could be brought to an end. It was a bright day, indeed, for my mother when it was announced that my father was coming to live with us. The old weary look faded from her face, and she worked as if her heart was in every task. But the golden days did not last long. The radiant dream faded all too soon.

In the morning my father called me to him and kissed me, then held me out at arms' length as if he were regarding his child with pride. "She is growing into a large fine girl," he remarked to my mother. "I dun no which I like best, you or Lizzie, as both are so dear to me." My mother's name was Agnes, and my father delighted to call me his "Little Lizzie." While yet my father and mother were speaking hopefully, joyfully of the future, Mr. Burwell came to the cabin, with a letter in his hand. He was a kind master in some things, and as gently as possible informed my parents that they must part; for in two hours my father must join his master at Dinwiddie, and go with him to the West, where he had determined to make his future home. The announcement fell upon the little circle in that rude-log cabin like a thunderbolt. I can remember the scene as if it were but yesterday;—how my father cried out against the cruel separation; his last kiss; his wild straining of my mother to his bosom; the solemn prayer to Heaven; the tears and sobs—the fearful anguish of broken hearts. The last kiss, the last good-by; and he, my father, was gone, gone forever. The shadow eclipsed the sunshine, and love brought despair. The parting was eternal. The cloud had no silver lining, but I trust that it will be all silver in heaven. We who are crushed to earth with heavy chains, who travel a weary, rugged, thorny road, groping through midnight darkness on earth, earn our right to enjoy the sunshine in the great hereafter. At the grave, at least, we should be permitted to lay our burdens down, that a new world, a world of brightness, may open to us. The light that is denied us here should grow into a flood of effulgence beyond the dark, mysterious shadows of death. Deep as was the distress of my mother in parting with my father, her sorrow did not screen her from insult. My old mistress said to her: "Stop your nonsense; there is no necessity for you putting on airs. Your husband is not the only slave that has been sold from his family, and you are not the only one that has had to part. There are plenty more men about here, and if you want a husband so badly, stop your crying and go and find another." To these unfeeling words my mother made no reply. She turned away in stoical silence, with a curl of that loathing scorn upon her lips which swelled in her heart.

My father and mother never met again in this world. They kept up a regular correspondence for years, and the most precious mementoes of my existence are the faded old letters that he wrote, full of love, and always hoping that the future would bring brighter days. In nearly every letter is a message for me. "Tell my darling little Lizzie," he writes, "to be a good girl, and to learn her book. Kiss her for me, and tell her that I will come to see her some day." Thus he wrote time and again, but he never came. He lived in hope, but died without ever seeing his wife and child.

I note a few extracts from one of my father's letters to my mother, following copy literally:

Deborah Willis, *Log Cabin Families*, 1992. Photography, quilt, 28 × 22 in.
Courtesy of the artist.

"SHELBYVILLE, Sept. 6, 1833.

"MRS. AGNES HOBBS.

"Dear Wife: My dear biloved wife I am more than glad to meet with
opportunty writee thes few lines to you by my Mistress who ar now about
starterng to virginia, and sevl others of my old friends are with her; in
compeney Mrs. Ann Rus the wife of master Thos Rus and Dan Woodiard
and his family and I am very sorry that I havn the chance to go with them as I
feele Determid to see you If life last again. I am now here and out at this
pleace so I am not abble to get of at this time. I am write well and hearty and
all the rest of masters family. I heard this eveng by Mistress that ar just from

theree all sends love to you and all my old frends. I am a living in a town called Shelbyville and I have wrote a greate many letters since Ive beene here and almost been reeady to my selfe that its out of the question to write any more at tall: my dear wife I dont feeld no whys like giving out writing to you as yet and I hope when you get this letter that you be Inncougege to write me a letter. I am well satisfied at my living at this place I am a making money for my own benifit and I hope that its to yours also If I live to see Nexet year I shall heve my own time from master by giving him 100 and twenty Dollars a year and I thinke I shall be doing good bisness at that and heve something more thean all that. I hope with gods helpe that I may be abble to rejoys with you on the earth and In heaven lets meet when will I am detemnid to nuver stope praying, not in this earth and I hope to praise god In glory there weel meet to part no more forever. So my dear wife I hope to meet you In paradase to prase god forever * * * * * I want Elizabeth to be a good girl
and not to thinke that becasue I am bound so fare that gods not abble to open the way * * * *

> "GEORGE PLEASANT,
> "*Hobbs a servant of Grum.*"

The last letter that my mother received from my father was dated Shelbyville, Tennessee, March 20, 1839. He writes in a cheerful strain, and hopes to see her soon. Alas! he looked forward to a meeting in vain. Year after year the one great hope swelled in his heart, but the hope was only realized beyond the dark portals of the grave.

HANDS:

FOR MOTHER'S DAY
Nikki Giovanni

I think hands must be very important . . . Hands: plait hair . . . knead bread . . . spank bottoms . . . wring in anguish . . . shake the air in exasperation . . . wipe tears, sweat, and pain from faces . . . are at the end of arms which hold . . . Yes hands . . . Let's start with the hands . . .

My grandmother washed on Mondays . . . every Monday . . . If you were a visiting grandchild or a resident daughter . . . every Monday morning at 6:00 A.M. . . . mostly in the dark . . . frequently in the cold . . . certainly alone . . . you heard her on the back porch starting to hum . . . as Black Christian ladies are prone to do . . . at threshold . . . some plea to higher beings for forgiveness and the power to forgive . . .

I saw a photograph once of the mother of Emmett Till . . . a slight, brown woman with a pillbox hat . . . white gloves . . . eyes dark beyond pain . . . incomprehensibly looking at a world that never intended to see her son be a man . . . That same look is created each year . . . without the hat and gloves, for mother seals are not chic . . . at the Arctic Circle . . . That same look is in vogue in Atlanta, Cincinnati, Buffalo . . . for much the same reason . . . During one brief moment, for one passing wrinkle in time, Nancy Reagan wore that look . . . sharing a bond, as yet unconsummated . . . with Betty Shabazz, Jacqueline Kennedy, Coretta King, Ethel Kennedy . . . The wives and mothers are not so radically different . . . It is the hands of the women which massage the balm . . . the ointments . . . the lotions into the bodies for burial . . . It is our hands which: cover the eyes of small children . . . soothe the longing of the brothers . . . make the beds . . . set the tables . . . wipe away our own grief . . . to give comfort to those beyond comfort . . .

I yield from women whose hands are Black and rough . . . The women who produced me are in defiance of Porcelana and Jergens lotion . . . are ignorant of Madge's need to soak their fingernails in Palmolive dishwashing

Laura Wheeler Waring, *Anna Washington Derry*, 1927. Oil on canvas,
20 × 16 in. National Museum of American Art, Smithsonian Institution,
Washington D.C. Gift of the Harmon Foundation.

liquid . . . My women look at cracked . . . jagged fingernails that will never be adequately disguised by Revlon's new spring reds . . . We of the unacceptably strong take pride in the strength of our hands . . .

Some people think a quilt is a blanket stretched across a Lincoln bed . . . or from frames on a wall . . . a quaint museum piece to be purchased on Bloomingdale's 30-day same-as-cash plan . . . Quilts are our mosaics . . . **Michelle-Angelo's** contribution to beauty . . . We weave a quilt with dry, rough hands . . . Quilts are the way our lives are lived . . . We survive on patches . . . scraps . . . the leftovers from a materially richer culture . . . the throwaways from those with emotional options . . . We do the far more difficult job of taking that which nobody wants and not only loving it . . . not only seeing its worth . . . but making it lovable . . . and intrinsically worthwhile . . .

Though trite . . . it's nonetheless true . . . that a little knowledge is a dangerous thing . . . Perhaps pitiful thing would be more accurate . . . though that too is not profound . . . The more we experience the human drama . . . the more we are to understand . . . that whatever is not quite well about us will also not quite go away . . .

Sometimes . . . when it's something like Mother's Day . . . you really do wish you were smart enough to make the pain stop . . . to make the little hurts quit throbbing . . . to share with Star Trek's Spock the ability to touch your fingertips to the temples and make all the dumb . . . ugly . . . sad things of this world ease from memory . . . It's not at all that we fail to forgive others for the hurts we have received . . . we cannot forgive ourselves for the hurts we have meted . . . So . . . of course . . . we use our hands to push away rather than to pull closer . . .

Cumulus clouds . . . we learn in the 5th grade . . . always travel in families . . . They appear to be a friendly group . . . If you see one

. . . others will soon follow . . . and you have to be very careful not to just lie on your back . . . putting aside all serious chores for the rest of the day . . . to watch the procession pass . . . I wish I were a cumulus cloud . . . then I could control the sunshine . . . Not the sun shining because it shines every day . . . it's just that some days we fail to see it . . . I don't want to be any of those altospheric clouds that lay a dark, threatening cover . . . I want to be a friendly cotton ball playing in the blue . . . calling, as all cotton clouds do . . . my family around me . . . It was very clever of nature to invent both cumulus clouds and mothers . . . Both would be nice to hold . . . but you can't squeeze too tight . . . They are not . . . after all . . . oranges or grapefruits . . . though a tough skin would probably be a help on days when daddy has a bear inside struggling to get out . . . and the kids have ants in their pants . . .

We look . . . in vain . . . for an image of mothers . . . for an analogy for families . . . for a reason to continue . . . We live . . . mostly because we don't know any better . . . as best we can . . . Some of us are lucky . . . we learn to like ourselves . . . to forgive ourselves . . . to care about others . . . Some of us . . . on special occasions . . . watch the ladies in the purple velvet house slippers with the long black dresses come in from Sunday worship and we realize **man** never stood up to catch and kill prey . . . **man** never reared up on his hind legs to free his front parts to hold weapons . . . WOMAN stood to free her hands . . . to hold her young . . . to embrace her sons and lovers . . . WOMAN stood to applaud and cheer a delicate mate who needs her approval . . . WOMAN stood to wipe the tears and sweat . . . to touch the eyes and lips . . . that woman stood to free the arms which hold the hands . . . which hold.

FROM ALL STORIES ARE TRUE
John Edgar Wideman

My mother is standing on her porch, May 10, 1991. Early morning and the street is quiet now, as peaceful as it gets here, as peaceful as it always stays in other neighborhoods, invisible, not a half mile away behind the tree-topped ridge that separates Tokay, Susquehanna, Dunfermline, Seagirt from their neighbors to the west. The litany of streets always sweet on my tongue. I think I murmur their names, a silence unless you are inside my skull, sing them as a kind of background music that doesn't break the quiet of morning. If I'm not reciting them to myself, I hear the names anyway coming from somewhere else, a place that also knows what lies within the sound of these streets said to oneself again and again. Footsteps, voices, a skein of life dragged bead by bead through a soft needle's eye. And knows the names of streets can open like the gates of a great city, everyone who's ever inhabited the city, walked its streets, suddenly, like a shimmer, like the first notes of a Monk solo, breathing, moving, a world quickens as the gates swing apart. And knows my mother is not alone on her porch this May morning. Knows she hears beneath the stillness enveloping her the sounds of street names, what is animated when they are recalled. The presence of other souls as palpable as light playing in the edges of her robe. Her mother and father and children. Her brother and sisters. Grands and great-grands. The man I have become and those whom I've lost becoming him. The song of street names a medium in which we all float, suspended, as if each of us is someone's precious, precious child who must never be allowed to slip from the arms cradling, rocking. And knows my mother is listening to time, time voiced in no manmade measurements of days or minutes or years, time playing as it always must, background or foreground or taking up all the space we have, a tape of the street names chanted that releases every Homewood footstep she's ever heard or dreamed.

I'm afraid for her. Experience one of those moments of missing her intensely, her gone, final good-byes said, though she is here, just ten feet away, through the front door screen, framed by two of the rusty wrought-iron columns supporting the roof. A moment where fear of losing her overwhelms me to such an extent that I am bereft, helpless, unconsoled even by her presence, one price I pay for other moments when she's thousands of miles away and I've needed her and she is there, *there* beside me. After nine months of chemo her hair has grown in again, softer, curlier. Many shades of bushy gray and a crown of lighter hair, nearly white, nearly spun of invisibility by morning. I'm aware as I seldom am of her dimensions, how tall, how wide, how much this woman on the porch with her newborn's hair weighs. I need what is tangible, no matter how small she turns out to be, to offset words like frail and vulnerable I can't help saying to myself, words popping up though I try not to think them. I hate words with the power to take her away. *Frail. Old.* The effort of denying them makes her disappear anyway. My eyes cross Tokay, counting cobblestones as they go, remarking the incredible steepness of the street slanting out of my field of vision, the broken curbs and littered gutters, settling on the gigantic tree islanded in the delta where Seagirt and Tokay converge and Bricelyn begins. If the downtown wedge of skyscrapers where three rivers meet is the city's Golden Triangle, this could be its Green Triangle. A massive tree centuries old holds out against the odds here across from my mother's house, one of the biggest trees in Pittsburgh, anchored in a green triangle of weeds and bushes, trunk thick as a Buick, black as night after rain soaks its striated hide. Huge spread of its branches canopies the foot of the hill where the streets come together. Certain times of day in summer it shades my mother's front porch. If it ever tore loose from its moorings, it would crush her house like a sledgehammer. As big as it is, its roots must run under her cellar. The sound of it drinking, lapping nourishment deep underground is part of the quiet when her house is empty. How the tree survived a city growing around it is a mystery. For years no more than a twig, a sapling, a switch someone could have snapped off to beat a balky animal, swat a child's behind. I see a dark fist exploding through the asphalt, thrusting to the sky, the fingers opening, multiplying, fanning outward to form a vast umbrella of foliage. The arm behind it petrifies, other thick limbs burst from knots of hardened flesh, each one duplicating the fan of leaves, the delicate network of branches, thinning, twisting as they climb higher and farther from the source. Full-blown in a matter of seconds, ready to stand here across from my mother's house forever, till its time to be undone in the twinkling of an eye, just the way it arrived.

I didn't say any of this to my mother as I pushed through the screen door with my cup of coffee to join her on the porch. Then it was just one quiet thing after the other, a matter of seconds, the sight of her standing still, her back to me, me thinking thoughts that flashed at warp speed but would take forever to unpack, the door creaking, her turning slowly towards the noise, *You up, Baby,* a quick welcoming smile before she turns back to whatever it was, wherever she was gazing when I saw her first, small, bathed in the soft, remorseless light of morning, when I heard the sound of Homewood street names playing, transforming a commonplace scene into something else, restoring the invisible omnipresence of time, the enabling medium, what brought you to this moment and will carry you away, how things begin and end, always, you about to step out onto your mother's porch, catching her staring off at something, somewhere, home again, morning again, steamy coffee mug in one hand, sure of what you will do next, your fingers press the doorframe, pushing, absolutely unsure, fearing what will happen next, wondering what's in her eyes, behind them this morning in May, and which ghosts crowd the porch, regretting her privacy you are invading with yours. Who will the two of you together summon if you steal her attention, if you are ready and willing to offer yours, if you can break away from the tune playing over and over in your head and maybe in hers of the street names, sorrow and loss in every syllable when you say them to yourself the way you must to locate yourself here, back home in Pittsburgh this morning, Tioga Susquehanna Seagirt Cassina, praying your mother won't move, won't be gone before you reach her.

You hug each other. Not hard, not soft. Briefly. Long enough to remember everything.

PATHWAY:
FROM SON TO FATHER
Lenard D. Moore

Father, how sharp you stand
in the mirror.
I see myself.
Your praise and love—
something any son weeps for—
overtake me.

I remember you young, teaching me
to set out tomato slips,
the earth already scooped
in the morning light,
thin roots and
water from the dripping bucket.

You taught me, hungry,
a finger pointing into the void
and you were Moses
leaning against the backyard fence.

You picked roses for mother to
put on the table with dinner.
A woman of grandeur

who'd go beyond ordinary cause for family.
Her dreams were large.

I am a man, your oldest son,
praying depths of silence,
for a son to show the pathway,
a daughter to pick the whitest rose.

LETTER—JAMES S. WATSON TO JAMES L. WATSON

MUNICIPAL COURT OF THE CITY OF NEW YORK

BOROUGH OF MANHATTAN

8 READE STREET

NEW YORK

JUSTICES' CHAMBERS
James S. Watson, Justice

January 23, 1943

Our fond son, Skiz:

You are leaving home and your loved ones to render patriotic service to your country, with the possibility of covering yourself with glory in paving the way for future achievements.

At all times and into whatsoever paths destiny may lead you, the fervent prayers of mother and dad, as well as those of your devoted sisters and brother, will be offered for your protection and guidance and for your safe return.

"In all thy ways acknowledge Him and He shall direct thy paths." Be true to your God, loyal to your country and a source of inspiration to your fellow soldiers.

We salute you in the name of Him who watches over all of us.

With the tenderest affection and devotion, we leave you into His hands.

Lovingly,
Dad and Mother

Private James L. Watson
No. *32720225 U.S. Army*

LETTER—JAMES L. WATSON TO JAMES S. WATSON

May 25, 1944

*M*y dear Father,

Well, Dad, by the time you receive this letter I imagine it will be your birthday. Dad, I just want to wish you the happiest birthday that a son could wish his father. I know that you will have many more. I only hope and pray that when your birthday rolls around again that I will be there to celebrate it with you.

Dad, I could go on and write volumes about just what having you as a father has meant to me, but I don't think it necessary. All I have to say is that you're all that a fellow, any fellow, could hope for. Your kindness, unselfishness, love, and devotion to not only me but the rest of the family leaves nothing else to be desired in a man and a father.

Many times before I've realized how fortunate I was to have a father like you and now that I'm in the Army I realize more than ever what a lucky fellow I am to have you as my Dad. Now, I'm not referring to your position in society as Justice James S. Watson. I'm just talking about Jimmy Watson the man and Dad the father. Even if you were just a street cleaner you would still be one of the great men of our race and you certainly couldn't be any better as a father. I cherish and hold dear to me the wisdom and advice which you have handed down to me and only hope that I can be half the man that you are.

You see I told you that I could write volumes and already I've started. I guess the only thing to say is, "Thanks for everything, Dad." Remember the words to that poem which says "Life has been much sweeter since I've had you as a friend."

Please give my love to Mother, Grace, Barbara and Doug. And all the rest. Tell Barb that I received the candy and the newspapers and I'll send her a letter soon.

Your devoted and loving son,
"Skiz"

P.S.

Say, Dad, I have saved fifty dollars. Now if you need it for anything, don't hesitate to call on me. I know how things are. And remember I'm a man now and I am a member of the Watson Family (share, share, share alike). Well, I'd like to share in some of the responsibility, too.

Hughie Lee Smith, *The Couple*, 1989. Oil on canvas, 36 × 42 in. Collection of Mrs. Al Roker. Courtesy of June Kelly Gallery, Inc., New York, NY. Photo: Manu Sassoonian.

FROM OUR CHILDREN ARE NOT THINGS
Howard Thurman

It is in order to think about children and our relationship to them. Often we underestimate both our influence and our responsibility with reference to children because they do not seem to be mindful of our presence except in terms of something to resist. The world of the adult is in some ways a different world from that of the child. We bring to bear upon life the cumulative judgment garnered from our years of living, of trial and error, of many, many discoveries along the way. It is from that kind of context that we judge the behavior of children.

But they have not lived and there is much that can be known and understood only from the harvest of the years. This fact should not blind us to the profound way in which we determine even in detail the attitudes and the very structure of the child's thought. If we are good to the child and to other people, he will get from us directly a conception of goodness more profound and significant than all the words we may use about goodness as an ideal. If we lose our temper and give way to hard, brittle words which we fling around and about, the child learns more profoundly and significantly than all the formal teaching about self-control which may be offered him.

If we love a child, and the child senses from our relationship with others that we love them, he will get a concept of love that all the subsequent hatred in the world will never quite be able to destroy. It is idle to teach the child formally about respect for other people or other groups if in the little ways we demonstrate that we have no authentic respect for other people and other groups. The feeling tone and insight of the child are apt to be unerring. It is not important whether the child is able to comprehend the words we use or understand the ideas that we may articulate. The child draws his *meaning* from the meaning which we put into things that we do and say. Let us not be deceived.

We may incorporate in our formal planning all kinds of ideas for the benefit of the children. We may provide them with tools of various kinds. But if there is not genuineness in our climate, if in little ways we regard them as nuisances, as irritations, as *things* in the way of our pursuits, they will know that we do not love them and that our religion has no contagion for them. Let us gather around our children and give to them the security that can come only from associating with adults who mean what they say and who share in deeds which are broadcast in words.

IMAGE OF MYSELF 3

Ira B. Jones

my sons and daughters are like the first twinkling of the stars
eternally embedded in beauty like their mother the sky Goddess
i watch them grow each day with wide watchful eyes
their lives glowing like moons caressed by my darkness
as the world blindly asks me if i am sensitive
i silently answer as i spin on my own axis
wrapping my arms around my children and kissing them
they become the universe

James A. Porter,
Playground, n.d.
Oil on canvas,
16 × 14 in.
Collection of
Professor and Mrs.
David C. Driskell.

NOW THAT I AM
FOREVER WITH CHILD
Audre Lorde

How the days went
while you were blooming within me
I remember   each upon each
the swelling changed planes of my body

how you first fluttered   then jumped
and I thought it was my heart.

How the days wound down
and the turning of winter
I recall   you
growing heavy against the wind.
I thought   now her hands
are formed   her hair
has started to curl
now her teeth are done
now she sneezes.

Then the seed opened.
I bore you one morning
just before spring
my head rang like a fiery piston
my legs were towers between which
a new world was passing.

Since then
I can only distinguish
one thread within running hours
you   flowing through selves
toward You.

(1963)

OF THE PASSING OF THE FIRST-BORN
W. E. B. Du Bois

O sister, sister, thy first-begotten,
The hands that cling and the feet that follow,
The voice of the child's blood crying yet,
Who hath remembered me? who hath forgotten?
Thou hast forgotten, O summer swallow,
But the world shall end when I forget.

SWINBURNE

"Unto you a child is born," sang the bit of yellow paper that fluttered into my room one brown October morning. Then the fear of fatherhood mingled wildly with the joy of creation; I wondered how it looked and how it felt,—what were its eyes, and how its hair curled and crumpled itself. And I thought in awe of her,—she who had slept with Death to tear a man-child from underneath her heart, while I was unconsciously wandering. I fled to my wife and child, repeating the while to myself half wonderingly, "Wife and child? Wife and child?"—fled fast and faster than boat and steam-car, and yet must ever impatiently await them; away from the hard-voiced city, away from the flickering sea into my own Berkshire Hills that sit all sadly guarding the gates of Massachusetts.

Up the stairs I ran to the wan mother and whimpering babe, to the sanctuary on whose altar a life at my bidding had offered itself to win a life, and won. What is this tiny formless thing, this new-born wail from an unknown world,—all head and voice? I handle it curiously, and watch perplexed its winking, breathing, and sneezing. I did not love it then; it seemed a ludicrous thing to love; but her I loved, my girl-mother, she whom now I saw unfolding like the glory of the morning—the transfigured woman.

Through her I came to love the wee thing, as it grew and waxed strong; as its little soul unfolded itself in twitter and cry and half-formed word, and as its eyes caught the gleam and flash of life. How beautiful he was, with his olive-tinted flesh and dark gold ringlets, his eyes of mingled blue and brown, his perfect little limbs, and the soft voluptuous roll which the blood of Africa had moulded into his features! I held him in my arms, after we had sped far away to our Southern home,—held him, and glanced at the hot red soil of Georgia and the breathless city of a hundred hills, and felt a vague unrest. Why was his hair tinted with gold? An evil omen was golden hair in my life. Why had not the brown of his eyes crushed out and killed the blue?—for brown were his father's eyes, and his father's father's. And thus in the Land of the Color-line I saw, as it fell across my baby, the shadow of the Veil.

Within the Veil was he born, said I; and there within shall he live,—a Negro and a Negro's son. Holding in that little head—ah, bitterly!—the unbowed pride of a hunted race, clinging with that tiny dimpled hand—ah, wearily!—to a hope not hopeless but unhopeful, and seeing with those bright wondering eyes that peer into my soul a land whose freedom is to us a mockery and whose liberty a lie. I saw the shadow of the Veil as it passed over my baby, I saw the cold city towering above the blood-red land. I held my face beside his little cheek, showed him the star-children and the twinkling lights as they began to flash, and stilled with an evensong the unvoiced terror of my life.

So sturdy and masterful he grew, so filled with bubbling life, so

tremulous with the unspoken wisdom of a life but eighteen months distant
from the All-life,—we were not far from worshipping this revelation of the
divine, my wife and I. Her own life builded and moulded itself upon the
child; he tinged her every dream and idealized her every effort. No hands
but hers must touch and garnish those little limbs; no dress or frill must
touch them that had not wearied her fingers; no voice but hers could coax
him off to Dreamland, and she and he together spoke some soft and unknown tongue and in it held communion. I too mused above his little white
bed; saw the strength of my own arm stretched onward through the ages
through the newer strength of his; saw the dream of my black fathers stagger
a step onward in the wild phantasm of the world; heard in his baby voice the
voice of the Prophet that was to rise within the Veil.

And so we dreamed and loved and planned by fall and winter, and the
full flush of the long Southern spring, till the hot winds rolled from the fetid
Gulf, till the roses shivered and the still stern sun quivered its awful light
over the hills of Atlanta. And then one night the little feet pattered wearily
to the wee white bed, and the tiny hands trembled; and a warm flushed face
tossed on the pillow, and we knew baby was sick. Ten days he lay there,—a
swift week and three endless days, wasting, wasting away. Cheerily the
mother nursed him the first days, and laughed into the little eyes that smiled
again. Tenderly then she hovered round him, till the smile fled away and Fear
crouched beside the little bed.

Then the day ended not, and night was a dreamless terror, and joy and
sleep slipped away. I hear now that Voice at midnight calling me from dull
and dreamless trance,—crying, "The Shadow of Death! The Shadow of
Death!" Out into the starlight I crept, to rouse the gray physician,—
the Shadow of Death, the Shadow of Death. The hours trembled on; the
night listened; the ghastly dawn glided like a tired thing across the lamplight.
Then we two alone looked upon the child as he turned toward us with great
eyes, and stretched his string-like hands,—the Shadow of Death! And we
spoke no word, and turned away.

He died at eventide, when the sun lay like a brooding sorrow above the western hills, veiling its face; when the winds spoke not, and the trees, the great green trees he loved, stood motionless. I saw his breath beat quicker and quicker, pause, and then his little soul leapt like a star that travels in the night and left a world of darkness in its train. The day changed not; the same tall trees peeped in at the windows, the same green grass glinted in the setting sun. Only in the chamber of death writhed the world's most piteous thing—a childless mother.

I shirk not. I long for work. I pant for a life full of striving. I am no coward, to shrink before the rugged rush of the storm, nor even quail before the awful shadow of the Veil. But hearken, O Death! Is not this my life hard enough,—is not that dull land that stretches its sneering web about me cold enough,—is not all the world beyond these four little walls pitiless enough, but that thou must needs enter here,—thou, O Death? About my head the thundering storm beat like a heartless voice, and the crazy forest pulsed with the curses of the weak; but what cared I, within my home beside my wife and baby boy? Wast thou so jealous of one little coign of happiness that thou must needs enter there,—thou, O Death?

A perfect life was his, all joy and love, with tears to make it brighter,— sweet as a summer's day beside the Housatonic. The world loved him; the women kissed his curls, the men looked gravely into his wonderful eyes, and the children hovered and fluttered about him. I can see him now, changing like the sky from sparkling laughter to darkening frowns, and then to wondering thoughtfulness as he watched the world. He knew no color-line, poor dear,—and the Veil, though it shadowed him, had not yet darkened half his sun. He loved the white matron, he loved his black nurse; and in his little world walked souls alone, uncolored and unclothed. I—yea, all men—are larger and purer by the infinite breadth of that one little life. She who in simple clearness of vision sees beyond the stars said when he had flown, "He will be happy There; he ever loved beautiful things." And I, far more ignorant, and blind by the web of mine own weaving, sit alone winding words and muttering, "If still he be, and he be There, and there be a There, let him be happy, O Fate!"

Blithe was the morning of his burial, with bird and song and sweet-smelling flowers. The trees whispered to the grass, but the children sat with hushed faces. And yet it seemed a ghostly unreal day,—the wraith of Life. We seemed to rumble down an unknown street behind a little white bundle of posies, with the shadow of a song in our ears. The busy city dinned about us; they did not say much, those pale-faced hurrying men and women; they did not say much,—they only glanced and said, "Niggers!"

We could not lay him in the ground there in Georgia, for the earth there is strangely red; so we bore him away to the northward, with his flowers and his little folded hands. In vain, in vain!—for where, O God! beneath thy broad blue sky shall my dark baby rest in peace,—where Reverence dwells, and Goodness, and a Freedom that is free?

All that day and all that night there sat an awful gladness in my heart,—nay, blame me not if I see the world thus darkly through the Veil,—and my soul whispers ever to me saying, "Not dead, not dead, but escaped; not bond, but free." No bitter meanness now shall sicken his baby heart till it die a living death, no taunt shall madden his happy boyhood. Fool that I was to think or wish that this little soul should grow choked and deformed within the Veil! I might have known that yonder deep unworldly look that ever and anon floated past his eyes was peering far beyond this narrow Now. In the poise of his little curl-crowned head did there not sit all that wild pride of being which his father had hardly crushed in his own heart? For what, forsooth, shall a Negro want with pride amid the studied humiliations of fifty million fellows? Well sped, my boy, before the world had dubbed your ambition insolence, had held your ideals unattainable, and taught you to cringe and bow. Better far this nameless void that stops my life than a sea of sorrow for you.

Idle words; he might have borne his burden more bravely than we,—aye, and found it lighter too, some day; for surely, surely this is not the end. Surely there shall yet dawn some mighty morning to lift the Veil and set the prisoned free. Not for me,—I shall die in my bonds,—but for fresh young souls who have not known the night and waken to the morning; a morning when men ask of the workman, not "Is he white?" but "Can he work?" When men ask artists, not "Are they black?" but "Do they know?" Some morning this may be, long, long years to come. But now there wails, on that dark shore within the Veil, the same deep voice, *Thou shalt forego!* And all have I foregone at that command, and with small complaint,—all save that fair young form that lies so coldly wed with death in the nest I had builded.

If one must have gone, why not I? Why may I not rest me from this restlessness and sleep from this wide waking? Was not the world's alembic, Time, in his young hands, and is not my time waning? Are there so many workers in the vineyard that the fair promise of this little body could lightly be tossed away? The wretched of my race that line the alleys of the nation sit fatherless and unmothered; but Love sat beside his cradle, and in his ear Wisdom waited to speak. Perhaps now he knows the All-love, and needs not to be wise. Sleep, then, child,—sleep till I sleep and waken to a baby voice and the ceaseless patter of little feet—above the Veil.

I WILL NOT LET THEM TAKE YOU

FOR JAWARA

Opal Palmer Adisa

tell them
them them loud and clear
i will not let them
take you
tell them
tell them your mother is
a crazy jamaican woman
who will wage war
for her children
so tell them
tell them now
i will not surrender
you to the streets
i will not give you over
to the dope dealers
i will not relinquish
you to the cops
who target you because
you are black and male
i will not let
you slip through
the school system
which acts as if
you are unteachable
so tell them

tell them
you have a mother
who remembers
all the fears
all the pain
all the discomfort
she endured in getting
you here
and she will not give you up
will not give you up
to no one but the love
of life and to help shape
the dreams
of our people

tell them

Aaron Douglas,
Boy with Toy Plane,
1938.
Oil on canvas,
22½ × 17 in.
Courtesy of
Walter O. Evans
Collection,
Detroit, MI.

FROM MISS EMILY'S GRANDSON WON'T
HUSH HIS MOUTH
Essex Hemphill

The last time I saw my grandmother was in the summer of 1986, in Columbia, South Carolina. I spent two cherished weeks with her. Columbia is the American ancestral home of my mother's family. To make this journey priceless, I brought along my niece, Shakira, who was seven at the time, and my nephew, Aaron, who was then two. It was their first time flying in a jet, but the last time they would see their great-grandmother alive. A year later, at the age of eighty-six, my grandmother died.

To all of her friends, neighbors, and church sisters, she was "Miss Emily," but to our family she was always "Mother," "Grandmother," or "Nana," names that are for us synonymous with faith, love, and selflessness.

During that two-week visit, the bond between Grandmother and me strengthened itself on pure love. It was the same love that disciplined me when I spent my summers with her as a youngster. And it was the same love that summoned me to Columbia with two great-grands in tow.

Although I promised my family I would not reveal my sexuality to Grandmother, I took a copy of *Earth Life* to give to her. On an early afternoon, a week after arriving in Columbia, while Grandmother sat rocking on the front porch, and while my niece and nephew settled into their afternoon nap, I pulled out the copy of *Earth Life* knowing the moment to give it to her had arrived. I considered it to be an innocent gift, although subconsciously I realized that she would learn more from it than I would ever be able to tell her in this life.

On that particular afternoon, I was going to the barber to get my hair cut. I gave Grandmother *Earth Life* before I left. I didn't think she would read it immediately, but she did, during the hour I was away. When I returned, she was still on the porch rocking. She complimented my haircut as I pulled up a chair to sit with her. *Earth Life* and her reading glasses were resting in her lap. She was rocking, gently, her eyes focusing straight ahead above the tops of the blossoming rose bushes growing around the porch. I thought she was focusing on the red rose petals or the sweet fruit on the fig tree across the yard. I carefully ventured to break the silence enveloping us. "Grandmother," I hesitantly began, "it looks as though you read *Earth Life* while I was at the barber."

"Yes, I did," she replied, and she continued to rock. After a pause, she said, "These are very good poems, Essex, but they're a bit disturbing." Another moment of silence enveloped us. "You know I'm so proud of all my grands," she continued, "all of you are doing so well." She then looked me directly in the eye and smiled just a little slyly before asking, "Essex, do the authorities know what you're writing about?"

Perched on the edge of tension as I had been, I was completely unprepared for her question. I threw my head and laughed deeply, and Grandmother joined me. When we regained our sobriety, I realized that her question was *very* serious, and that our laughter had helped us both to mask the implications.

"I guess they know what I'm writing about, Grandmother, but I can't really be concerned with the authorities," I offered.

"Some of this is very disturbing," she said, "and I just want you to be careful. I don't want you getting hurt out here."

"But Grandmother, isn't it important to tell the truth?"

"Yes, it is *always* important to tell the truth, but truth means different things to different people. Some people can't handle the truth, Essex. I just want you to be careful. I will always love you, and I will always be so proud of you and all of my grands. Each of you is special to me. It would break my heart to see any harm happen to any one of you."

"I'll always love you, too," I said, then I leaned over and kissed her on the cheek and hugged her.

Of the many things that I remember about Grandmother, her question "Do the authorities know what you're writing about?" and her cautioning me to be careful are the words that come back to me ringing with all the intensity and conviction of her love and concern. She could formulate such a question only because she had witnessed how dangerous it is for Black people to be outspoken in America.

Archibald J. Motley, Jr., *Mending Socks*, 1924. Oil on canvas, 43⁷/₈ × 40 in.
Ackland Art Museum, The University of North Carolina at Chapel Hill,
Burton Emmett Collection, Chapel Hill, NC.

LETTER—CLAUDE A. AND ETTA M. BARNETT TO MARIA BARNETT TINNIN

October 14, 1954

Dear Maria Barnett Tinnin:

Your grandmother and I send you the warmest sort of welcome. We are so glad you came to join our family circle. Both of us are anxious to see you and will do so at the very earliest moment.

Your Aunt Sue and Cousin Etta Sue both think you are wonderful.

What we really wanted was to be there when you were all together. I am disappointed that things turned out to prevent that happening next week.

As I think of all the little girls of our hue who come into the world, I am especially happy for you. You have been born to two parents who will love and cherish you, who will surround you not only with affection but with their brilliance of mind and infinite charm of personality.

They will guide you in paths which will make your life one of happiness and beauty and offside your grandmother and grandfather and all your other relatives will be praying that only that which is good and lovely may ever traverse your path.

Welcome again and tell your broad-shouldered Brother Freeman that we give him the special trust of looking after you.

With all our love,

Your Grandma & Grandpa

PART III

*A Jewel
for a Friend*

As children we have a dozen "best friends"; our choosing and unchoosing of them changes with the wind and is as fickle as a spring rain. Yet, as we grow older, we realize that a good friend is a treasure beyond compare precisely because we *can* choose them, unlike family who are dealt to us by the fates, like it or not. But a friend's counsel, given out of love not duty, is to be prized. Their loving advice can straighten our paths, their listening ear can help to preserve our sanity. When Ntozake Shange says so poignantly, "please come talk to me" in the poem "Pages for a Friend," we know the added dimension that beloved counsel can bring to our lives.

The melody of friendship is contained in these stories, letters, and poems. Sometimes the melody is wistful and longing, like Shange's poem. Or it is the praises of a friend joyfully sung by a mature voice like Sue Bailey Thurman, one that recognizes the value of an earthly beloved counselor. But often, as Toi Derricotte, J. California Cooper, and Saundra Murray Nettles tell, friendship is about an emotional connection that transcends the pain we cause each other or the world inflicts upon us. And when that pain is sometimes too great, it is friends like Gloria Wade-Gayles who bring us back to a recognition of the love we still have left to give. And how our friendships and romantic loves interrelate can be the field for jealousy or healing, as Cooper's and Wendell Hooper's tales illustrate.

Both Hooper and poet Peter J. Harris speak of a special bond between African-American men that too often is ignored or misunderstood in the words our sisters so readily summon to speak of friendship. But read their testimony and hear the notes of profound love and healing to be found in the true brotherhood of Black men.

Sometimes friendship turns to love. In our case, ten years' worth of sharing popcorn while watching "Saturday Night Live," recipes via long-distance telephone and gifts of cookbooks, secrets, dreams, and plans began to expand to our seeing each other as essential to the happiness we both wanted in life and love. Nikki Giovanni's "Poem of Friendship," then, strikes a special chord for us, one we believe is essential to success if friends should become lovers.

PAGES FOR A FRIEND
Ntozake Shange

letters from friends used to be an art form
literary exquisite observations of the soul
aesthetics and compulsions to give
order to whatever this life is
pages for a friend kept many a prairie
woman / lingering by her fire in a sod house
from committing suicide / some prairie
women killed themselves anyway
the letters from their friends
crushed in their fists / the same
fists that beat walls trying to
keep up enough anger not to die
not to burn the kettle swinging
over the fire / the ladle too hot to handle
loneliness stalking the
       farmyard a warring Comanche

pages for a friend fluttering off
in the wind / lost breaths wishes
dying for someone to loom over the horizon
anyone / come talk / please come talk to me / now
i've no one to write
i'm so lonely i'm not sure i remember
how it is you read
you see i've memorized all the letters
my woman friends sent me

i could recite some to you
let me make some coffee &
we could sit & talk
please, mister, let's just talk
before i forget how & become silence.

LETTER — MRS. SUE BAILEY THURMAN
TO META W. FULLER

San Francisco
[before February 14, 1965]

earest Meta,

You know me so well (in the deep recesses of your being) that I did not need to write you about the outcome of the hasty trip to Florida and return to San Francisco, the closing days of the old year. Howard and Madaline (who has recovered through music so beautifully) took over for all the holiday festivities and I betook me to bed, coming out only for extensive medical tests required to track down a thyroid disorder, the causes of which have just been discovered.

All of this has deferred my return to Boston to see you and get all the information about your own progress which I'm so eager to hear.

As it stands now, I shall be coming in a few weeks, perhaps the first of March, to remain until late spring (in Boston and environs).

Today, I want to have you know how much joy and happiness your very existence and personal friendship have brought to me. Maybe it is a way of sending you an early "Valentine." Quoting from one rare poet that both of us have loved: "We are never far apart. . . . Have not the fates associated us in a thousand different ways? Is it of no significance that we have so long partaken of the same loaf, drank at the same fountain, breathed the same air, summer and winter, felt the same heat and cold, that the same fruits have been pleased to refresh us both, and we have never had a thought of different fibre the one from the other!"

So you know that I am always in the little room where you live, that *we are never far apart.*

I thought you would like this letter from Mrs. M.L. King, Jr., referring to your [sculpture] "Mother and Child." I told Coretta that she should be writing something in a diary every day—significant sentences that measure exact times in the symphony. . . .

Aren't you glad that your hands have so inspired her days? She will doubtless write you whenever she gets a moment from the exhausting life she lives.

Anne [Thurman, Sue and Howard Thurman's daughter] is coming to see you soon. Give Coretta's letter to her to return to me.

A kiss, a hug, and warmest love,
Sue

Lois Mailou Jones, *Sue Bailey Thurman*, 1944. Oil on canvas, 25 × 21½ in.
Courtesy of June Kelly Gallery, Inc., New York, NY.

A Jewel for a Friend
J. California Cooper

I have my son bring me down here to this homegrown graveyard two or three times a week so I can clean it and sweep it and sit here among my friends in my rocking chair under this Sycamore tree, where I will be buried one day, soon now, I hope. I'm 90 years old and I am tired . . . and I miss all my friends too. I come back to visit them because ain't nobody left in town but a few old doddering fools I didn't bother with when I was younger so why go bothern now just cause we all hangin on? Its peaceful here. The wind is soft, the sun is gentle even in the deep summer. Maybe its the cold that comes from under the ground that keeps it cool. I don't know. I only know that I like to rest here in my final restin place and know how its gonna be a thousand years after I am put here under that stone I have bought and paid for long ago . . . long ago.

After I eat my lunch and rest a bit, I gets down to my real work here in this graveyard! I pack a hammer and chisel in my bags and when I's alone, I take them and go over to Tommy Jones' beautiful tombstone his fancy daughter bought for him and chip, grind and break away little pieces of it! Been doin it for eleven years now and its most half gone. I ain't gonna die til its all gone! Then I be at peace! I ain't got to tell a wise one that I hate Tommy Jones, you must know that yourself now! . . . If I am killin his tombstone! I hate him. See, his wife, my friend, Pearl, used to lay next to him, but I had her moved, kinda secret like, least without tellin anyone. I hired two mens to dig her coffin up and move her over here next to where I'm going to be and they didn't know nobody and ain't told nobody. It don't matter none noway cause who gon pay somebody to dig her up again? And put her back? Who cares bout her? . . . and where she lay for eternity? Nobody! But me . . . I do.

See, we growed up together. I am Ruby and she is Pearl and we was jewels. We use to always say that. We use to act out how these jewels would act. I was always strong, deep red and solid deep. She was brown but she was all lightness and frail and innocent, smooth and weak and later on I realized, made out of pain.

I grew up in a big sprawling family and my sons take after them, while Pearl growed up in a little puny one. Her mama kissed her daddy's ass til he kicked her's on way from here! That's her grave way over there . . . Way, way over there in the corner. That's his with that cement marker, from when he died two years later from six bullets in his face by another woman what didn't take that kickin stuff! Well, they say what goes around . . . But "they" says all kinda things . . . can't be sure bout nothin "they" says. Just watch your Bible . . . that's the best thing I ever seen and I'm 90! Now!

Anyway, Pearl and me grew up round here, went to school and all. A two room school with a hall down the middle. Pearl nice and everybody should of liked her, but they didn't. Them girls was always pickin on her, til I get in it. See, I was not so nice and everybody did like me! Just loved me sometime! I pertected her. I wouldn't let nobody hurt her! Some of em got mad at me, but what could they do? I rather fight than eat! Use to eat a'-plenty too! I was a big strong, long-armed and long-legged girl. Big head, short hair. I loved my eyes tho! Oh, they was pretty. They still strong! And I had pretty hands, even with all that field work, they still was pretty! My great-grandchildren takes care of em for me now . . . rubs em and all. So I can get out here two or three times a week and hammer Tommy Jones' gravestone. Its almost half gone now . . . so am I.

When we got to marryin time . . . everybody got to that, some in love and some just tryin to get away from a home what was full of house work and field work and baby sister and brother work. I don't know how we was all too dumb to know, even when we got married and in a place of our own, it was all headin down to the same road we thought we was gettin away from! Well, I went after Gee Cee! He was the biggest boy out there and suited me just fine! I use to run that man with rocks and sticks and beat him up even. He wouldn't hurt me, you know, just play. But I finally got him to thinkin he loved me and one night, over there by the creek behind the church, way behind the church, I gave him somethin he musta not forgot . . . and we was soon gettin married. I didn't forget it . . . I named it George, Jr. That was my first son.

In the meantime the boys all seem to like Pearl and she grinned at all of em! She seem to be kinda extra stuck on that skinny rail, Tommy Jones, with the bare spot on the side of his head! He liked everybody! A girl couldn't pass by him without his hand on em, quick and fast and gone. I didn't like him! Too shifty for me . . . a liar! I can't stand a liar! His family had a little money and he always looked nice but he still wasn't nothin but a nice lookin liar what was shifty! Still and all, when I had done pushed Pearl around a few times tryin to make her not like him, he began to press on her and every way she turned, he was there! He just wouldn't let up when he saw I didn't like him for her! He gave her little trinkets and little cakes, flowers, home picked. Finally she let him in her deepest life and soon she was pregnant and then he got mad cause he had to marry her! I fought against that and when he found out it made him grin all the way through the little ceremony. I was her best lady or whatever you call it, cause I was her best friend.

Then everything was over and we was all married and havin children and life got a roll on and we had to roll with it and that took all our energies to survive and soon we was back in the same picture we had run away from cept the faces had changed. Stead of mama's faces, they was ours. And daddy's was the men we had married. Lots of times the stove and sink was the same and the plow was the same. In time, the mules changed.

Well, in time, everything happened. I had three sons and two daughters, big ones! Liked to kill me even gettin here! Pearl had one son and one daughter. Son was just like his daddy and daughter was frail and sickly. I think love makes you healthy and I think that child was sickly cause wasn't much love in that house of Pearl's, not much laughter. Tommy Jones, after the second child, never made love to Pearl again regular, maybe a year or two or three apart. She stayed faithful, but hell, faithful to what? He had done inherited some money and was burnin these roads up! He'd be a hundred miles away for a week or two, whole lotta times. Pearl worked, takin them children with her when I could'n keep em. But I had to rest sometimes, hell! I had five of my own and I had done told her bout that Tommy Jones anyway! But I still looked out for her and fed em when she couldn't. Yet and still, when he came home he just fall in the bed and sleep and sleep til time to get up and bathe and dress in the clothes he bought hisself and leave them again! If she cry and complain he just laugh and leave. I guess that's what you call leavin them laughin or somethin!

One day he slapped her and when he saw she wasn't gonna do nothin but just cry and take it, that came to be a regular thing! For years, I mean years, I never went over her house to take food when she didn't have some beatin up marks on her! I mean it! That's when she started comin over to the cemetery to clean it up and find her place. She also began savin a nickel here and a dime there to pay for her gravestone. That's what she dreamed about! Can you imagine that?!! A young, sposed to be healthy woman daydreamin bout dyin!!? Well, she did! And carried that money faithfully to the white man sells them things and paid on a neat little ruby colored stone, what he was puttin her name on, just leavin the dates out! Now!

My sons was gettin married, havin babies, strong like they mama and papa, when her son got killed, trying to be like his daddy! He had done screwed the wrong man's daughter! They put what was left of him in that grave over there, behind that bush of roses Pearl planted years ago to remember him by. Well, what can I say? I'm a mother, she was a mother, you love them no matter what! The daughter had strengthened up and was goin on to school somewhere with the help of her father's people. And you know, she didn't give her mother no concern, no respect? Treated her like the house dog in a manger. I just don't blieve you can have any luck like that! It takes time, sometime, to get the payback, but time is always rollin on and one day, it will roll over you! Anyway even when the daughter had made it up to a young lady and was schoolin with the sons and daughters of black business people, she almost forgot her daddy too! She was gonna marry a man with SOMETHIN and she didn't want them at the weddin! Now! And tole em! Her daddy went anyway, so she dressed him cause he was broke now, and after the weddin, got his drunk ass out of town quick as lightnin cross the sky and he came home and taunted Pearl that her own daughter didn't love her! Now!

Well, time went on, I had troubles with such a big family, grandchildren comin and all. Love, love, love everywhere, cause I didn't low nothin else! Pretty faces, pretty smiles, round, fat stomachs, and pigtails flying every-

Richard Mayhew, *Spiritual Space Series #1*, 1993. Watercolor/pastel on paper, 29 × 36½ in. Courtesy of Alitash Kebede Fine Art, Los Angeles, CA.

where and pretty nappy-headed boys growin up to be president someday, even if they never were . . . they was my presidents and congressmen! I could chew em up and swollow em sometimes, even today, grown as they are! We could take care of our problems, they was just livin problems . . . everyday kinds.

Pearl just seem to get quiet way back in her mind and heart. She went on, but she was workin harder to pay for that tombstone. The name was complete, only the last date was open and finally it was paid for. With blood, sweat and tears for true . . . seem like that's too much to pay for dyin!

One night I had bathed and smelled myself up for that old hard head of mine, Gee Cee, when a neighbor of Pearl's came runnin over screamin that Tommy Jones was really beatin up on Pearl. I threw my clothes on fast as I could and ran all the way and I was comin into some age then, runnin was not what I planned to do much of! When I got there, he had done seen me comin and he was gone, long gone, on them long, narrow, quick to run to mischief feet of his! I had got there in time to keep him from accidently killin her, but she was pretty well beat! He had wanted her rent and food money, she said, but she would not give it to him, so he beat her. She cried and held on to me, she was so frail, so little, but she was still pretty to me, little grey hairs and all. She thanked me as I washed her and changed the bed and combed her hair and fed her some warm soup and milk. She cried a little as she was tellin me all she ever wanted was a little love like I had. I cried too and told her that's all anybody wants.

When I was through fixin her and she was restin nice and easy, I sat by the bed and pulled the covers up and she said, "Hold my hand, I'm so cold." Well I grabbed her hand and held, then I rubbed her arms tryin to keep her warm and alive. Then, I don't know, life just kept rollin and I began to rub her whole little beautiful sore body . . . all over . . . and when I got to them bruised places I kissed them and licked them too and placed my body beside her body in her bed and the love for her just flowed and flowed. One minute I loved her like a child, the next like a mother, then she was the mother, then I was the child, then as a woman friend, then as a man. Ohh-hhh, I loved her. I didn't know exactly what to do but my body did it for me and I did everything I could to make her feel loved and make her feel like Gee Cee makes me feel, so I did everything I could that he had ever done to me to make me feel good, but I forgot Gee Cee . . . and I cried. Not sad crying, happy cryin, and my tears and my love were all over her and she was holding me. She was holding me . . . so close, so close. Then we slept and when I wakened up, I went home . . . and I felt good, not bad. I know you don't need nothin "forever," just so you get close to love sometime.

Well Pearl got better. When we saw each other, we weren't embarrassed or shamed. She hit me on my shoulder and I thumped her on her head as we had done all our lives anyway. We never did it again, we didn't have to!

Pearl wasn't made, I guess, for the kind of life she had somehow chosen, so a few years later she died and Tommy Jones picked her plot, right over there where she used to be, and put her there and the tombstone man put that old-brand-new ruby colored gravestone on her grave. The preacher said a few words cause there wasn't much to pay him with and we all went home to our own lifes, of course.

Soon, I commence to comin over here and sweepin and cleanin up and plantin plants around and this ole Sycamore tree, Pearl had planted at her house, was moved over here before Tommy Jones got put out for not payin rent. I planted it right here over where Gee Cee, me and Pearl gonna be. I likes shade. Anyway I was out here so much that's how I was able to notice the day Pearl's tombstone disappeared. Well, I like to died! I knew what that tombstone had gone through to get there! Right away I had my sons get out and find out what had happened and they found out that Tommy Jones was livin mighty hard and was mighty broke and had stole that tombstone and took it way off and sold it for a few dollars! You can chisel the name off, you know? But I can't understand what anyone would want a used tombstone for! I mean, for God's sake, get your own!! At least die first-class even if you couldn't live that way! Well, we couldn't find how to get it back so that's when I started payin on another one for her, and yes, for me and Gee Cee too. They's paid for now.

In the meantime, liquor and hard livin and a knife put Tommy Jones to rest, and imagine this, that daughter of theirs came down here and bought ONE gravestone for her DADDY!!! To hold up her name I guess, but that's all she did, then she left! Ain't been back!

Well, life goes on, don't it! Whew!

Now I come here over the years and chip away and chisel and hammer away cause he don't deserve no stone since he stole Pearl's. He never give her nothin but them two babies what was just like him and then he stole the last most important thing she wanted! So me, I'm gonna see that he don't have one either! When it's through, I'm gonna be through, then the grave-stone man can bring them two stones over here, they bought and paid for! And he can place them here beside each other, for the rest of thousands of years. I'm in the middle, between Gee Cee and Pearl, like I'm sposed to be. They don't say much, but Ruby and the dates and Pearl's on hers, and the dates. Then my husband's name and the children on mine and her children's on hers. And that's all. I mean, how much can a gravestone say anyway?

Afterword

After Ruby died at 91 years of age, Gee Cee was still living at 90 years of age and he had a marker laid across the two graves saying "Friends, all the way to the End." It's still there.

THE DRUGSTORE

Toi Derricotte

I'm sure most people don't go around all the time thinking about what race they are. When you look like what you are, your external mirrors reflect back to you an identity that you take for granted. However, for me those mirrors are broken, and my lack of consciousness takes on serious implications. Am I not conscious of my blackness because, like everyone else, I am just thinking of other things, or is it because I don't want to be conscious, am I mentally "passing"? In fact, in situations where I am not only conscious of being black but speak of it, I am taken to be white. Because of this I see things people recognizable as black don't see, for example, a salesperson who treats a darker person in a totally different manner. Often the occurrence is subtle, more sensed than provable, like the slightest breeze, and the other person, perhaps without the same basis for comparison, seems unaware.

That moment when I sense myself to be other than what people think I am, I often experience a feeling of isolation, fear, and self-consciousness. The emotions that sweep through me are painful and alarming, and this emotional state can happen many times, twenty or thirty, throughout a usual day.

When we moved into Upper Montclair, there were almost no black people who frequented the stores. When I went into the drugstore, I wondered if word had spread, if the pharmacist and clerks knew I was a member of the black family that had moved in—or if I was invisible, if they thought I was just another housewife. I didn't want to be treated "differently"; if they treated me differently, it meant they thought I was less, inferior. I felt my way through months, alert, like a worm taken out of the dirt, my head lifted, sniffing the air with my whole being.

I was afraid to ask for credit, even though the other women asked for a charge on their first visit, I was terrified to be rejected. I didn't say much; my personality wasn't exactly like theirs. I laughed at slightly different things. I thought they would be able to sense my fear.

One day, after I had spent several hundred dollars in the store, I asked for credit. The clerk didn't blink an eye. Maybe she doesn't know, I thought.

Archibald J. Motley, Jr., *Octoroon (Portrait of an Octoroon, The Octoroon)*, 1922.
Oil on canvas, 37¾ × 29¾ in. Collection of Hon. Norma Y. Dotson.

Slowly I began to bring myself into the store—my friendliness, my neighborly questions, "How is your wife doing?" I asked for advice: "Can you suggest a cold pill?" All the time I was charging, paying my bill on time, building bridges I walked on tentatively, holding my hat, watching for the escape route.

Months went by. I brought my jokes into the store, kidded the pharmacist. He laughed. Would he go over the line and say something belittling? I loosened up. We had worked out a way to speak to each other, not like the manager of the fruit store who found out I was black and started pinching my arm.

Months went by.

Toni Snead moved into Upper Montclair. She is dark, married to a doctor. We became friends because she was having many of the same self-doubts I was having. We talked together several times a week. We helped each other through hard times. We both saw a therapist.

I could go to her house when I had no place else to go, stop in her kitchen for a cup of coffee and sit with the dishes undone. She could see me in my torn bathrobe and dirty house shoes. There was so much we laughed about—like the time the couple from across the street came for dinner (I was showing off my remodeled kitchen) and, just as the doorbell rang, I stepped with my long gown into the deluxe Jenn-air fry pan full of grease that I had put, for a moment, on the floor. I had to go to the door dragging my soaked skirt, leaving a trail of slime like a mummy. I invited them into the kitchen and, as I mopped up the congealing grease and they sat with vodka and lime, large drops of water started to plunk on their heads. We looked up—a leak through the light fixture from upstairs where my husband had taken a shower.

We took delight in stories like that. We sat in our kitchens and howled, tears streaming down our faces. We were so glad to have found each other. I loved her because I felt so comfortable loving her, so unafraid that I would say the wrong thing. I knew no matter how much I hurt, she wouldn't hurt me more because of it.

Months went by. She was the only one who mattered. Let the others sink in the earth, let them be swept underground by earthquakes—every white house, neat lawn, every station wagon full of clean children, every cherry tree and rhododendron. Let them go to hell. She was the only one who mattered.

One day I was in the drugstore, shopping without thinking. I walked down the aisle like a known customer. I had a smile on my face. I felt someone touch my shoulder and it was Toni. When I saw her dark face, inside I felt my arms that were reaching for her pull away. My heart shrank, and everything came back—the months, the years, the fear of being recognized. As if I hated her! As if she were not the only living being in the world. I greeted her warmly, but my heart was a cold thing that could have been plucked out of my chest and eaten.

Years passed.

I told a white woman, a friend, what I had done. "Terrible," she said. "Terrible to deny someone in your heart you love." And she looked at me as if I were an ugly thing.

Years passed.

I told Toni—how I had hated to see her standing before me. How I had wanted her to disappear. She said she had known nothing of this when I touched her. I told her how I hated myself.

She held my hand. She did not say I was an ugly thing. She knew my black girl fear, even when it was her I hated.

She cried with me and loved me well.

FOR A FRIEND
WHO CONSIDERS SUICIDE
Gloria Wade-Gayles

I have no right to ask you to live
when you have already sharpened the blade
and found the strongest pulse.

You have fought the serpents longer than
the best of us, wrestling with their
thrashing tails and speaking sane above
the sound of their rattlers in your head.

When their fangs pierced your skin again
and again, it was your mouth
not mine
that found the marks
and cleansed your veins,
sucking hard
to stay alive.

But that was then,
you tell me,
and this is now.

You have prepared the poison.
It is your life

and your pain
and your right
to end it all.

End it
if you must
but in your note
write in a clear hand
that in the other world
you will remember
these things:

the velvet touch of friendship
the sound of laughing children
the sight of men and women
in their winter years smiling spring
and the feel of lovers you have known
who delivered on their promise
to take you to the heavens.

Before you leave,
tell me you will remember
that you were the loving sister
who prepared feasts for others
from a cupboard bare.

Write that note,
my friend.

It is your antidote.

WAR STORIES

Saundra Murray Nettles

They sit on edge
telling tales of lost battles.

His:
I told them not to send me back
in pieces

feel my body
it still works through my mind
remembers the man just ahead
of me
ambushed
and the day we had to help a brother
go away.
You know what I mean?

Hers:
My first battle was on a piece of virgin
ground, mine

feel my body
it still works though my mind
says no to memories
of me
fighting

willing strange, familiar men to
go away.
You know what I mean?

They sit on edge
gazing at each other through shards of pain
hoping for the grace of mirrored peace.

THE LETTER
Wendell Hooper

It was all so sad, she thought, as she threw his letter in the trash. The way he went on about this Joe fella, it sounded like he'd gone all fruity. God no, she thought. Not her man Frank. He could make love like makin' a bed, but it was still all so disturbing the way he went on and on about this Joe, and the way he talked about how they were expanding each other's minds.

Shit! It sounded like he was in group therapy, not jail. The truth was, he was in motherfuckin' jail, probably talkin' jailhouse shit and talkin' big talk about what he was gonna do when he got out. But the truth was, he was gonna do what he always did, and that was go back to jail. So why was she gittin herself all upset about his ranting on about some jailhouse prophet she didn't know. And couldn't know.

There was nothing to do but sit down and cry.

Frank could remember as clear as water what it felt like the first time he looked up into Joe's big ol' brown eyes. It was in chow, and Frank was still keyed up and nervous from spending three days in jail after a fifteen-minute trial with a lawyer he had only met once, and then for only five lousy minutes.

In twenty minutes of justice, he'd been handed five years. He was angry and tired, and he hadn't even had time to talk to her. And now he was staring into the calmest pair of big brown eyes he'd ever seen. Eyes that seemed to say "Hey, baby, everything's gonna be all right." Frank took his chow and ambled off to his seat and waited. A man learned to wait in jail. After all, everyone had time.

Later that day, after chow, Joe sauntered over to Frank. Frank stood still smoking, waiting, watching. Joe said, "You look like you gonna bite the head off a rattlesnake."

"And I will too, if I run across one," Frank countered.

"Well, we usually see in others what we have in ourselves," Joe answered, and stuck out his hand. "Hey, partner, my name's Joe. Come on and tell me about it—who you done done wrong, and who done did you wrong."

Frank felt like a rat on a sinking ship, done for. And then, strange enough, he opened his mouth and spoke. His was the first sentence in the millions of sentences that would be spoken between them—in line to chow, or sittin' between Joe's legs as he got his hair plaited. Whispers late at night, after everything around them had long ago fallen asleep.

God knows how the words filled the time and space: never stupid or angry, never boastful, but sweet words. Words that moved him and shaped

Hughie Lee Smith, *The Letter*, 1989. Oil on canvas, 26 × 32 in.
Courtesy of June Kelly Gallery, Inc., New York, NY. Photo: Manu Sassoonian.

him, held him secure like a lover's embrace. And so he was moved to share his new words with his girl, writing long and thick passages to share what he was now experiencing with the one with whom he could not experience it. And as the world woke around him, and Frank heard Joe's soft snores, he wondered if she had received his letter. And how she had received his letter.

"Sometimes it's as if you've spent your whole life blind, and you think, hell, that's the way it goes, and then someone walks up and pulls the blinders, the shades, right off your eyes, and you begin to see everything for what it is, and the way things really are. And you become so powerfully grateful that you don't even know how you made it through until this point." Had she lost her mind to go and pull that letter out of the trash and to sit reading it like she was some lonely, insane, jealous housewife? Bebe started laughing. She really started to chuckle to herself, and that chuckle turned into a good ol' roll. God, she was howling with laughter. Oh, to think what Frank would say if he knew that she had pulled this letter back out of the trash to read it over and over, to sit contemplating it like it held some secret. Her laughter nearly choked her as it rolled from somewhere deep inside, bubbling up deep from within that spring of emotion that turned itself into a river.

Bebe found herself sitting there, clutching that letter like it was life itself, and her laughter died down, and her tears began to flow soft and gentle like the soft patter of rain on a murky, cloudy day.

Blinders. What did she know about blinders? Fifteen years of waiting and not seeing what was right in front of her eyes. Had she ever talked about blinders? No children, no family. Ratty old couch that she could never see as anything but beautiful, nothin' to hold on to except the intangible.

Her blinders were being removed too, washed clean by the hot tears of years of sadness and remorse that had never been spoken or felt. And now she wanted to see. What did he see?

The phone's ring interrupted her reverie and she softly answered, "Hello?" and his voice flowed rich and deep, "How's my girl?" shaking her already fragile sensibilities. "Fine," she answered, trying to tuck away the emotions still so near the surface. "Did you get my letter?" he queried. "Yes, baby," she answered, stilling the hundreds of questions racing through her mind.

"I've said I'm sorry too many times. I've only begun to really see how badly I must've disappointed you all these many years. If only there was some way I could erase them all," he said, then paused, caught his breath. "But I can't. And so I hope my letter lets you know that I want you to be happy, and if you want to move on with your life, then I want you to. I want you to be happy and know that I love you with all my heart. But, baby, if I really love you, I must be willing to let you go."

Never in fifteen years had he said that, and silence hung in the air as it never had before.

"Thank you," she said, her voice thick with emotion. "And if I should ever need to take you up on that offer, you'll be the first to know. But as things sit, they're fine with me."

His sigh of relief was the first indication she had that she had made the right choice. He hung up after a brief conversation of softly mumbled love.

"Silly woman," she chided herself. To think she had almost thrown away fifteen years behind a silly ol' letter.

AIN'T TOO PROUD TO BEG

Peter J. Harris

rom all I've ever read about The Tempts, David Ruffin, the *man,* not the singer, was crazy. Considering his career moves—leaving The Tempts at their peak for the abyss of a solo career—Homeboy should about had the *patent* on begging by the time of his tragic death in a Philly hospital in 1991, after a late-night limousine ride, with thousands of dollars stuffed in a briefcase, to what the cops had tabbed as a crack house.

So it's just like life that a motherfucker who could wring the pain out of a line, or stir up the joy in a ditty, or make a simple raspy wail a signature sound, would actually be off. It's just like life that a cat who could sing that he ain't too proud to beg—providing a whole generation of teenage boys with the soundtrack for getting back into their babies' arms—would be the last man you'd invite over the house to meet your sister.

Still, David is in on this one, 'cause if it wasn't for songs like "My Girl," or "Since I Lost My Baby," or even "What Now My Love" from *The Temptations in a Mellow Mood* LP, I don't think I would have ever met Melvin, my main man, my Ace Boon Coon, my boy, my best friend.

Let me rephrase that. I might have *met* Melvin anyway—after all, Baltimore is a small town and poetry got a way of bringing like souls together. But without David Ruffin, me and Melvin might not have got tight. Tight enough to be each other's "rock against the wind," speaking of some poetry. (Etheridge Knight, to be exact, from a love poem of the same name that's right up there, come to think of it, with something Smokey might have written for The Tempts).

When Melvin and I met in 1978, him an Eastside native of Charm City, me a transplant from D.C. one year out of Howard, it was David who shifted me and Melvin from acquaintances to friends. Mmmm-hmmm, yep, that's right, it was David Ruffin, Paul Williams, Eddie Kendricks, Melvin Franklin, and Otis Williams, The Tall Talented Ones, The Tempting Temptations, the original and, to those of us who've lip-synched since the '60s, the *only* Temptations, who helped me and Melvin crack into the marrow of friendship.

Shit, at first, Melvin didn't even want me to ride in his car. He was teaching over at Sojourner-Douglass College, which at the time held its classes at Dunbar High School off Orleans Street. I was working as a reporter with the *Afro-American* newspaper. I wanted to write about Baltimore's Black poets. I was told that Melvin E. Brown, poet, teacher, and editor of the literary magazine *Chicory,* published by the Enoch Pratt Free Library, was the source for all live information.

So I called Mr. Brown and he said I could sit in on his class, that it was okay for *Afro* photographer Robin McGinty to take pictures of him and for me to interview him after class. When the class was over, me and Melvin walked to our cars, and I suggested I ride with him to the little restaurant he had in mind, and after the interview he could drive me back to my parked car.

Oh no, he said bluntly, "I don't want to do that."

By now his cigarette was lit, and smoke was curling ominously, disdainfully (at least to my nonsmoker's eyes), around his head. He paused to calculate the depth of inconvenience my suggestion was causing him, and would cause him two, maybe three, hours from now. It was already about 9 P.M.

"You follow me," he said.

And I did, over to this now absolutely forgettable Chinese food joint on Charles Street in downtown. The food sucked. And actually Melvin wound up interviewing me, cautioning me, turning down the volume on my idealistic enthusiasm.

But he did agree to be a source for my series of articles on Baltimore's Black poetry scene. At that time, the scene included people like Lucille Clifton, whose short poetry and children's stories and loving encouragement would make her an internationally known writer and sage; Avon Bellamy,

whose love poetry was earthy and candid and made me buy whole cases of
Bic cigarette lighters for even my *thoughts* about writing a love poem; Laini
Mataka ("I Usta B Wanda Robinson"), whose uncompromising work challenged us to decide *when,* not whether, we were going to build Black Institutions, love Black people, if not haul off and *pimp-slap* the next white
Maryland farmer who even looked sideways at you; Gina Gregory, whose
tender, weirdly-punctuated poems about life, love, and spirit were as delicate as her voice, whose meanings were as deep as she was tall; and Otis
Williams (not to be confused with the Temptation of the same name), whose
blues poems made audiences laugh and sing and clap hands, even as they
taught us about the Dixie Hummingbirds, or Lightning Hopkins, or Jimmy
Reed.

At that time, these were among the folk Melvin published in *Chicory,* and
Chicory was the book that made Melvin the heart and soul of a hip, attractive
community of sincere People of the World.

And Melvin's own work, collected in his book, *In the First Place,* with its
quiet tones, tough *Blackpolitic* and caring for common folk, was important
enough to make him a critical contact for me, as I struggled to figure out
how to like Baltimore, after growing up with a D.C. sneer on my face about
this riverport town thirty-some miles to the north.

Beyond our work as poets, though, Melvin became my best friend.

That first night over bland shrimp fried rice, his friendliest gesture was
giving me a copy of his book. And while reading that, I came upon a poem
called "Gettin' Ready (for Shabaka & Kenya)," and that's when I found a
soulmate.

When I called Melvin the next time, I got around quickly to saying:
"I didn't know you was into The Tempts!" This time without tempering any
of my idealistic enthusiasm. Melvin smiled deeply, genuinely, right there
over the phone. 'Cause I had tapped into the deep Black chord of this singing
group thing. Me and him been tapping it ever since. Even getting silly about
the whole thing one night in '87, wondering whether, like baseball teams,

you could trade members of groups and still come up with a winning vocal combination.

In a follow-up postcard, he wrote:

> Hey man: Look, I'll trade you two Ink Spots for one Spinner, one Manhattan, two Delfonics and a Miracle. The Spots obviously having a high trade value because they're dead(?). This newly discovered Doo Wop free agency poses certain serious questions: can a Smokey be backed up properly by some Main Ingredients? Can three Tops out-Pip the Pips behind Gladys? Are three Emotions an equal trade for two Vandellas plus Martha? Love, Brown.

Silly, huh? Two urban brothers, two *grown* city brothers, cracking up about shit many cats leave behind in their teens. That's what happens when you got myth up inside you.

Singing groups just happen to be one of the purest icons of our thang. Elemental. Joyous. I've looked through Black literature for the past twenty-five years and I ain't never seen the groups used for nothing but symbols of harmony between Black men, Black male high style, professionalism, interpersonal intimacy, and community togetherness.

Once I read an essay by playwright and producer Woody King, called "Searching for the Brothers Kindred, Rhythm and Blues of the Fifties." King was talking about how he and two friends wound up in the territory of a rival Detroit gang, the Chilli-Mac. They were looking for some girls we had met at the Madison Ballroom.

"As we approached the corner of Davison and Lumpkins," King wrote, "we heard the Chilli-Mac's singing as pretty as Clyde and the Drifters themselves. . . . We were drawn over to them; forgetting that they were ass kickers. We asked them if they knew 'Adorable' and 'Money Honey.' They knew all the Drifters' songs. They knew some of the routines because the group had recently appeared at the Olympia on Grand River. We sang on the corner with them for over two hours. We started laughing and shaking hands. . . ."

Melvin and me were never enemies, but our love for The Tempts, for The Groups, for Black Folk and their popular culture, had us spending more and more time on the phone talking about writing and creativity. How we were trying hard to be ourselves while saying something that resonated with as many Bloods as we could reach.

Taking off from The Tempts, we began to talk about family, children, love, friendship, Baltimore. We began to hang out together, meeting at readings, getting together over his house to listen to favorite records or watch films he'd bring home from his job at the library. We talked about so much more than Baltimore's Black poetry community—in fact, I never did write that damn series.

We talked mostly about ourselves. I don't know what I've taught Melvin, but let me tell you the most basic, useful thing he taught me: He taught me how to sacrifice some of my own lead singing, so I could become an adult listener. He taught me how to listen like a good background singer, blending my intensity into harmonious, thoughtful, even contrary affirmation for whoever's got the spotlight.

See, Melvin is a very deliberate Virgo, who don't get rushed by too many or too much. During our phone calls or the times we hung out, I used to speak real fast, my Taurus—*Aries-rising*—ass determined to impress him and bust him at the same time, I'd drown him out or interrupt the silences between his words and sentences. It got so I was the only one talking. Impress him? No, pissing him off was more like it. He didn't say anything, but I definitely sensed his impatience that our conversations were becoming my monologues. I felt shame because I really enjoyed what he had to say. (In fact, my excitement was driving my raps.) But I knew I had to learn to shut up or this friendship would die on the vine.

To control my urges, I literally began to hold the phone away from my mouth while he talked. I started sitting when I talked to him, instead of pacing. I began to feel myself slowing and breathing and listening, biting my tongue, gritting my teeth and listening. Melvin would start a thought, pause, sip a drink, puff a cigarette, continue, begin to use one word, stop, sift the possibilities, then speak again. Eventually, my patience replaced my straitjacket and I was swaying within his molasses flow toward confessions about his dreams and passions, his molasses flow toward testimony about his regrets and lessons. Swaying and finding hip times to interrupt, perfect moments to interject. To hear when I could slip in an *amen, mmmm-hmmm,* or *uh-oh* without damming up his train of thought. I also began to realize that certain pauses meant he really needed me to take over the microphone.

He still carries his end of our conversations like this. Of course, long

Archibald J. Motley, Jr., *The Jazz Singers*, ca. 1937. Oil on canvas, 32⅛ × 42¼ in. Permanent Collection, Western Illinois University Art Gallery/Museum, Macomb, IL.

ago I learned to love the creative tensions between our styles, to love his
delicious delays, because the boy is smart, funny, will quote a Tempts song
to make just the right point, will slip in some classic Richard Pryor for good
measure, and will own up to his deepest feelings about family, children,
love, friendship.

Melvin is a lead singer who ain't too proud to beg.

Harmonizing behind him, or stepping with him right in the center of a
spotlight, is food for me. Our conversations now, over transcontinental
phone lines, are happy marathons. Sometimes we talk so long he'll put me
on hold to go piss, or I'll just carry the phone into the bathroom and take
care of my business right in the middle of listening to his blue-light-and-
grind eloquence on one subject or another.

Or we'll admit we sleepy, but then he'll say, "One more thing, man. You
hear . . . ?" and we'll get a shot of adrenaline that keeps us talking until one
of us will look at the clock and say "damn, we been on this phone for another motherfucking hour!"

But this my man we talking about and it's become so understandable.
Our friendship is one of the foundations of my life.

Back in our early Baltimore days, once I worked hard enough to learn
to listen, me and Melvin wound up becoming part of a magnetic group of
men whose love for poetry, music, ideas, laughter, and social contribution
convinced us we could be friends. All of them, but me, were Baltimore na-
tives.

I met Avon Bellamy, poet, raconteur, and devoted husband and father
through Melvin. I met Kinya Kiongozi, a printer, photographer, and Black
book collector through Melvin. I met Daki Napata, community activist and
griot, through Melvin. I met Ralph Moore, at the time a counselor at a low-
income housing nonprofit, through Melvin.

In 1979 we all started meeting over Ralph's downtown apartment once a
week. The meetings started loosely for us, then became indispensable. We
gathered as if we were a singing group dedicated to rehearsals and dreams

for the big time. We gathered because we were Black men who had found a place where we could be lovely together.

Oh man, I learned to love Baltimore then.

I learned about love affairs of the past and relationships going on right now. I learned about what it was like to grow up in Baltimore when there were Black businesses everywhere, live music at The Royal, and a copy of *The Afro* in every pocket. Man, we played records in Ralph's apartment. We rolled on the floor laughing in Ralph's apartment. We talked politics and culture, bullshit and pussy, heartbreak and triumph in Ralph's apartment. We listened reverently to each other in Ralph's apartment. And when a mother-fucker was caught skimming the surface, we unleashed powerful, adult dozens on him till he got to cracking up at his own self and decided to come clean like he as supposed to from the git.

None of the brothers at Ralph's apartment was too proud to beg. None of the brothers was too proud to be lead singers. None of the brothers was too proud to be background singers.

This group of men came together of their own free will, in the spirit of common ground, to be friends with each other. We didn't all think the same way either.

Avon would say *nigger* with the eloquence of Mudbone (Richard Pryor's gritty alter ego) and, despite a burnished religiosity about him that would lead him to the ministry, he would tell the most secular tales about *getting some* I'd ever heard this side of Redd Foxx. Kinya hardly talked at all, but when he did, he used words like "concretize" and "in terms of" a lot, in sentences that needed blueprints to help us understand where the stairways and twisting hallways and trapdoors led.

Daki was a straight-out Pan Africanist, Black Nationalist, who defined the term "firebrand," and was known to *hijack!* a city hall meeting or public lecture, stalk Baltimore's streets passing out flyers from his always-stuffed briefcase, and quote anybody from Sterling Brown to John Henrik Clarke to Lucille Clifton at the drop of a hat. And Ralph, our host and convener, leaned left, was open to hip, committed white folks if they came without colonialism in their eyes, and was grounded more in a contemporary American populism than any straight up Black thang.

There we were, though, turning Ralph's living room into a damn amphitheater or something. For a year solid we locked ourselves into an interpersonal pocket. God! It was a sacred time.

Then the real world intruded.

Daki and his wife separated and it cracked something whole in him and sent him to Chicago to commune with the community of folks who operated the Institute for Positive Education and Third World Press. We were pulled by our other friends, even welcoming into our circle one or two we thought could click. But no outsiders ever really did. Eventually we stopped meeting. With no hard feelings or nothing. We just, as The Tempts might say, faded away.

Metaphysically speaking, though, the last meeting I remember was when Daki returned from Chicago, stronger, feeling better, but clearly still in need of our charging. Shit, he barely came out to this last set. He was subdued. Couldn't even take our ribbing when he pulled an empty potato chip bag out his case, and we jokingly jammed his vegetarian ass about having a good time with some *Bon Temps* behind his boys' backs. He protested in this uncharacteristically defensive, official voice that he had only picked it up as unsightly litter off the ground.

But he stuck it out and we decided to write a group poem. One of our little rituals, where we passed around a blank sheet of paper, the first man wrote a snatch of words, and the next man had to riff until we'd built a piece of writing that was genuine, if not necessarily going to win no awards. We wrote a long one that night, and I kept my section 'cause it was dedicated to Daki and called "And the Men Were Waitin'."

> Home is
> coming is
> Homecoming among us
> You back with us

The Welcome is the memory
The Bonds are the results
The wishin whispered

& whisked you home
& whisked you home

And the men were waitin'
Arms wide & willin
With time to spare

& space here,
slide in next to me
I'll tell you of my missin . . .

I hope you see and hear Melvin in there. It had got like that by then. Brother to brother. Even riding in each other's cars. Having each other's backs when the big shifts in our lives occurred. His father died. I was there. He got married. I was there, hands full with a gift and a poem. My marriage died. He was there, with open ears, no judgment, and a spare bedroom. His marriage died. I was there with open ears, no judgment, and invitations to my new home in the San Francisco Bay area. My mother died. He was there to pick me up at BWI and take me to eat before driving me to my parents' sorrowful home in D.C.

I love Melvin E. Brown. He loves me.

Know how I know?

'Cause he tells me just before he hangs up the phone, or while we're hugging whenever we get together.

Because of our love, and because we sang David Ruffin among friends, I will never be too proud to beg.

Never.

A Poem of Friendship

Nikki Giovanni

We are not lovers
because of the love
we make
but the love
we have

We are not friends
because of the laughs
we spend
but the tears
we save

I don't want to be near you
for the thoughts we share
but the words we never have to speak

I will never miss you
because of what we do
but what we are
together

Betye Saar, *Couple in the Garden*, 1992. Mixed media on paper,
15½ × 12½ in. Courtesy of the artist. Photo: Stephen Peck.

PART IV

For
Better,
For Worse

alentine's Day 1992 we cooked a romantic dinner for some loving couples we knew. It was to be a "celebration of love." But as Priscilla and Guy, Reggie and Virginia were relaxing with their coffee, someone innocently mentioned Anita Hill and Clarence Thomas. The temblor that ran through the room was bigger than an earthquake. As the cacophony of discussion and accusation swirled around the room, fuel, in the name of Mike Tyson, was added to the fire. The resulting conflagration left bodies literally scattered about the room and highlighted an ever-growing rift between Black men and women on the subject of romantic love and relationships.

What we witnessed that night made a profound impact on us; it made us think seriously about how we could go about healing the discord among Black men and women when it comes to romantic love. How could we reassemble, remember the positive feelings of our love, attraction, and commitment to each other? What makes those connections so strong for some that neither Anita, Clarence, Mike, nor Armageddon itself can turn one from the other?

Our search led to the words and images you'll find in the following pages, testimony to the richness and variety of the love we Black folk have. Our initial guide is poet Paul Laurence Dunbar, who drops the mask of Southern dialect he often wore to invite us to the seasons of love. And whether it's formal letters between sweethearts of over a hundred years ago that hint at the mysteries of feeling and affection society of the time was too polite to speak out loud, the simplicity of Henry Dumas' words or the thrill of a twelve-year-old's first kiss, we are reminded of the giddy, intoxicating first taste of love we've all had in our lives.

As we reconstruct love from our collective memories, we see tactile, erotic images, too—love, as Pinkie Gordon Lane says, "the color of light," water that refuses to leave the beloved's body, a woman awash in the sweetness of love's afterglow in Romare Bearden's inner landscape of love, being loved by another with all our supposed imperfections. And however love reaches us, honeysuckle fragrant, with a young artist's passion and intensity, or rich with years of loving, it's all here to be celebrated and remembered.

But romantic love is more than the thrill of it all, it is a sacred recognition of the beloved as an integral part of our lives. That sense of the sacred can be not better stated than by Malcolm X as he reflects on Betty Shabazz in his autobiography, or by Gwendolyn Brooks, who gives a wise benediction over our wedding days. How we come to those days, beautiful, passionate, but *aware* of what it takes to heal and grow within our unions, is explored here with humor and caring by devorah major and Saundra Sharp from both sides of the aisle, bride and groom. The art, a rarely seen painting by William H. Johnson, enhances the joyful, humorous, yet solemn mood of the moment.

Romantic love in its highest form is a sacred celebration of the highest order, a never-ending party where we dance with our beloved, as in Marilyn Waniek's poem "Epithalamium and Shivaree," drunk after years of loving. Dr. Charles Drew, whose love for Lenore Robbins is expressed in his early letters, brings together that sense of the profoundly sensual and spiritual in his desire for a mate.

We sit at the feet of our elders and ask many questions, seeking their insight on the riddles of the ages. As we seek their wisdom on the great issues of our time, we must also ask, How does it all come together in love and marriage? How do the dreams, desires, goals, passions in our lives cohabitate with the person we choose to love? How did these elders and, by extension, how can we make it all work? No less a sage than noted historian John Hope Franklin and his wife Aurelia answer that question for their own forty-five years together, and thereby show what the joys of a shared life can be when love, friendship, trust, and mutual respect are at its core.

INVITATION TO LOVE
Paul Laurence Dunbar

Come when the nights are bright with stars
Or come when the moon is mellow;
Come when the sun his golden bars
Drops on the hay-field yellow.
Come in the twilight soft and gray,
Come in the night or come in the day,
Come, O Love, whene'er you may,
And you are welcome, welcome.

You are sweet, O Love, dear Love,
You are soft as the nesting dove.
Come to my heart and bring it rest
As the bird flies home to its welcome nest.

Come when my heart is full of grief
Or when my heart is merry;
Come with the falling of the leaf
Or with the redd'ning cherry.
Come when the year's first blossom blows,
Come when the summer gleams and glows,
Come with the winter's drifting snows,
And you are welcome, welcome.

LETTER—LONEY BUTLER
TO SOPHRONIA COLLINS

Hazlehurst, Miss.
9/2/1889

*D*ear Sophronia, —the impression you have made upon me is so deep and powerful that I cannot forbear writing to you, in defiance of all rules of etiquette. Affection is sometimes of slow growth, and sometimes, too, it springs up in a moment.

In one moment after I saw you, my heart was no longer my own. I have not the assurance that I have been fortunate enough to create any interest in yours; you will remember that I told you in my last letter, that moments seem hours, and hours seem days while I am absent from you, altho I saw you yesterday, but did not have the chance to talk with you, as you were so busily engaged with others, but my intention was to see you when you got ready to retire, and as you disappeared secretly, I did not get to see you still. Oh! Sophronia, only a momentary conversation with you would lessen the burden of my heart. Darling, as I cannot get to talk with you, please hasten a letter to remove all doubts. You will remember that I told you in my last letter, that every word you write would be a comfort to me, I just feel at a loss to conjecture the cause of your preliminary silence. I can remember the time when I could receive precious notes from you regularly, but now it seems there are some new actors in the field of Simpson.

If you have a previous engagement, or if your affection is occupied otherwise, please comply at your earliest convenience. Your appearance of yesterday seemed to be far away, but if you had only knew my feeling, you would not have returned to your school satisfied. Dear—I think you are the sweetest girl on the globe, and unless I greatly deceive myself, I believe you

Betye Saar, *Friends and Lovers*, 1974. Mixed media assemblage, 13¼ × 11¼ in. Courtesy of the artist. Private collection. Photo: F. J. Thomas.

are a permanent girl. I hope you will comply with this epistle, if I could only have a conversation with you momentarily, I would be the happiest of beings. Just to talk with you one moment. Please write and tell me when you are coming again, and tell me how you are getting along with those wearisome scholars and how is Mr. Hunter.

During the time you was over here I had a letter ready to send to you by Mr. Evans, but after I knew you were here, of course I would not send it. So I have appealed to another letter—hoping it will satisfy your fancy. Dearest, let me hear from you very soon, and in the old vein, anxiously awaiting the result of your consideration on this important and interesting subject,

Believe me dearest

Sophronia

I am your sincere lover,

Direct to   Loney Butler

Carpenter, Miss.
August 10, 1892

ear Pet—

I got the letter that you mailed from Perkinston, Miss., and you wanted to
know why I had not wrote. My dear, I wrote you two letters, one to
Handsborough and one to Hazlehurst. The one I wrote to Handsborough
returned to me last week from the dead letter office (unclaimed), you know;
and I could not hear from the one I wrote to Hazlehurst and so I had given
you up. I am glad you thought enough of me to write me again.

Well, Darling, your loving letter stated that you were still in love with
me and when I read and reread your loving epistle I had to give vent to my
feelings by shedding tears. I want to see your sweet face again. I would give
a world to see you now. Oh! that I could recall that eve I spent with you in
Hazlehurst. Darling, you spoke in your letter as if I had forsaken you.
But never will I forsake such a friend.

I love you more and more each day. I think of you every hour, yes,
every moment . . .

Love,
Sophronia Collins

VALENTINES

Henry Dumas

Forgive me if I have not sent you
a valentine
but I thought you knew
that you already have my heart
Here take the space where my
heart goes
I give that to you too

Stephanie E. Pogue,
Love Flux, 1971.
Color viscosity etching,
12 × 10¾ in.
Courtesy of the artist.
Photo: Stephen Peck.

My First Kiss
Dexter Rivens

Last year when I was in the seventh grade was when I had the most significant experience of my life. At that time I was in a relationship with a girl. She was the first girl to give me a real kiss. The kiss set off fireworks in my body. It was so amazing because for the first time I had someone who cared enough to kiss me. All the times before it was just holding hands and hugging. Now it was the real thing and the only thing that was left was sex. Which would probably never happen and was fine with me because all I wanted was a true relationship that I knew would last. The kiss seemed like it lasted for weeks but was only a few minutes. The kiss that was so different and unique still managed to break my heart. It lasted for a while but hurt so bad. I still managed to find someone else, but it was different. The kiss was moist as the dew on an early morning's leaf, sweet like the taste of strawberry shortcake with whipped cream, gentle like a bear with a sweet little face, and kind with a feeling of a nice day. She touched my tongue with her sweet and wet curious tongue, and I slithered my tongue in like the strong feeling of a snake creeping up on a prey. As our body temperature reached the boiling point, we were happy but in a scared way, pulled back as if we had started a new day. That was so surprising to me because in elementary school we talked but never got that close. I can still remember how it felt and I'm trying to work on it again. No one I have ever kissed yet has given me the same feeling that I had then. As we saw each other the next day we gave each other a hug that would make me never let go of the feeling the kiss gave us. I guess sometimes things aren't meant to last, because soon after we kissed we only spent one more week together.

After that she was back with her old boyfriend who doesn't treat girls very well because everyone he goes with ends up not talking to him as a friend or

Hughie Lee Smith, *Offering*, 1989. Oil on canvas, 12 × 24 in. Collection of the artist.
Courtesy of June Kelly Gallery, Inc., New York, NY.

anything. He doesn't respect people. It's amazing what happened, because afterward I didn't love her the way I did before. The way we treated each other had a lot to do with the breakup. The girl who gave a new meaning to the word "love" to me seemed to always get herself into trouble and never get a break. She was so sad and pitiful. She was a convincing little girl that always got her way. Somehow she didn't talk a lot to people and kept her mouth closed to students but not to the teachers.

My friend is the one that really got us together, which on her part was a miracle. My friend and I always seemed to disagree with each other and sometimes would say that we would never talk to each other ever again. To me she came through when things were about to fall apart. The sweetest girl that I have ever known that really doesn't say much to anybody, afraid that she might say the wrong thing. Don't get me wrong, because when the girl is not having a good day she can be something else. What I'm saying is that looks may be deceiving.

One day I hope the relationship we learned from will amount to a lasting marriage because I still have feelings for the girl who kissed me. Every time we look deep into each other's eyes we fall in love, and she may deny it but it's the truth. I think we could have around two kids and raise them. One boy and one girl, so we can each have one for ourselves.

Lyric: I Am Looking at Music

Pinkie Gordon Lane

It is the color of light,
the shape of sound
high in the evergreens.

It lies suspended in hills,
a blue line in a red
sky.

I am looking at sound.
I am hearing the brightness
of high bluffs and almond
trees. I am
tasting the wilderness of lakes,
rivers, and streams
caught in an angle
of song.

I am remembering water
that glows in the dawn,
and motion tumbled
in earth, life hidden in mounds.

I am dancing a bright
beam of light.

I am remembering love.

WATER OF YOUR BATH

Ahmasi

I WISH I COULD BE
THE WATER OF YOUR BATH
    I WOULD SURROUND YOU
    WITH MELLOW WARMTH
    LIQUID LOVE
LIKE A FROLICKING / CHILDISH WAVE
ON THE SANDY SHORE
    I WOULD DASH AND BREAK
    UPON THE FIRMNESS OF YOUR BODY
    ENGULF AND MOISTEN
    THE PLACES I DREAM OF

IF
I
WERE
THE WATER OF YOUR BATH
    I WOULD MEMORIZE
    EACH AND EVERY MUSCLE
AND BEING LIQUID
    I WOULD TAKE YOUR SHAPE
    MOLD MYSELF TO YOUR EVERY CURVE
    YOUR EVERY INDENTATION
I WOULD ROLL ON / OVER / AND OFF YOUR SATIN SKIN

Romare Bearden, *Reclining Nude*, 1979. Collage on board, 15½ × 23½ in.
Courtesy of Walter O. Evans Collection, Detroit, MI, and the estate of Romare Bearden.

IF

I

WERE

THE WATER OF YOUR BATH

    I WOULD SEND PART OF ME

    TO GATHER IN THE RECESS

    OF YOUR NAVEL

THERE MY TEMPERATURE WOULD RISE TO MATCH YOURS

    AND LIKE PLANTS OF

THE SEA

    I WOULD MOVE YOUR BODY HAIRS

    IN AND OUT WITH THE TIDE

    CREATED BY YOUR MOVEMENTS

PLAYFULLY

I WOULD SLOSH AGAINST YOUR
THIGHS
AND BECOME VERY INTIMATE
WITH YOUR NATURE

IF
I
WERE
THE WATER OF YOUR BATH
    I WOULD CLEANSE YOU
    AS MY ANCESTORS
THE NILE & CONGO
CLEANSED YOUR ANCESTORS
BUT EVEN MORE
        WHEN YOU LEAVE ME AND
        PULL THE PLUG
    I WOULD DEFY THE NATURAL ORDER OF THINGS
        AND STAY & WAIT
    FOR YOUR NAKED RETURN

FROM AND DO REMEMBER ME
Marita Golden

"Can I be that bold tonight? Will you let me?" Noble asked softly, reaching across the length of the sofa, pulling her close to him. "I don't feel like being a gentleman," he whispered in her ear. "And, Macon, I don't want you to be a lady."

As soon as they walked into her bedroom, Macon turned off the lights, but Noble quickly turned on the lamp beside her bed. He unbuttoned her blouse, his fingers nimble and quick, as Macon stared at a corner of the room, afraid to look at his eyes when he saw her chest. He gently pushed the blouse over her shoulders and kissed her on her neck, whispering, "Relax, please, don't fight me, not now."

His plea was so deep, so real, that Macon gave in. She rested her arms on his shoulders as he unfastened her bra in the back. The prosthesis came off easily, and Noble laid it on the bed beside them. He kissed her there, kissed her there first, on the place where she had thought for so long that she was empty. Dead. Noble made tiny circles of kisses around the place where her breast had been and then gazed up at Macon and kissed her eyes, stalling the onslaught of tears. They lay in her bed for a long time, Noble simply running his hands over her body, caressing her. When Macon reached for him, Noble said, "No, wait, let me make love to you."

Beneath his touch she was renewed, her body a continent he joyously discovered. Later, lying in his arms, Macon asked quietly, "Does it matter to you?"

"Not one bit," he said, letting his hand again rest there and gently fondle her. "One day it won't matter to you either," he assured her.

"Noble, I want to live," she sighed. "I want to live a long time."

"So do I, Macon, so do I."

Charles Burwell, *Subterranean View No. 2*, 1988. Oilstick,
crayon, and pencil on canvas, 60 × 48 in. Courtesy of Sherry
Washington Gallery. Collection of United American
Healthcare Corporation, Detroit, MI.

BE SOMEBODY FRAGRANT

Peter J. Harris

I wanna be somebody
fragrant
in your life
wanna cloud you with my scents

overcast as pine
overcast as pine

I wanna be a
bouquet
in your mouth
wanna flavor you
with my mists

flowers like honeysuckle
flowers like honeysuckle

I wanna bloom in your fingerprints
sprout a weak willingness
entangle your grinning heart
till it blossoms & pumps sweet fertilizer
into our unending high country

perfume rises from our breathless footsteps

your sugar ripens my touch
my syrup honeys your skin

I wanna float in your memories
melt on your horizon
I wanna be somebody
fragrant
in your time
wanna wisp of me to defy dilution

dew can't
storm can't

I wanna be invisible
so I can seep into the back door of your pores

LETTERS—AARON DOUGLAS
TO ALTA SAWYER

[before Sept 1925]

*S*weetheart:

I have been reading an interesting volume on the history of painting. The book is nearly as fascinating as a novel. But, dear, before I had read ten pages I find that you begin to appear at the end of each sentence. I was forced finally to lay the book aside and write you.

I was happy yesterday. I am always happy when you are near. You are so beautiful, you are so sweet, you are so lovely. And then you are mine. That is where the real joy begins.

Shouldn't we be ashamed dear to drag our friends into the intimate magic of our emotional madness? I felt sorry for Orvetta. She was so patient and considerate. I mailed her letter okay. Tell her I think her brown outfit pretty.

Sweet, don't forget that you are engaged in an intense love affair. And that the two people involved are two ordinary human beings. And that susceptibility to err is the most constant peculiarity of man. And as intelligent educated people we must see beyond the pitfalls that engulf most lovers. And that a wholehearted confidence in me naturally calls for a reciprocal confidence in you. But remember above all, dream girl, that doubt is the best fertilizer for discontent. And that the man you love thinks you are the last word in womanhood. And that your errors or possible faults are consumed in his heart as by fire. I regret that the fairy fanciful dream tones of our letters have changed, but life full and joyous must be a harmonious combination of fact and fancy.

Edwin A. Harleston, *Portrait of Aaron Douglas*, 1930. Oil on canvas, 32¼ × 28¼ in.
Gibbes Museum of Art/Carolina Art Association, Charleston, SC.

My program is six hundred dollars and Paris by September 1925. I can't go like a prince on such a sum nor can I live in Paris like an ambassador, but I feel that if I get there I will get on by some means or other. Do you approve of my program dear? Tell your daddy just how you feel about the plan.

I saw Thelma and she ask[ed] me if you and yours had separated. She said she had heard it a great many times. She has heard that you said you were tired of married life. I ask[ed] her if she had heard my name mentioned in the affair. She said no. I am sure she falsified. I ask[ed] her in order to destroy in her mind the idea that my implication was of sufficient seriousness to warrant my concealing it.

Write me quickly. I need to hear from you after such an unnatural weekend.

Your Daddy

Aaron Douglas,
Untitled (Woman with Tray, Alta),
1937. Oil on canvas,
28 × 24 in.
Schomburg Center for Research
in Black Culture, Art and
Artifacts Division.
The New York Public Library,
Lenox, Astor, and Tilden
Foundations, New York, NY.
Photo: Manu Sassoonian.

*S*weetheart:

I looked at the moon last night. I wondered at it. What a beautiful thing it was. How full of mystery. How full of life. How full of love. It seemed to reek with voluptuousness. What a sensitive thing it seemed last night. How charming. But the most fascinating thing about it was that it seemed to give me an unusual sense of your presence. I could feel you. I lived in the memory of all moons. Last night I saw the happiness and beauty and love of all moons crowded into the memory of that most glorious of all moonlight nights. The night that I shall never forget. The night that we rode from Topeka to K.C. last June. I can see it now. We were one with nature that night as we sped along oblivious of everything except our own happiness and the flood of moonlight that spread over us a soft canopy of love.

We had a stag party last night. After listening to Langston read his poems yesterday afternoon at the Civic Club, we came up town and had dinner. There were five of us in the crowd. Harold Jackman, a suspiciously good looking fellow, a school teacher. Bruce Nugent, a poet and artist, good too; eccentric, a little fairylike, somewhat egotistic, a good Charleston dancer. Wallace Thurman, acting editor of *Messenger* magazine and a writer of talent. Langston Hughes himself. And me myself personal. We went to Small's cabaret. The music was rotten. The crowd was uninteresting. About 2 o'clock we wandered into Bamboo Inn where we remained until four. Home and bed.

Your letter was interesting. Tell me some more. Remember me to your mother. Estrella is teaching in Trenton.

St. Joe? It doesn't appeal to my fancy. The East is so much more interesting. Don't forget June. Love me little one[?].

Daddy

From The Autobiography of Malcolm X

Malcom X,

with the assistance of Alex Haley

I guess by now I will say I love Betty. She's the only woman I ever even thought about loving. And she's one of the very few—four women—whom I have ever trusted. The thing is, Betty's a good Muslim woman and wife. You see, Islam is the only religion that gives both husband and wife a true understanding of what love is. The Western "love" concept, you take it apart, it really is lust. But love transcends just the physical. Love is disposition, behavior, attitude, thoughts, likes, dislikes—these things make a beautiful woman, a beautiful wife. This is the beauty that never fades. You find in your Western civilization what when a man's wife's physical beauty fails, she loses her attraction. But Islam teaches us to look into the woman, and teaches her to look into us.

Betty does this, so she understands me. I would even say I don't imagine many other women might put up with the way I am. Awakening this brainwashed black man and telling this arrogant, devilish white man the truth about himself, Betty understands, is a full-time job. If I have work to do when I am home, the little time I am at home, she lets me have the quiet I need to work in. I'm rarely at home more than half of any week; I have been away as much as five months. I never get much chance to take her anywhere, and I know she likes to be with her husband. She is used to my calling her from airports anywhere from Boston to San Francisco, or Miami to Seattle, or, here lately, cabling her from Cairo, Accra, or the Holy City of Mecca. Once on the long-distance telephone, Betty told me in beautiful phrasing the way she thinks. She said, "You are present when you are away."

A Black Wedding Song

First Dedicated to
Charles and La Tanya
Allen and Glenda
Haki and Safisha

Gwendolyn Brooks

I

This love is a rich cry over
the deviltries and death
A weapon-song. Keep it strong.

Keep it strong.
Keep it logic and Magic and lightning and Muscle.

Strong hand in strong hand, stride to
the Assault that is promised you (knowing
no armor assaults a pudding or a mush.)

Here is your Wedding Day.
Here is your launch.

Come to your Wedding Song.

II

For you
I wish the kindness that romps or sorrows along.
Or kneels.
I wish you the daily forgiveness of each other.
For war comes in from the World
and puzzles a darling duet—
tangles tongues,
tears hearts, mashes minds;
there will be the need to forgive.

I wish you the jewels of black love.

Come to your Wedding Song.

THE DAY KENNY DID IT

Saundra Sharp

Mostly, Kenny looked nervous.

As he entered, all of us looked around and gave nods, thumbs up, and heads down. Heads rocking from side to side in disbelief at what we were about to witness. It was *the* event of the year, and we had carpooled, gift-pooled, and shot pool for money to make sure everybody who could stand it could make the forty-five-mile trip from the university to the city to see it.

He looked good, of course. Real good, standing up there in white on white, satin on silk. Umph, umph, umph! But then, Kenny was naturally fine! And warm with folks, which made everything he did kind of okay. He wore life lightly. Wore it with easy beauty. So young women felt his smile and were in love, young mothers baked him sweet potato pies and wished they were younger.

Nervous. Tiny little beads of sweat popped out along his creamy forehead and above his eyebrows. And, was that a . . . a little tick? Yep! Kenny, the sweet one, the lover, the girls-come-running, unchallenged number-one playboy was . . . shaking.

The music provided the cue and heads turned to the other end of the church. God, was she beautiful! Who could compete with that? Kenny reached out for her like he thought maybe she wasn't going to show up today. Fat chance! Dozens of girls in two cities would have surrendered their virginity to be in her place. Problem was, dozens had.

The officiating pastor, a husky, middle-aged man with a bolt of gray through his eyebrows, sent his voice out among us so we understood what he wanted us to understand. That this was *his* domain, and the couple of the hour was only half the glory. We held a collective breath. He cleared his throat and the organist stopped playing.

Kenny didn't bolt. We exhaled and settled into the solemnity of the timeless ritual. "Who gives this woman? . . ."

The good reverend was well into the "do-you-takes" when suddenly his voice lurched to the right and his body followed. "Now, Kenny—?!" The detour was so strong that the entire church seemed to shift starboard.

"Now, Kenny—?!" he repeated. Folks' antennas sprang up. The elder in the third row woke with a start. If a wish had dropped you would have heard it. Where was the good reverend going from here??

To the point, evidently. He lowered his head and peered across the upper rim of his glasses deep into the child become man who stood before him. "Now, Kenny," he roared, "I *knooows* you, boy!!" It was an elongated "knoooowws" that spun us all the way back to short pants, snotty noses, and pure young devilment scampering through the house of the Lord.

"I kno-oo-oows you, boy," he enunciated again with even more music in the knowing. "Now, Kenny—?!?" The boat rocked to the other side. "You gonna have to stop all that rrrunning around. And Kenny—?!?"

He paused, waiting for that half—our half—of the congregation that had fallen under the pews and into the aisles, howling or holding our mouths trying not to. Kenny's salmon rose flush spread all the way to the back of the church where the young ushers pranced on tiptoe and slapped five. Ted, the best man (and runner-up for the title of number-one playboy), fell back into the lilac lace slap of one of Kenny's aunts.

Our reaction to the unbelievable did not daunt the good reverend. "You gonna have to come hooooome at night," he continued. "You gonna have to be there, Kenny, in sick! ness! and in hea! lth! and you gonna have to *give up* your ooolllldd ways. 'Cause I knows you, boy! And I want you to hear me this afternoon, in the presence of these witnesses. This is not a light thing that you do here today, boy."

A chorus of grunts and amens rose from the other half of the witnesses, those who had already been there.

Then, as if he and Kenny had been having a private conversation all along, the good reverend lowered his voice to a whisper, a whisper just this side of a threat, and asked Kenny, "Am I making myself clear?"

Now he turned his attention to the bride. He opened his mouth to call her name but then turned back, giving Kenny one last look across the rim of experience, waiting for a promise from this, the most beautiful and wayward of his flock.

Kenny looked up finally. Smiled. Meekly. And the good reverend nodded acceptance.

And we, awed, wondered quietly how it would all turn out.

William H. Johnson,
Wedding Couple, ca. 1942.
Tempera, pen and ink
on paper, 17½ × 13¾ in.
National Museum of
American Art,
Smithsonian Institution,
Washington, D.C.
Gift of the
Harmon Foundation.

SHOWERS AND CREPE PAPER
devorah major

Charlene was sitting so soft and easy, looking like a maple syrup fairy-tale princess. I mean, she had her hair puffed around her face like the wind was frozen, wisping its breath under her eyebrows so they'd arch just so. She was flushed, or blushing, it's hard to tell with cool, serene Charlene, and her lips were painted in these sharp pomegranate lines that drew both voluptuous and innocent around her teeth. She was, as usual, immaculately dressed in a pastel dress of spring flowers that swung around her calves and teased the ties of her espadrilles.

Actually everyone was done pretty that afternoon. Charlene was opening the gifts and oohing and aahing at all the pretty pretties. Most everyone was getting giggly from too much white wine and too few tea sandwiches. It was a sufficiently pleasant, not too exciting wedding shower. Charlene, well, she was in love, a young blossom with her petals spread and fragrant, and we were like mother hens primping and preparing her for the leap. That is, all of us except Dawa. You can expect Dawa to come in with her mumbo jumbo and turn everything inside out. Sometimes it's nice because it's like hot sauce on some bland beans, but other times it's a sharp razor slashing at your tendons leaving you crumpled and helpless in the middle of the floor.

Charlene was on the couch opening the package we had bought from one of those sex-in-a-suitcase parties. We had gotten the massage oils, perfumed bath soap, ostrich feathers, and raunchy fantasy postcards. There was some specific discussion around the comfort or awkwardness of certain strategies, and Charlene sat turning and grinning as if she and Jermaine hadn't been humping and bumping for the last two years. Sometimes this girl is just too proper. But we were really working up to the spirit of things;

all except Ms. Keisha, who is very upright and doesn't demean herself by talking about "such a private and special act." Lord, that child need to get out and dance once in a while.

Brenda, on the other hand, was getting hot and nervous scrunching up on the couch and kind of snatching cards from our hands. Brenda was waiting to fall in love again and hasn't had any for over a year, so she kept kind of edgy. You should of seen her face when Dawa called out, "Honey, just go get you a piece, I mean, love be damned, sometimes you've got to keep your joints oiled." She didn't know whether to cry or jump up and strangle Dawa, so she just looked at the cards even harder. Denise was settling into the fun of it all talking about rocking and rolling, twirling her hips and keeping the records changing with a d.j's ease and timing. She and I had pitched in for some good Jamaican rum, finding white wine just a little dreary for a real party. Dawa had gone to the kitchen to fix some of what she calls "real" food. She turns up her nose at white bread and tuna fish. She came out with some kind of spiced bean curd (she calls it tofu, I call it toe food) fried in sesame oil with red peppers and acts as if it comes express from the motherland. I'm always here to remind the sister that we were confirmed meat eaters long before we was frying crackling and cleaning out pig guts. Well, like I said, Dawa is always manifesting herself in ways that amuse and offend. I love her dearly but this time she just went too far.

There was Charlene laughing and enjoying herself. "Next Sunday is going to be the best day of my life!" And here came microphone-ears Dawa out the kitchen with her chef's surprise, "You'd better hope not!" Now, I know the sister too well, so I quickly shook out this pretty lace chemise that Denise bought and talked about how seductive Charlene is going to look on her honeymoon, trying to move around the corner from Dawa's crooked road. But here came the steam roller, never you mind. "Girl, if that's the best day it goes downhill from then on, and it's not like you've seen too much of the world. I mean, you just turn to maid and baby-maker and receptionist and before you know it, you turn around and he'll be complaining about you taking a crap at the wrong time. Just you wait. I mean, marriage is cool if you into it, but you can't be thinking it's the pinnacle of your woman-ness or you're in for one swift and very hard fall."

Charlene was sitting with her mouth falling open just staring. Dawa is not really her friend anyway. She was there more because she's my running buddy, and usually brings a nice spice to a party, but who was she to start berating Jermaine? Brenda was stuffing another sandwich into her mouth and laughing. "Child, back off and put away your whips. She'll find out soon enough."

Now, you've got to understand, Charlene is really nice. One of those women everyone always says "What a sweet girl" about. One of those ones that everyone wants their son to marry. She's real pretty in a neat wrapped-up kind of way. She trained to be a model and ended up as a re-

ceptionist for the agency she schooled with. She speaks in a soft kind of purring and is like a bright red balloon just bop-ping around in the wind. She's full of dreams and ideals, and I for one didn't see why she shouldn't be allowed to keep them.

Denise started to snapping her fingers and singing the "oldies but goodies," singing along with Martha and the Vandellas' "Dancing in the Street." Keisha was folding up

Fern Logan, *The Wedding*, 1986.
Gum bichromate print, 10 × 8 in.
Courtesy of the photographer.

the gift wrapping paper real serious like, and Dawa was standing with her hands on her hips in these wide African-pattern harem pants, her head thrown back getting ready to bite off more behind.

"Now, you all just ain't being fair sitting here talking about sex kitten games when this child here is about to go off the deep end and ain't had one serious swimming lesson. I mean, dating is fine, and looping the loop is fun, but living with a man, honey, that's a whole different kettle of fish."

I came up on Dawa to try to quiet her mouth and suggest that the wine had got her tongue wagging out a hole in her cheek, and maybe she might want to go out on the back porch with the alley cats. She ignored me! Dawa's got this manner of just hearing what it suits her to hear, she's got selective editing. She keeps her mind on video playback with no commercial breaks.

Charlene had closed her mouth and was smiling porcelainlike. "Dawa, I understand it's not all good times. I mean, Jermaine and I have had arguments. Anyway I'm saying it's the most important moment in *my* life, not yours. I know that from next Sunday on I'm going to be a different person."

"You sure will, honey, with that attitude."

Now I was beginning to see that Dawa was going to launch into one of her tirades about woman space and freedom road and asserting and African woman strong and all of that, so I tripped right next to her and spilled my drink on her blouse.

"Jeanine, you are one awkward sister when you want to be. Now you got me all wet and sour."

Keisha breathed something about how Dawa was all sour anyway and I felt things rapidly going flat, but Dawa didn't have time for pettiness, she called out to Brenda who was getting down in the corner, "Honey, throw me that tea towel near your hand," and Brenda obliged but added, "I think that was a not-so-subtle message, girl, which you seem determined to miss."

Dawa rolled her eyes to the ceiling like she was once again being told something she's known since she was two and sponged off her blouse. I knew it felt uncomfortable because I could see it hanging around her bust and waist, but she wouldn't leave the room and let me get her a dry top so I could tell her to just be cool.

Cindy was busy putting on different scents of perfume, over her eyebrows, behind her earlobes, and between her breasts. She looked up suddenly, aware that a fog has rolled into the room, chilling everyone, and used her squeaking throat to contribute "Well, of course, Cheryl, I mean, Dawa is right . . . but what's life without your fantasies? You go right on ahead, Charlie, and have your day, so on hard times you can look back at the pictures and remember one day of being Cinderella," and back she went to primping and smelling. I swear, before she left she was a version of a Woolworth's cosmetic counter overrun by precocious preteens.

Dawa was still dabbing at herself and sat right next to Charlene. "It's just a matter of arithmetic, honey. I mean, if this is the top, you can only go down. You can't define your future and hopes on the back of a man you don't really know. You should be ashamed to give someone else the power of all your happiness. Jermaine doesn't want it either. He doesn't want to know that you're going to blame him if it rains and praise him when it's warm, because he really don't have that much control over the situation."

Charlene, calm and crisp, came back: "But I want it to be the best day of my life. It's my right!" I noticed despite the picture-perfect face her voice was trembling just a little and her well-manicured hands moved through the air like a butterfly whose wings had been tattered.

"Years from now I'm going to open my photo album and remember what I dreamed of and how I felt. I want this hallmark, this rite of passage, and you, Dawa, have no right to say I shouldn't want it."

The room was still and Dawa looked at each one of us real cold, I mean, cold steel, and said real quiet, "Naw, it ain't like that. I'm not saying don't get married. I'm just saying it ain't the top and you got to be ready. Sisters, where's the stories, not the fantasies, the stories? Come on, Brenda, how come you ain't had a piece since Sam left? Tell her. Tell her how he made you have that abortion 'cause he didn't want no more babies and then came home and accused you of sleeping with his best friend. What about those bruises you carried round your neck for two weeks? Tell her!"

"Dawa, shut up, that's my business."

But Dawa just kept on. "And you, Cindy, you work five days a week, keep a spotless home, and politely turn your head to Kwaku's running all over town. Men will be men, right?

"And you, Jeanine, my sister at the soul, tell her how hard it is. Tell her how many times you think of chucking it with you and Hank. Tell her about the time you told him you wouldn't wash no more dirty drawers of anyone but you who was over the age of ten or under the age of sixty. Tell her about the dragons, Ms. Happily Married."

"Dawa," I said, "she knows all that."

"No, she doesn't. No, she's not saying the right things to know."

"Dawa"—Charlene gasped—"haven't you ever been in love?"

"Honey, I am always in love, or just out of love. But love doesn't carry you. Love is a warm blanket that moths keep eating. Love . . ."

Now Keisha stood up as righteous as you please and walked over to Dawa and said, "Look here, Ms. High and Mighty Know-it-all. We are all sick of your crap. Those stories are ours to keep inside. They are private moments of hurting, and telling really just doesn't change the score. You need to take your loud-mouth, tough-bitch behind out the door, because we aren't interested in your blacker-than-black feministic antagonistic man-hating psychology."

I about leaped over to the couch and threw my arms around sister love, whose wild left—and I mean wild (I have seen it in action)—was about to grab a hold to Keisha's laid-out collar bone and shake it hard. "Ladies, ladies, this is a celebration, not a time to fight and quibble. Why, we don't even have any mud for a good wrestling match. Brenda, baby, put on Sam Cooke about 'Change Gonna Come.' Come on now, let's all just take it down a little."

Dawa was sputtering and crying and waving her arms and then she just looked at Keisha real hard. "Okay, Jeanine, let me be. I'm not going to bloody up your little 'tea to tea.' But you all aren't being fair. The stories aren't just yours. They all of ours. If we don't know how we all share hurt and bury pain, if we don't circle around and rock in memories, how are we going to change things? How you gonna throw out a rope to this sister when you too busy tying up your own past with tape so nobody will see? It's not about hating men, it's about keeping a balance on. It's about giving up the old lies. You know that if you had held your ground here, or had the right words there, or just been a little more patient, or been a whole lot more in a hurry, you know if someone had told any of us a little bit more, a little bit sooner, it might not have made the road any easier, but at least you'd a known how to navigate the curves and climb past the boulders with a little less damage. Charlene, it just isn't the best day or the top day, it's another day when you dress up, look pretty, and get given to the lions by your all-so-honorable maids.

"You know it's always been the women bound the feet, the women who infibulated their daughters, the women who cut off the clits. Always the women holding in the stories and celebrating the best goddamn day of their lives! Damn all of you."

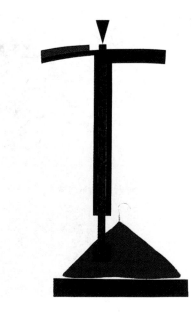

And with that, Dawa picked up her bag, grabbed her jacket from the rack at the door, and left.

"And good riddance!" Keisha shouted after her. The room was so hot we all just swayed in the sweat, and then Charlene, in the most quiet voice I have ever heard, says, "She's right, you know."

Juan Logan, *Sacrifice*, 1990.
Acrylic on canvas, 60 × 48 in.
Courtesy of Jerald Melberg Gallery,
Charlotte, NC.

Just like that, Miss Don't-Rock-the-Boat agreeing with Dawa. We just held our breaths and stared, and she kept right on whispering.

"She's right and that's what I want besides the other presents, everybody give me one story from each side of the roller coaster, two memories, one look at the road ahead. Tell me, tell me the real stories."

Well, I could of just fell all over myself. At first no one would talk so I started about my years and how I learned what new kind of monsters I could be, and saw new kinds of anger I didn't know. About when I finally learned to enjoy blood flowing down my thigh because it meant I wasn't pregnant and the moon and me were still working together. Then Brenda came in with lies she told herself to keep from seeing or believing that she really did play a punching bag as someone else's therapy, and then finally even Keisha broke down and there we were all in a circle holding each other and crying.

After about the longest time Brenda started humming a pretty tune. Just humming and we were all rocking and then Charlene, who for hours had just been listening, offered her own crooked bruised memory to the pile and laid on top the promise of a better time with Jermaine. Then she stood up and smoothed out her skirt. "I'm really scared, but I'm a little more ready now. Come on, who wants some more sandwiches or drink?" She turned to me and said real smooth, "You tell Dawa thanks. But next time, she needs to improve her timing."

"Fat chance of that." Brenda laughed. "Then she wouldn't be Dawa."

Then Denise jumped up and put on "Going to the Chapel" and we all laughed and grabbed each other off the floor and couches and danced into the sunset.

I swear that was the strangest shower I ever was a part of. That Dawa, I keep saying I'm not ever going to bring her with me again, she is always raising so much cain, but of course I always do. I tell you, if you need some reading glasses, that gal is sure to give you a specially created prescription.

EPITHALAMIUM AND SHIVAREE

FOR LINDA AND DEBBIE

Marilyn Waniek

All Cana was abuzz next day with stories:
Some said it had a sad aftertaste; some said
its sweetness made them ache with thirst.
Years later those who had been there
spoke of it with closed eyes, and swayed
like the last slow-dance of the prom.
The village children poked each other's ribs
when they reeled past, still drunk at eighty.

Lovers know what that drunkenness is:
It makes a festive sacrament of praise
for the One who loans us each other
and this too-brief time.
One sip of the wine of Cana
and lovers become fools. And fools lovers.
The willows are drunk tralala; they shimmy
in the silly wind of Spring,

lovers sing noisily. With a little pink parasol
a lover pedals out to the halfway point on the wire.
Below, a silver thread of river. She waves, blows kisses,
wavers, and oops,
her unicycle disappears into mystery.
Her face mimes our gasp.

We hear an unseen slide-whistle chorus.
She sings: *Tralala, the willows are drunk;*

they shimmy in the silly April wind.
And I'm just a kitten in catnip, a pup
rollin' in some ambrosial doggie cologne.
Why settle for less than rapture?
Your pulse against my lips, your solitude
snoring next to mine. The wine we drink from each other.
She leaps. And now there are two of them out there,
jitterbugging on shimmering air.

William H. Johnson,
Jitterbugs IV,
1939–40.
Gouache,
pen and ink on
paper,
12⅞ × 10⁹⁄₁₆ in.
National Museum of
American Art,
Smithsonian
Institution,
Washington, D.C.
Gift of the
Harmon Foundation.

Easter Sunday
at Twilight

enore,

With a heart that's full with a new found joy my thoughts turn to you as the day closes, and a sigh rises as an evening prayer to ask whatever gods there be to keep you safe for me. Since first seeing you I have moved through the days as one in a dream, lost in reverie, awed by the speed with which the moving finger of fate has pointed out the way I should go. As the miles of countryside sped by on our return trip I sat silent and pondered on the power that lies in a smile to change the course of a life; the magic in the tilt of a head, the beauty of your carriage and the gentleness that struck so deeply.

Later, when I become more coherent, I shall say perhaps many things but tonight this one thing alone seems to ring clearly,

I love you.

Charlie

Washington, D.C.
April 9, 1939

Sunday Morning am
April 16, 1939

$\mathcal{M}$y Sweet,

Man at his best is an odd creature and I as the least of men am the oddest of creatures at best, but never have I, even at my worst, acted as strange as I have for the past week. For years I have done little but work, plan and dream of making myself a good doctor, an able surgeon and in my wildest moments perhaps also playing some part in establishing a real school of thought among Negro physicians and guiding some of the younger fellows to levels of accomplishment not yet attained by any of us. I have known the cost of such desires and have been quite willing to do without many of the things that one usually regards as but natural. Then I met you and for the first time mistress medicine met her match and went down almost without a fight. Life suddenly widened its horizons and took on new meaning. I knew clearly just how lonely I had become, just how badly I needed *some one,* rather than just something to cling to, some one to work for, rather than just a goal to aim at, some one to dream with, cherish from day to day, and share the little things with, the smiles and if need be the tears that will sometimes come. When I first kissed your hand it was almost reverently done for even then I felt an inward surge that was inexplicable. When you walked I felt lifted by the graciousness of your carriage; when you talked it was your gentleness that struck so deeply; when you smiled there was sweetness that only a fortunate few can carry over from an unspoiled childhood to full glorious womanhood; poised but vibrant, there was something which responded in me and left a glow which still suffuses my whole being and warms my heart. It's a grand feeling Lenore. The only rash, unplanned, unpremeditated thing I've done for years is already paying dividends in a thousand delightful ways.

Like Elizabeth Browning I feel that a new source of strength has come to me, and I am grateful.

"How do I love thee? Let me count the ways.
I love thee to the depth and breath and height
My soul can reach, when feeling out of sight
For the ends of being and ideal grace.
I love thee to the level of every day's
Most quiet need, by sun and candle light
I love thee with the breath, smiles, tears
Of all my life."

And so

  My love

    Goodnight,

      Charlie

Claude Clark, Sr., *Iris*, 1954.
Oil on canvas, 20 × 16 in.
Courtesy Bomani Gallery,
San Francisco, CA.

May 3, 1939

*D*ear Lenore,

What's the matter with your hand? Hope it's very minor. Don't write if it bothers you—but don't forget who I am.

Glad your soldier boy play went over so well, or is it that one?

I suppose I do write incoherently from time to time and fail to get the things over that I want to say but I didn't know that I had put anything into my last letter which would make you say, "Frankly, I'm not sure a wife would help you." If I did I take it back.

May I attempt again? It's not just a wife for the sake of having a wife that's important to me Lenore. I've ducked, dodged and squirmed away from would-be wives for a long time, it's become almost an art. I don't need a wife just to have a woman,—the streets are full of them, the drawing rooms too, with feminine allure galore. Intellectual companionship may be had without marriage and there are those gentle souls who will gladly listen to the tales of trials and woe with relish, and even a rare spiritual bond may be firmly welded outside of the bounds of matrimony. Yet all of these things are a part of a harmonious wedded existance and I decry none of them. These are the things that one receives in some measure or degree.

When I think of you Lenore I think more largely in terms of the things I'd freely give what love there is in me unstintedly, my inner thoughts, my dearest dreams, my fondest hopes. My head strongness would listen to your council *[sic],* my fears I'd tell you, my weaknesses confess. This must sound silly but these are the things I don't do. I've walked alone it seems for so long that perhaps it's just loneliness, but it's a very specific kind of loneliness, the kind that only you, out of the many people I've met, seem capable of doing anything about. People have expected me to be strong and rather than disappoint them I've been strong, when I much rather would be weak. I'd not be ashamed to admit my weakness before you for there is no place for vanity in the presence of those we love and in the presence of those who love us, even weakness becomes strength. One must have faith in himself and go forward with a sure step but too much sureness may lead to arrogance—a word from one near and trustworthy may prevent this if the word is heeded. I feel that I could trust you always and heed you as the better part of my own conscience.

More than the things you'd bring to me and the small measure in which I'd be able to repay you in terms of care and devotion are the things we could do, build, dream together. Really I think I have possibilities if someone like you took the raw material in hand. A devil of a job I'll admit but if entered in the right frame of mind might keep you not too unhappily employed for years, and I'd love it.

When you were a little girl you must have thought of growing up some day and meeting some guy and marrying him, etc. (how many?) What was he like, what did you want to be, what did you want him to be, what would your house be like? I asked you before but you ignored me. Then you next said you didn't see how you could help. I almost dread your next letter but I'll await it with trembling knees.

Goodnight, loveliest of creatures,
Charlie

Sunday Night
June 25, 1939

ear Lenore,

I went to hear an all-Wagner program tonight. I enjoyed it most simply
because I thought that had you been here you would have enjoyed it. I liked
it but to say that I was carried away would be affectation. Nothing in my
background makes Wagner dear to me. I did not hear it when I was small—
hence there is no recrystallization of old faded images, I have never had any
experiences with this music forming the backdrop so that its melodies do
not call up hauntingly scenes whose grandieur has gone, but whose
impressions remain imperishable; none whom I have loved have loved this
music and passed its essence on to me; so I remain untutored and
untouched—except for "Lawnhauser" which my father used to sing—
waiting only to be guided to and through the inner portals of its power to
the edge of the clear proof at its source and drink in its beauty through
your eyes.

The moon here was lovely tonight and in its quiet passage through the
heavens there was something to still the murmur of unrest that swells within
me as I sit alone,——and the words of the song to the moon slowly force their
way into the melody.

> "The same silver moon
> Shining down through the trees,
> The same night in June,
> The same cool breeze.
> Though we are apart,
> We've the same stars above,
> You have my faithful heart,
> You're the one I love."

See, I too grow sentimental under the spell of the soft Summer's night—
but I open my heart and speak to myself in you and tell you what I feel,
while you close your heart and lay your pen aside with a sharp straight-line
to stop such thoughts, to pick it up again in the clear light of day to write of
the economy of textiles—not that I have anything against them, heaven
forbid—but I do wonder why you must save all the good things, the sweet
things, the little nothings that perhaps don't make sense but mean so much.
Is this the way of a maid in love? To lead one on to the bottom of the page
with "something clicked, it was just so marvelous—shall I tell you about it?"
Then I turn over with baited breath to find the subject completely dropped,
and here I hang in suspense and all the beauty that the moon engendered as
you gazed half dreaming in the sweet fragrance of magnolia and honeysuckle
dies with the night when some of its fragrance might have scented a little
world that is largely yours so many miles away. An opportunity lost that robs
us both of a moment which could have been like a pearl in the long chain of
ties that bind with the strong unseen bonds of communion which the days
that come will add to as we share the joys and sorrows of their passing.

So tonight, my loved one, with memories' arms, I reach out and hold
you through the miles as though close to me and kiss you goodnight.

Charlie

Sunday Afternoon
[undated ca. 1940]

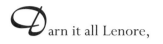arn it all Lenore,

I'm supposed to be here [Columbia University-College of Physicians and Surgeons] working, but work is the farthest thing from my mind. I'm simply no good at it. It's terribly disturbing, disorganizing, inefficient, demoralizing, upsetting, frustrating, understandable—delightful. The sap has gone crazy, grins at himself, preens, struts, blushes, smiles, laughs, whistles, sings and then just sits in a daze. Got heartburn, palpitation, indigestion, anorexia, psychasthenia, euphoria and delusions of grandeur. Hallucinations by day and insomnia by night. Got misery and ecstasy. Dear Dr. Robbins what is my trouble? Only you can tell me. Please answer soon. I'm in bad shape.

Charlie

Sunday
First Anniversary
[June 11, 1940]

Dear Lenore,

This time a week ago you were here and things were different. I wish that it had been possible to have you stay. I am much more upset now than I was then. The whole question resolves itself into the amount of money we need to live on and how to get it. I feel that $100 a month is probably not enough. I have no way of increasing it and feel that it would be wrong to borrow money—it's a bad way to start a life's work. I should feel badly if my wife was deprived of the things she is used to. I should be hurt just a bit, it's unreasonable I know, if my wife had to go to a friend's house to hear phonograph records if she felt that they were essential to her happiness. It would be worse if she didn't go to hear them simply because she felt I wouldn't like it. I don't like martyrs. This isn't pessimism, it's realism.

My cousin, Yvonne Walker, (incidentally she knew you at Columbia) married last Fall. Kirk Jackson, her husband, and she were working, all went well for a while, then she lost her job because both she and her husband were working on the same project and that is against the law. For a while everything went O.K. then bills began to pile up. Kirk started to crack a bit under the strain, they gave up the apartment, went into a room, then Yvonne went home. You [know] her father and mother both have large salaried jobs at home and an easy life is assured. I don't know what Kirk is doing—haven't been able to get in touch with him.

I don't doubt your ability to "take it" if the going gets rough, but I doubt my right to ask you to take that chance. It's so terribly important that happiness isn't throttled at the start. The world is too full of so called sacrifices which are in part nothing but impositions. Always before I have done things with the knowledge that should I fail no one but myself would feel it. Actually, I'm afraid to ask anyone to take chances with me, the type I've always taken without a second thought. You know your own makeup, what you want out of life, what you are willing to pay for it, for everything costs something. I'd like nothing better than having you here with me permanently from now on.

If you feel it, the [better] part of wisdom and the safer course to stay at Atlanta until next January, do so. If you feel that you can pull in your belt, do without for a while some of the things you are used to and not feel that you have prejudiced your own future, then come back here to stay. Perhaps you could find something here to help out. I'll love to write that there are no problems—there is in fact only one. If I could only throw caution to the wind—but I'm not built that way. This is the biggest issue of my life and for the first time I'm scared, not for myself, but for what might happen to one with whom I'm very deeply in love.

Charlie

FOR BETTER, FOR WORSE
Aurelia and
John Hope Franklin

In September 1931 we arrived as freshmen at Fisk University from opposite sides of the country—Aurelia from Goldsboro, North Carolina, and John Hope from Tulsa, Oklahoma. We met during the first month, but it was not a case of love at first sight. We were gradually drawn together by common experiences and by going out together for walks, to lectures and concerts, to dances and other social occasions at the college. We were never in class together except the large freshman courses, such as Contemporary Civilization and the general science survey. We continued to find time to be together, nevertheless, even if only to study in the library in the evenings and then to walk together to the women's dormitory.

The 1930s were years of economic stress, and we, with our parents, suffered from a lack of resources to enjoy our college years free of anxiety about finances. John Hope worked at several jobs in the college, and for part of the time Aurelia also worked. What few pennies we had for recreation we shared. There just was not enough money for any show of gallantry on John Hope's part, so we pooled our resources and pioneered in the practice of expecting no more from the man than from the woman. The lack of resources also meant that we had no opportunity to return home for holiday periods such as Christmas and Easter or even to call home to share with our parents our joys and our disappointments. This meant that we spent our holidays together on campus and, perhaps more important, began to develop an intimacy that made possible the sharing of confidences that under other circumstances we would have shared with our parents and other members of our families. Thus we became close friends. At least as early as we began to realize that we were in love.

If experiences during the college term caused us to grow closer together, the summer season imposed a separation that became more painful with every passing year. While we exchanged letters, there were no opportunities to see each other between June and September, and not even a telephone conversation was a real possibility. Consequently, we looked forward to the reunion each fall, and it became clearer and clearer that we meant a great deal to each other. We took each day at a time, however, and made no unequivocal commitments to each other. The future was too uncertain. There was graduate or professional school for both of us, and if there was the thought or the hope that "something" would eventuate, it remained unspoken.

Aurelia's plans for the future seemed more certain and stable than John Hope's. She planned to major in English, then following graduation to teach for a while in order to finance her pursuit of graduate studies in library science. John Hope went to college determined to follow his father into the legal profession. An encounter with Theodore S. Currier, professor of history, changed all that in his sophomore year. By that time he hoped to emulate Currier and become a historian. It was during our third year at Fisk that our career plans seemed to become fairly well set, but our personal plans remained uncertain, even undefined.

Despite that uncertainty, our relations with each other had deepened and our affection for each other had grown stronger. It manifested itself in a variety of ways. There was not much spare time, but what there was we spent together. As John Hope became more involved in campus politics, Aurelia evinced an interest in his progress and well-being that showed how much she cared. When John Hope was elected president of the Student Council in the spring of their third year, the dean of the college tried to persuade him to yield the post to one whom the dean regarded as more worthy and was certain should have been elected. When Aurelia learned of the proposal to bypass John Hope, her outrage was controlled but quite obvious. She made it clear to John Hope that she expected him to reject the dean's suggestion out of hand not only because it was unseemly but also because John Hope had a clear obligation to the students who had voted for him. He was grateful to her for expressing her opinion, and if he had not made a final decision before hearing her views, he now had no difficulty in declining the dean's suggestion. It was the first time that we had made a critical decision together. In the future we would continue the practice.

When we graduated in 1935 we did not know when we would see each other or, indeed, if we would ever see each other again. John Hope was trying to find funds to go to graduate school. When he found them, thanks to a loan secured for him by Theodore S. Currier, he was off to Harvard in the autumn. The classwork was difficult, the outside work to make ends meet was time-consuming, and it was difficult to adjust to the new environment. It was the loneliness, however, that was devastating. Meanwhile, Aurelia

Robert Scott Duncanson, *Roses, Still Life*, ca. 1842–48.
Oil on canvas, 24 × 19 in. National Museum of
American Art, Smithsonian Institution, Washington,
D.C. Gift of Leonard Granoff.

secured a teaching position in a small town in northeastern North Carolina, where her hard work and loneliness were not even relieved by the distractions of an exciting intellectual community such as Harvard or a huge metropolitan area such as Boston. We corresponded more or less regularly, but not daily or weekly; and there were no phone conversations at all. We seemed not to need letters or telephone contact to sustain our devotion and loyalty to each other.

During the five years between our graduation from college and our marriage in 1940, we saw each other only a few times. Christmas 1936 was the first time we had seen each other since we graduated some eighteen months earlier. John Hope was in the midst of a one-year stint of teaching at Fisk. His mother had died in November, and the trauma left him emotionally and financially depleted. Consequently, Aurelia came to Nashville to visit John Hope and her sister, who was a student at Fisk. During that week late in 1936, it seemed easy to resume where we had left off in the middle of 1935. The ten days went by all too rapidly. It was just a visit with no future plans. The next time we were together was in the summer of 1937, when John Hope taught for six weeks at A. and T. College in Greensboro and Aurelia came there to take some courses for teacher certification. That was a *real* reunion that meant much to our relationship. We were together daily, and there were even visits to Goldsboro on weekends. The next meeting did not come until the spring of 1939, when Aurelia was completing her first degree in library science at Hampton Institute and John Hope visited her there en route to North Carolina to work on his doctoral dissertation. It was a brief but meaningful encounter where we began to talk seriously about a future together.

The following academic year was the most critical in our relationship. John Hope began his first regular teaching job in September 1939 at St. Augustine's College in Raleigh. Aurelia became the librarian at the Dillard High School in Goldsboro. For the first time since we graduated from college, we were close enough—fifty-two miles—to see each other with some regularity. The big obstacle was our work. Aurelia was in a new, time-consuming job with additional demands on her time by the community where she had been born and reared. John Hope, teaching five different courses covering a wide range of historical fields, was also in the throes of completing the research on his dissertation. For a while it appeared as if we were no closer to an irrevocable decision about our future than we had been in June 1935. We seemed not quite able to take the next step.

Then in the spring of 1940 it happened. We reasoned that Aurelia had attained a measure of professional independence with her library science degree. John Hope, with his first regular teaching position and on the threshold of completing his doctorate, moreover, could be optimistic about the future. We concluded that even in another year or so we would be no better prepared for marriage than we were at that time. Thus we reached the momentous decision and were married on June 11, 1940. Almost simultaneously Aurelia secured the position of librarian of Washington High School in Raleigh. At the time we married, therefore, there was no immediate prospect of separation due to our work being in different locations. This contributed to getting our marriage off to a better start than we had anticipated. Despite the fact that both of us were career-oriented, Aurelia voluntarily conceded that John Hope's career should take precedence over hers. Thus she never hesitated about giving up her position and moving on if a better opportunity for John Hope was in the offing. Three years after we were married, we moved to Durham, where John Hope was to take an attractive position at North Carolina College. During our third year there, by which time Aurelia had become librarian at the law school, John Hope suggested that we purchase a lot in a new development and build a home. It was Aurelia who demurred, with the prediction that we would be there only a year or so longer. Her prediction was accurate, for in 1947 John Hope was invited to Howard University as a full professor. Aurelia cheerfully resigned her position and was ready to move at the appointed time.

As a young couple work was an important ingredient in our lives, and we early learned to respect each other's intellectual and professional interests. Four days after we were married we were in Washington working in the Bureau of the Census collecting data for John Hope's doctoral dissertation, which he completed the following year. We believed even then that work took precedence over play, although we fully appreciated the importance of the latter. Play could wait; work could not. When John Hope was working on his second book and needed to spend several months in Washington, Aurelia remained in Durham, working and helping support him on his research trip. When Aurelia decided to return to school and obtain a second degree in library science after we moved to Washington, John Hope encouraged her and helped her as she had helped him. When she decided to become a housewife after we moved to Brooklyn when our son was four years old, John Hope encouraged her to do so. We had a practice of discussing our work with each other. We felt that each could offer suggestions or advice to the other as well as lend moral support. Aurelia read virtually everything that John Hope wrote, beginning with his dissertation, and always felt free to offer criticisms. John Hope read Aurelia's master's thesis and, to the extent that he understood it, he offered comments. We have always felt that anything as important as one's professional activities must be shared in order for a couple to have a full appreciation of each other's work and activities.

As long as we both worked, we shared the duties in our home. We shared the cleaning as well as the cooking. The one who arrived home first began the evening meal. If Aurelia had to go to work earlier than John Hope, he prepared the breakfast, a practice that he continued for many years. We enjoyed sharing the work in the house, the garden, and the greenhouse. We never developed any precise division of labor at home, although it must be admitted that John Hope never learned to operate the washing machine and dryer.

Matters of finance were never serious for us, not because we did not have financial problems but because we refused to let them affect our lives. We never lived beyond our means, even when we had very little. We cheerfully waited until we could afford what we wanted and never opened charge accounts simply because it was possible. The few charge accounts we have had have been for convenience and not to spend what we had not earned.

Whatever our resources, we shared them completely. We have never had separate bank accounts or other financial arrangements that excluded one or the other. Realizing that the financial area is one in which there can easily be a misunderstanding, we early resolved never to have any secrets about the way in which we spent money or for what. Consequently, except for gifts for each other, there are no secret expenditures in our family.

Both of us believe that a relationship can be shattered if one violates the rights, dignity, or privacy of the other. We also believe that a healthy relationship rests on absolute trust on both sides. Consequently, we enjoy an independence not sullied by suspicion. We tend to be open and free about our activities, but sharing is voluntary and is never forced. We tell each other where we have been and what we have done, but we would not approach the line that raises suspicion by asking. We never open each other's mail nor do we read opened mail addressed to the other unless invited to do so. We share the view that mutual respect is as essential in a marriage as it is in other relationships.

Happily, we have mutual interests in many areas. We enjoy the same kinds of music, art, and literature. We enjoy travel, especially if we are able to make the journey together. We delight in having friends in our home, in small groups and, on occasion, in large groups. Because we have been closely associated since our mid-teens, we cannot be certain how much is the result of a commonality of interests and how much is the result of accommodation over the years. We like to believe that we are two quite independent people, reaching points of view and having tastes that are individually our own. After all this time, we do not know, and we are certain that now it really does not matter.

As we look back on some forty-five years of married life, several cardinal factors—love, friendship, mutual respect, complete trust—stand out as major considerations. We do not mention these factors as keys to success, for we make no public qualitative judgment of our marriage. We know what we have meant to each other, and we do not designate the relationship as successful or unsuccessful. Indeed, were we to describe it in such terms, others might well have other opinions. The only thing that matters to us is that the relationship has been satisfactory and that is because we have worked hard to make it so. We never take anything for granted, nor do we assume that one's actions should be acceptable to the other if the actions were taken unilaterally. The only unilateral action we feel free in taking is for one of us to do something in the hope that it will bring joy to the other. Full reward comes in the expression of gratitude on the part of the recipient. Our greatest joy has come in the sharing of experiences, whether a trip to Europe, Asia, or Africa or a tour of our flower garden at home. After all, it is the sharing that is the very essence of any close relationship.

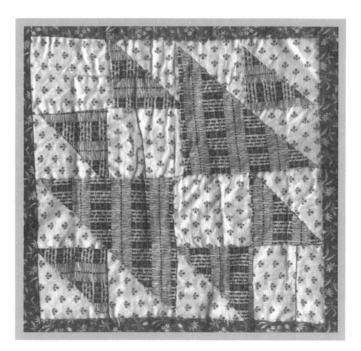

PART V

See the Heart

The world can be a hard and fearful place, with streets so mean they almost spit on *us*. Carjacked or skyjacked, faced with ecological disaster or urban blight, we sometimes just want to run—to the suburbs, to the South of our parents' memory, to the once fabled golden West of opportunity, to a corner of our rooms, somewhere, *any*where, and just close the door and pull the covers over our heads. But we cannot run away, cannot hide from the pain without missing the joy. We must pry open our eyes and reassemble, remember for ourselves and our children, the love before us.

Our streets, our town, our buildings have love within them that we must embrace and emulate. Women who watch the street to be sure the people who walk up and down it "belong there." Or the men who sat in our fathers' barbershops or auto parts stores and nurtured and cajoled our boys into a steady manhood. You know who they were and are in your life, on your block, in your community. Remember the love they gave and continue to give as you read bell hooks, Elizabeth Alexander, Wanda Coleman, Nayo Barbara Malcolm Watkins, and the other voices assembled here. As you read the poetry of Lucille Clifton, Jean Toomer, and Gloria Wade-Gayles, honor as part of our community the ones among us who struggle. And know that whatever pain we see in the faces of those in our communities, beneath it lie hearts that have not ceased to need, that can be touched by love.

SEE THE HEART

Jean Toomer

Those who have ceased to love
Have not ceased to need,
Those who have ceased to care
Have not ceased to bleed;
Do not weigh the words that
Never ask, the minds that never
Seek, nor mark the averted faces,
But see the heart

Juan Logan, *Inverted Heart*, 1991.
Acrylic on canvas, 45 × 36 in.
Courtesy of Jerald Melberg Gallery,
Charlotte, NC.

THE CHITLIN CIRCUIT

ON BLACK COMMUNITY

bell hooks

One of the most intense, vivid memories of childhood relives itself in my mind often, the memory of school desegregation, which meant then the closing of black schools, our beloved Booker T. Washington and Crispus Attucks, schools in segregated black neighborhoods. We loved going to school then, from the moment we rushed out of the door in the morning to the lingering strolls home. In that world, black children were allowed innocence. We did not really understand the meaning of segregation, the brutal racism that had created apartheid in this society, and no one explained it. They wanted us to live childhood life not knowing. We only knew the world we lived in, and as children we loved that world in a deep and profound way.

It was the world of Southern, rural, black growing up, of folks sitting on porches day and night, of folks calling your mama 'cause you walked by and didn't speak, and of the switch waiting when you got home so you could be taught some manners. It was a world of single older black women school-teachers, dedicated, tough; they had taught your mama, her sisters, and her friends. They knew your people in ways that you never would and shared their insight, keeping us in touch with generations. It was a world where we had a history. There grandfathers and great-grandfathers, whose knees we sat on, gave us everything wonderful they could think about giving. It was a world where that something wonderful might be a ripe tomato, found as we walked through the rows of Daddy Jerry's garden, or you thought it was his garden then, 'cause you did not know that word you would learn later—

"sharecropper." You did not know then that it was not his property. To your child mind it had to be his land, 'cause he worked it, 'cause he held that dirt in his hands and taught you to love it—land, that rich Kentucky soil that was good for growing things. It was a world where we had a history. At tent meetings and hot Sunday services we cooled ourselves with fans that waved familiar images back to us. Carried away by pure religious ecstasy we found ourselves and God. It was a sacred world, a world where we had a history.

That black world of my growing up began to fundamentally change when the schools were desegregated. What I remember most about that time is a deep sense of loss. It hurt to leave behind memories, schools that were "ours," places we loved and cherished, places that honored us. It was one of the first great tragedies of growing up. I mourned for that experience. I sat in classes in the integrated white high school where there was mostly contempt for us, a long tradition of hatred, and I wept. I wept throughout my high school years. I wept and longed for what we had lost and wondered why the grown black folks had acted as though they did not know we would be surrendering so much for so little, that we would be leaving behind a history.

Scenes in Paule Marshall's novel *Praisesong for the Widow* remind me of that loss; there the black couple is so intent on "making it" economically in the white world that they lose the sense of who they are, their history. Years later, older, and going through a process of self-recovery, the black woman has the insight that "they had behaved as if there had been nothing about themselves worth honoring." Contemplating the past, she thinks:

> Couldn't we have done differently? Hadn't there perhaps been another way! . . . Would it have been possible to have done both? That is, to have wrested, as they had done all those years, the means to rescue them from Halsey Street and to see the children through, while preserving, safeguarding, treasuring those things that had come down to them over the generations, which had defined them in a particular way. The most vivid, the most valuable part of themselves.

That line "they had behaved as if there had been nothing about themselves worth honoring" echoes in my dreams. She could have been writing about us back then when we let our schools go, when no one talked about what we would be losing, when we did not make ways to hold on.

With no shame, I confess to bearing a deep nostalgia for that time, for that moment when I first stood before an audience of hundreds of my people in the gymnasium of Crispus Attucks and gave my first public presentation. I recited a long poem. We had these talent shows before pep rallies, where we performed, where we discovered our artistry. Nostalgia for that time often

Archibald J. Motley, Jr., *The Picnic*, 1936. Oil on canvas, 30⅛ × 36⅛ in.
The Howard University Gallery of Art, Permanent Collection, Washington, D.C.

enters my dreams, wets my pillow (for a long time the man lying next to me, whose skin is almost soot black like my granddaddy's skin, woke me to say "stop crying, why you crying?"). I cannot imagine daily life without the brown and black faces of my people.

Nostalgic for a sense of place and belonging and togetherness I want black folks to know again, I learn anew the meaning of struggle. Words hardly suffice to give memory to that time, the sweetness of our solidarity, the heaviness of our pain and sorrow, the thickness of our joy. We could celebrate then; we knew what a good time looked like.

For me, this experience, of growing up in a segregated small town, living in a marginal space where black people (though contained) exercised power, where we were truly caring and supportive of one another, was very different from the nationalism I would learn about in black studies classes or from the Black Muslims selling papers at Stanford University my first year there. That nationalism was linked to black capitalism. I had come from an agrarian world where folks were content to get by on a little, where Baba, mama's mother, made soap, dug fishing worms, set traps for rabbits, made butter and wine, sewed quilts, and wrung the necks of chickens; this was not black capitalism. The sweet communion we felt (that strong sense of solidarity shrouding and protecting my growing-up years was something I thought all black people had known) was rooted in love, relational love, the care we had toward one another. This way of loving is best described by Linell Cady in her essay "A Feminist Christian Vision":

Love is a mode of relating that seeks to establish bonds between the self and the other, creating a unity out of formerly detached individuals. It is a process of integration where the isolation of individuals is overcome through the forging of connections between persons. These connections constitute the emergence of a wider life including yet transcending the separate individuals. This wider life that emerges through the loving relationship between selves does not swallow up individuals, blurring their identities and concerns. It is not an undifferentiated whole that obliterates individuality. On the contrary, the wider life created by love constitutes a community of persons. In a community, persons retain their identity, and they also share a commitment to the continued well being of the relational life uniting them.

It is this experience of relational love, of a beloved black community, I long to know again.

At this historical moment, black people are experiencing a deep collective sense of "loss." Nostalgia for times past is intense, evoked by awareness that feelings of bonding and connection that seemed to hold black people together are swiftly eroding. We are divided. Assimilation rooted in internalized racism further separates us. Neonationalist responses do not provide an answer, as they return us to an unproductive "us against them" dichotomy that no longer realistically addresses how we live as black people in a postmodern world. Many of us do not live in black neighborhoods. Practically all of us work for white people. Most of us are not self-sufficient; we can't grow, build, or fix nothing. Large numbers of us are educated in predominantly white institutions. Inter-racial relations are more a norm. The "chitlin circuit"—that network of black folks who knew and aided one another—has been long broken. Clearly, as Marshall suggests in her novel, things must be done differently. We cannot return to the past. While it is true that we lost closeness, it was informed by the very structure of racist domination black civil rights struggle sought to change. It is equally true that this change has meant advancement, a lessening of overt racist brutality toward all black people. Looking back, it is easy to see that the nationalism of the sixties and seventies was very different from the racial solidarity born of shared circumstance and not from theories of black power. Not that an articulation of black power was not important; it was. Only it did not deliver the goods; it was too informed by corrosive power relations, too mythic, to take the place of that concrete relational love that bonded black folks together in communities of hope and struggle.

Black women, writing from a feminist perspective, have worked hard to show that narrow nationalism with its concomitant support of patriarchy and male domination actually helped erode an organic unity between black women and men that had been forged in struggles to resist racism begun in slavery time. Reinvoking black nationalism is not an adequate response to the situation of crisis we are facing as a people. In many ways, ours is a crisis of identity, not that "I need to find out who I am" lifestyle brand. The identity crisis we suffer has to do with losing a sense of political perspective, not knowing how we should struggle collectively to fight racism and to create a liberatory space to construct radical black subjectivity. This identity has to do with resistance, with reconstructing a collective front to re-vision and renew black liberation struggle.

In his provocative book *The Death of Rhythm and Blues* Nelson George sees this crisis as informed by a split between assimilationists and those black folks who wish to be, as he calls it, self-sufficient. This simplistic account is problematic. There are many black people who are not positioned to be self-sufficient, who are also not assimilationist. It is not simply a matter of personal choice. Much of the "new racism" bombarding us undermines black solidarity by promoting notions of choice and individual rights in ways that suggest "freedom" for a black person can be measured by the degree to which we can base all decisions in life on individualistic concerns, what feels good or satisfies desire. This way of thinking militates against bonding that is rooted in relational love, nor is it countered by nationalism.

When black people collectively experienced racist oppression in similar ways, there was greater group solidarity. Racial integration has indeed altered in a fundamental way the common ground that once served as a foundation for black liberation struggle. Today black people of different classes are victimized by racism in distinctly different ways. Despite racism, privileged black people have available to them a variety of life choices and possibilities. We cannot respond to the emergence of multiple black experiences by advocating a return to narrow cultural nationalism. Contemporary critiques of essentialism (the assumption that there is a black essence shaping all African-American experience, expressed traditionally by the concept of "soul") challenge the idea that there is only "one" legitimate black experience. Facing the reality of multiple black experiences enables us to develop diverse agendas for unification, taking into account the specificity and diversity of who we are.

Teaching Black Studies, I find that students are quick to label a black person who has grown up in a predominantly white setting and attended similar schools as "not black enough." I am shocked and annoyed by the growing numbers of occasions where a white person explains to me that another black person is really "not black-identified." Our concept of black experience has been too narrow and constricting. Rather than assume that a black person coming from a background that is not predominantly black is assimilationist, I prefer to acknowledge that theirs is a different black experience, one that means that they may not have had access to life experiences more common to those of us raised in racially segregated worlds. It is not productive to see them as enemies or dismiss them by labeling them "not black enough." Most often they have not chosen the context of their upbringing, and they may be suffering from a sense of "loss" of not knowing who they are as black people or where they fit in. Teaching students from these backgrounds (particularly at Yale), I found myself referring often to traditional black folk experience and they would not know what I was talking about. It was not that they did not want to know—they did. In the interest of unity, of strengthening black community, it is important for us to recognize and value all black experiences and to share knowledge with one another. Those of us who have a particularly rich connection to black folk traditions can and should share.

Years ago I would begin my introduction to African-American literature classes by asking students to define blackness. Usually they simply listed stereotypes. Often folks evoke the experience of Southern rural black folks and make it synonymous with "authentic" blackness, or we take particular lifestyle traits of poor blacks and see them as "the real thing." Even though most black folks in the United States have Southern roots (let's not forget that for a long time ninety percent of all black people lived in the agrarian South), today many know only an urban city experience. A very distinctive black culture was created in the agrarian South, by the experience of rural living, poverty, racial segregation, and resistance struggle, a culture we can cherish and learn from. It offers ways of knowing, habits of being, that can help sustain us as a people. We can value and cherish the "meaning" of this experience without essentializing it. And those who have kept the faith, who embody in our life practices aspects of that cultural legacy, can pass it on. Current trends in postmodernist cultural critiques devaluing the importance of this legacy by dismissing notions of authenticity or suggesting that the very concept of "soul" is illusory and not experientially based are disturbing. Already coping with a sense of extreme fragmentation and alienation, black folks cannot afford the luxury of such dismissal.

Philosopher Cornel West, an influential black scholar committed to liberation struggle, calls attention to the crisis we are facing in his discussions of postmodernism. Commenting on the nihilism that is so pervasive in black communities, he explains:

> Aside from the changes in society as a whole, developments like hedonistic consumerism and the constant need of stimulation of the body which make any qualitative human relationships hard to maintain, it is a question of a breakdown in resources, what Raymond Williams calls structures of meaning. Except for the church, there is no longer any potent tradition on which one can fall back in dealing with hopelessness and meaninglessness.

West is speaking about the black underclass, yet the patterns he cites are equally manifest among black people who have material privilege. Poverty alone does not create a situation of nihilism; black people have always been poor. We need to re-examine the factors that gave life meaning in the midst of deprivation, hardship, and despair. I have already cited relational love as one of these forces; that way of being can be consciously practiced.

We can begin to build anew black communal feelings and black community by returning to the practice of acknowledging one another in daily life. That way "downhome" black folks had of speaking to one another, looking one another directly in the eye (many of us had old folks tell us, don't look down, look at me when I'm talking to you), was not some quaint country gesture. It was a practice of resistance undoing years of racist teachings that had denied us the power of recognition, the power of the gaze. These looks were affirmations of our being, a balm to wounded spirits. They opposed the internalized racism or alienated individualism that would have us turn away from one another, aping the dehumanizing practices of the colonizer. There are many habits of being that were a part of traditional black folk experience that we can re-enact, rituals of belonging. To reclaim them would not be a gesture of passive nostalgia; it would reflect awareness that humanizing survival strategies employed then are needed now.

Another important practice we need to reconstruct is the sharing of stories that taught history, family genealogy, and facts about the African-American past. Briefly, during the contemporary black power movement, tremendous attention was given to the importance of learning history. Today young black people often have no knowledge of black history and are unable to identify important black leaders like Malcolm X. The arts remain one of the powerful, if not the most powerful, realms of cultural resistance, a space for awakening folks to critical consciousness and new vision. Crossover trends in black music, film, etc., that require assimilation have a devastating anti-black propagandistic impact. We need to call attention to those black artists who successfully attract diverse audiences without pandering to a white supremacist consumer market while simultaneously creating a value system where acquisition of wealth and fame are not the only measures of success.

The most important agenda for black people concerned with unity and renewed struggle is the construction of a visionary model of black liberation.

To complete this task we would need to examine the impact of materialist thinking in black lives. Nowadays many black folks believe that it is fine to do anything that will make money. Many of us have lost a needed sense of ethics, that morality Mama evokes in *A Raisin in the Sun* when she asks Walter Lee, "Since when did money become life?" Black people must critically examine our obsession with material gain and consumer goods. We need to talk about the way living simply may be a necessary aspect of our collective self-recovery. We need to look at the way addiction to drugs, food, alcohol and a host of other substances undermines our individual sense of self and our capacity to relate to one another. Addiction must be seen politically as both sickness and a manifestation of genocidal practices that have a grip on black life and are destroying it.

In *Freedom Charter,* a work which chronicles resistance strategies in South Africa, the phrase "our struggle is also a struggle of memory against forgetting" is continually repeated. Memory need not be a passive reflection, a nostalgic longing for things to be as they once were; it can function as a way of knowing and learning from the past, what Michael M.J. Fischer in his essay "Ethnicity and the Art of Memory" calls "retrospection to gain a vision for the future." It can serve as a catalyst for self-recovery. We are talking about collective black self-recovery. We need to keep alive the memory of our struggles against racism so that we can concretely chart how far we have come and where we want to go, recalling those places, those times, those people that gave a sense of direction. If we fall prey to the contemporary ahistorical mood, we will forget that we have not stayed in one place, that we have journeyed away from home, away from our roots, that we have lived drylongso and learned to make a new history. We have not gone the distance, but we can never turn back. We need to sing again the old songs, those spirituals that renewed spirits and made the journey sweet, hear again the old testimony urging us to keep the faith, to go forward in love.

AFFIRMATIVE ACTION BLUES

Elizabeth Alexander

Right now two black people sit in a jury room
in Southern California trying to persuade
nine white people that what they saw when four white
police officers brought batons back like
they were smashing a beautiful piñata was
"a violation of Rodney King's civil rights,"
just as I am trying to convince my boss not ever
to use the word "niggardly" in my presence again.
He's a bit embarrassed, then asks, but don't you know
the word's etymology? as if that makes it
somehow not the word, as if a word can't batter.
Never again for as long as you live, I tell him,
and righteously. Then I dream of a meeting
with my colleagues where I scream so loud the inside
of my skull bleeds, and my face erupts in scabs.
In the dream I use an office which is overrun
with mice, rats, and round-headed baby otters
who peer at me from exposed water pipes (and somehow
I know these otters are Negroes), and my boss says,
Be grateful, your office is bigger than anyone
else's, and maybe if you kept it clean you wouldn't
have those rats. And meanwhile, black people are dying,
beautiful black men my age, from AIDS. It was amazing
when I learned the root of "venereal disease"
was "Venus," that there was such a thing as a disease

of love. And meanwhile, poor Rodney King can't think straight;
what was knocked into his head was some addled notion
of love his own people make fun of, "Can we all
get along? Please?" You can't hit a lick with a crooked
stick, a straight stick made Rodney King believe he was
not a pinata, that *amor vincit omnia.*
I know I have been changed by love.
I know that love is not a political agenda, it lacks sustained
analysis, and we can't dance our way out of our
constrictions.
I know that the word "niggardly" is "of obscure etymology" but
probably derived from the French Norman, and that Chaucer
Milton and Shakespeare used it. It means "stingy," and
the root is not the same as "nigger," which derives from
"negar," meaning black, but they are perhaps, perhaps,
etymologically related. The two "g"s are two teeth
gnawing; rodent is from the Latin "rodere" which means "to
gnaw," as I have said elsewhere.
I know so many things, including the people who love me and the
people who do not.
In Tourette's syndrome you say the very thing that you are
thinking, and then a word is real.
These are the words I have heard in the last 24 hours which fascinate
me: "vermin," "screed," "carmine," and "Niggardly."
I am not a pinata, Rodney King insists. Now can't we all get along?

FIGHTING MY HOMOPHOBIA

FOR MY STUDENTS WHO SHARED

Gloria Wade-Gayles

What
else
could they expect from me,
a natural woman,
who loves the nights (and days)
when my natural man
holds me naturally
getting and giving pleasure
naturally?

My logic was the logic
of the universe.
Beyond challenge.
Unalterable.
In the divine plan.
In the birthing of the species.

Naturally
I rejected them
straight-up
for creating a way
not created to be the way
to love.

Betye Saar, *Five Friends*, 1992. Mixed media collage on paper, 15½ × 12½ in. Courtesy of the artist. Photo: Stephen Peck.

I marched with the righteous
who sought them out
(to straighten them out).
I indicted them wholesale
(my gavel was made of steel)
sure in the logic of my logic
they had no defense

until . . .

names and faces
and voices and eyes
journeyed straight to my heart
with memories of the time when
I knew not, and
loved them.

Gave them praisenames
because I
loved them:
eagleminds
chosen ones
children of the Ancestors
young revolutionaries
straight-up sure
about changing the world.

Nothing had changed,
they told me,
except my eyes
clouded by a logic
which rejected truth:

They
compose symphonies
paint murals
write poems
head nations
start revolutions
birth babies
and prepare the dead for homecoming.

Wherever we are, so may they be also:
in the halls of justice,
in the annals of history,
in the pulpits of churches
and
in
heaven.

Their breath, like mine, is in the
wind of the universe
and in the eye of god
there, too, is their image.

Why, then,
can we judge whom
or how they love?

We can
not.
We should
not.
I will

not
ever again.

     I knew not,
     and loved them.

     I love them still.
     Naturally.

Moving Toward the Light
Recovery in Our Communities
Cecil Williams

Now, there is only one Glide; it can't be duplicated. Yet the Glide attitude is one that can be chosen and adapted to any church, community, or city. Anyone, especially you, can take the risk of telling the truth and living in the Spirit.

Begin today. Take a chance on yourself. Risk extending a hand and being honest with your brothers and sisters. Put your whole life into the present moment. Let go of the past and take your eyes off of the future.

To cultivate the Glide attitude you must first come to see that all people are made in God's likeness. Then you must begin to wrestle with your previous conclusions and labels about people. Perhaps you once thought you could identify who was "in" with God and who was "out" by categorizing people.

Maybe you thought drug addicts or gay people were "out" no matter the content of their hearts or character. Perhaps you thought that white, middle-class, or married people probably were "in" regardless of the quality of their love or care for one another.

Our appearances or labels are not what count with God or with one another; it's who we are and how we live our lives that truly matters.

Over the years, people have labeled me as a crazy minister, a touched man, or a holy fool. None of what others call me matters much. What matters is that I live out the likeness of God that is found in my humanity. I must be who God created me to be. So must you.

The kind of attitude I'm talking about leads to true spirituality, which is discovered through self-revelation and self-definition. The power of the Spirit is set free when the truth is exposed. When someone stands up and tells the truth, others can feel it. The divine likeness that we all share enables us to recognize the truth and the Spirit when they are shared. When the truth is felt, the Spirit moves to action in those who hear it. Living rightly, acting in love, and then reflecting are more important than believing any certain way.

Telling the truth does something to you. Have you tried it lately?

Telling the truth builds community; it creates a new extended family where people can find love and healing. It is critical for people who hurt to know it is okay to stand up and be vulnerable. If we're honest we must admit that no one in the world, however downtrodden, has done anything so terrible that the rest of us wouldn't do it or at least think about it if put in his or her circumstances for a while.

Once a community catches the Glide attitude, it is natural to want to share it. The gift that the Glide attitude offers is the ability to survive. This gift allows me and you to carry on, endure, and live through suffering. This gift tells me never to give up.

Many years ago, when I was a boy, my mother and my father took me to the church, and the church was the only place that ever told me never to give up. Through the testimonies, the stories, the songs, and the hardship, I heard the community saying, *Look, we have to live across the tracks and deal with racism and segregation. We don't have good jobs. We don't always have enough to eat or decent clothes to wear, but you are goin' to go to school, boy. You are going to learn something. You are going to be somebody. Don't you ever give up. Don't ever give in. Keep on goin'. One of these days things will be different.*

The belief of that community propelled me on. Today the New Generation of young people needs a community like that, too.

I have a need to survive; so do you. Those of you who have been through addiction or incest, just think about the fact that you are still here. You somehow have held on to a thin thread of survival. Keep on living one day at a time. If you did it today, you can do it tomorrow.

To survive means to choose life every moment and every day. Hold on, don't give up. Choose life, then offer the gift you have to your community.

When we as a community of people in recovery offer what we have together, then everything begins to change.

I especially believe that the African-American community has something important to offer to our troubled society. Because of the fact of slavery, because of the truth that our ancestors tilled the soil and in many instances died due to inclement weather and beatings and humiliation, we've learned the importance of faith and resistance.

In the end our ancestors held fast to something that allowed them to survive, to choose to live, love, and go on. They made sure that they never gave up.

My grandfather, who was an ex-slave, once said to me, "I could have given up a long time ago, but I had to make sure that my sons and my daughters made it somehow. I wanted to do what I could to make sure my grandsons and granddaughters made it somehow. I had a strategy for survival."

The community at Glide is committed to seeing the New Generation survive. But we also want more than survival for them and for ourselves.

There is more to life than just making it. We want liberation and empowerment for all. Liberation means choosing freedom. Empowerment means claiming your power to change.

The power of decision allows movement; it lets us move beyond what we have always been and lets us change and do things we have never done before. We can overcome some things we have never overcome before. That's when recovery takes place.

We need to keep telling those all around us who are caught in addiction, "You can be stronger than before. You can turn in a new direction. If you've been beaten down all your life, those beaten-down days are over. Stand up for yourself."

Liberation is really redemption. You reclaim your life and live it. You release your brothers and sisters to be themselves.

Liberation is not the loss of tradition; it is the renewal of a lost tradition. I think some of the early Christians and Jews might have acted like some of us act at Glide. In the early Christian era people of different classes and races came together.

Glide also hearkens back to the Early American underground railroad, which told those who were caught in slavery, "You don't have to be a slave any longer; there is a freedom train and we will help you catch it."

There are still so many people who are waiting for the freedom train. They are just inches away from being captured by addiction, violence, and victimization.

The underground railroad, yesterday and today, works because of faith and resistance. Faith and resistance are the fuels that power the train of freedom and transformation.

Young folks, middle-aged folks, and old folks addicted to crack and mired in misery need to know that they can be free. The freedom train passes by where each of us lives. We can all catch it. There is room on that train for me and for you. There is a seat reserved for each of us.

Walter W. Ellison, *Train Station*, 1936. Oil on canvas, 20.3 cm × 35.6 cm.
Charles M. Kurtz Charitable Trust, Barbara Neff and Solomon Byron Smith funds; estate of
Celia Schmidt; through prior gifts of Florence Jane Adams, Mr. and Mrs. Carter H. Harrison,
The Art Institute of Chicago, Chicago, IL.

Black, red, yellow, brown, and white folks, street folks, hustlers, and those who secure themselves behind their money—all need to catch a new train.

As a people and as a society, we've been going in the wrong direction for too long. We've believed that the differences and the social problems that divide us are unsolvable. We have waited too long for a savior to come from afar. We are the ones we have been waiting for. It is up to us to break free and extend a hand to others who long to be free themselves.

Today I say to you, *Go down and catch the freedom train for yourself. Then reach out your hand to your brothers and sisters and bring them on into freedom, too.*

I remember when I used to ride the train with my brothers when I was a kid. One time my mother gave my brothers and me a brown bag full of chicken and biscuits. We were going to ride seventy-five miles or so across Texas.

The conductors lead us to the Colored car and pulled the curtain. As the curtain hid us from the view of the white folks in the other cars, my brothers and I started laughing. The conductor and all those white folks couldn't figure out why we were laughing; they probably thought we were crazy. But we laughed because we knew that we were free. That curtain had not closed off our lives. That curtain did not take away our choice to be who we were. The curtain did not take away our humanity; it only tried to hide it, to beat us down.

But the likeness of God, the Spirit born deep inside us, could not be shut out. We knew that curtain would be pulled back one of these days. Someday things would be different.

Decades later we still have much to do to pull back that curtain for ourselves and for our brothers and sisters. I still have a long way to go as a recovering person. Glide has a long way to travel, too. You and yours probably do, too.

As for me, I'm going to keep on moving.

Join me at the New Generation—we are already on board and traveling toward our freedom. The train of freedom and recovery chugs on daily. Claim your place on this train.

The freedom train is passing by you. Catch it.

Then listen. Listen carefully. Those on the train are singing. Can you hear the voices of the New Generation? They are singing and shouting with unchained abandon.

> *Lift your voice; raise your fist.*
> *You sing, too.*
> *There's no hidin' place down here.*
> *There's no hidin' place down here.*
> *Oh, I went to the rock to hide my face.*
> *The rock cried out, "No hidin' place."*
> *There's no hidin' place down here.*

ALL ABOUT MY JOB

Alice Childress

Marge, I sure am glad that you are my friend. . . . No, I do not want to borrow anything or ask any favors and I wish you'd stop bein' suspicious everytime somebody pays you a compliment. It's a sure sign of a distrustful nature.

I'm glad that you are my friend because everybody needs a friend but I guess I need one more than most people. . . . Well, in the first place I'm colored and in the second place I do housework for a livin' and so you can see that I don't need a third place because the first two ought to be enough reason for anybody to need a friend.

You are not only a good friend but you are also a convenient friend and fill the bill in every other way. . . . Well, we are both thirty-two years old; both live in the same building; we each have a three-room apartment for which we pay too devilish much, but at the same time we got better sense than to try and live together. And there are other things, too. We both come from the South and we also do the same kinda work: *housework.*

Of course, you have been married, and I have not yet taken the vows, but I guess that's the only difference unless you want to count the fact that you are heavier than I am and wear a size eighteen while I wear a sixteen. . . . Marge, you know that you are larger, that's a fact! Oh, well, let's not get upset about it! The important thing is that I'm your friend, and you're mine and I'm glad about it!

Why, I do believe I'd lose my mind if I had to come home after a day of hard work, rasslin' 'round in other folks' kitchens, if I did not have a friend to talk to when I got here. . . . Girl, don't you move, 'cause it would be terrible if I couldn't run down a flight of steps and come in here to chew the fat

William H. Johnson, *Still Life*, ca. 1927. Oil on canvas, 32 × 25⅛ in.
National Museum of American Art, Smithsonian Institution, Washington, D.C.
Gift of the Harmon Foundation.

in the evenin'. But if you ever get tired of me, always remember that all you have to do is say, "Mildred, go home," and I'll be on my way! . . . I did not get mad the last time you told me that! Girl, you ought to be ashamed of yourself! . . . No, I'm not callin' you a liar but I'm sayin' you just can't remember the truth.

Anyhow, I'm glad that we're friends! I got a story to tell you about what happened today. . . . No, not where I work although it was *about* where I work.

The church bazaar was open tonight and I went down to help out on one of the booths and, oh, my nerves! you never saw so many la-de-da fancy folks in all your life! And such introducin' that was goin' on. You shoulda *heard* 'em. "Do meet Mrs. So-and-so who has just returned from *Europe*," and "Do meet Miss This-and-that who has just finished her new *book*," and "Do meet Miss This-that-and-the-other who is on the Board of Directors of everything that is worthwhile!"

Honey, it was a dog! . . . Oh, yes, it was a real snazzy affair, and the booths was all fixed up so pretty, and they had these fine photographs pinned up on the wall. The photographs showed people doin' all manner of work. Yes, the idea of the pictures was to show how we are improvin' ourselves by leaps and bounds through the kinda work that we're doin'.

Well, that was a great old deal with me except that if they was talkin' 'bout people doin' work, it seemed to me that I was the only one around there that had took a lick at a snake in years! . . . No, it wasn't a drag at all because I was really enjoyin' the thing just like you'd go for a carnival or a penny-arcade once in a while.

My booth was the "Knick-Knack" corner and my counter was full of chipped-china doo-dads and ash trays and penny banks and stuff like that, and I was really sellin' it, too. There was a little quiet lady helpin' me out and for the life of me I couldn't figure why she was so scared-like and timid lookin'.

I was enjoyin' myself no end, and there was so many bigwigs floatin' around the joint 'til I didn't know what to expect next! . . . Yes, girl, any second I thought some sultan or king or somebody like that was gonna fall in the door! Honey, I was how-do-you-doin' left and right! Well, all the excitement keeps up 'til one group of grand folks stopped at our booth and begun to chat with us and after the recitation 'bout what they all did, one lady turned to my timid friend and says, "What do *you* do?"

Marge, Miss Timid started sputterin' and stammerin' and finally she outs with, "Nothin' much." That was a new one on me 'cause I had never heard 'bout nobody who spent their time doin' "nothin' much." Then Miss Grand-lady turns to me and says, "And what do *you* do?" . . . Of course I told her! "I do housework," I said. "Oh," says she, "you are a housewife." "Oh, no," says I, "I do housework, and I do it every day because that is the way I make my livin' and if you look around at these pictures on the wall you will see that people do all kinds of work, I do housework."

Marge, they looked kinda funny for a minute but the next thing you know we were all laughin' and talkin' 'bout everything in general and nothin' in particular. I mean all of us was chattin' except Miss Timid.

When the folks drifted away, Miss Timid turns to me and says, "I do housework too but I don't always feel like tellin'. People look down on you so."

Well, I can tell you that I moved on in after that remark and straightened her out! . . . Now, wait a minute, Marge! I know people do make nasty cracks about houseworkers. Sure, they will say things like "pot-slingers" or "the Thursday-night-off" crowd, but nobody gets away with that stuff around me, and I will sound off in a second about how I feel about my work.

Marge, people who do this kinda work got a lot of different ideas about their jobs, I mean some folks are ashamed of it and some are proud of it, but I don't feel either way. You see, on accounta many reasons I find that I got to do it and while I don't think that housework is the grandest job I ever hope to get, it makes me *mad* for any fools to come lookin' down their nose at me!

If I had a child, I would want that child to do something that paid better and had some opportunity to it, but on the other hand it would distress me no end to see that child get some arrogant attitude toward me because I do domestic work. Domestic workers have done a awful lot of good things in this country besides clean up peoples' houses. We've taken care of our brothers and fathers and husbands when the factory gates and office desks and pretty near everything else was closed to them; we've helped many a neighbor, doin' everything from helpin' to clothe their children to buryin' the dead.

. . . Yes, man, and I'll help you to tell it! We built that church that the bazaar was held in! And it's a rare thing for anybody to find a colored family in this land that can't trace a domestic worker somewhere in their history. . . . How 'bout that, girl! . . . Yes, there's many a doctor, many a lawyer, many a teacher, many a minister that got where they are 'cause somebody worked in the kitchen to put 'em there, and there's also a lot of 'em that worked in kitchens themselves in order to climb up a little higher!

Of course, a lot of people think it's *smart* not to talk about *slavery* anymore, but after freedom came, it was domestics that kept us from perishin' by the wayside. . . . Who you tellin'? I know it was our dollars and pennies that built many a school! . . .

Yes, I know I said I wasn't particular proud about bein' a domestic worker, but I guess I am. What I really meant to say was that I had plans to be somethin' else, but time and trouble stopped me from doin' it. So I told this little Miss Meek, "Dear, throw back your shoulders and pop your fingers at the *world* because the way I see it there's nobody with common sense that can look down on the domestic worker!"

MISS JONES
Wanda Coleman

she was the great baby sitter—tall dignified
rich warm brown

we'd scream her name pretend to be endangered
run and hide in mama's clothes closet
she'd search house and yard
get angry and upset when she couldn't find us
we'd pop out laughing while
she scolded us for wolfing

delicately she reported on our bursts into puberty
and experiments in sex

on visits to her home she made us family
after play with her nieces and nephews fed us
the best tuna sandwiches on the planet

love and love always for the only person
to ever comb my thick black kinks
without taking my hair out
in handfuls

i loved her coffee stained teeth flashing gold
her thick british honduras croon
how she always called her lover "Mr."

so pretty inside
there was a joy about her i had to be a woman
to understand

MIZ CULCHURE LADY
Nayo Barbara Malcolm Watkins

I've seen her everywhere. Wearing her hats, walking and talking fast, taking care of business. No doubt, she is universal. And sometimes she is not a she at all, but a he of a certain nurturing, fostering, marshaling spirit. Keeper of the culture. Missionary and visionary. Making sure things are done "like they s'pose to be done." And sometimes, she is not walking at all, but in a wheelchair, or maybe sight-impaired. Often, she has silver hair; but she may be 21. One thing is for sure, we can always count on her. At least the children can, for they are the objects of her attention. Even the ones who think they're grown. She is about the business of "taking care."

I began to take notice of Miz Culchure Lady a few years ago when I traveled the state of Mississippi providing "technical assistance" to "emerging arts organizations." I'd arrive in some small town to consult with some dear soul who'd called or written my office in Jackson about the arts program she was trying to get going. Invariably, she'd tell the story. "Honey," she'd say, "we've got to get this arts program going, just got to. 'Cause these girls are getting pregnant every which way you turn, and the boys, they ain't doing nothing but hanging out and getting mixed up with that ole dope. The trouble is they don't know nothing 'bout who they are, their history, or nothing, 'cause they don't teach that in these schools no more." She was consistent, predictable, and so like all the stewards of our communities we've ever known.

After a while, I began to know I'd seen her before. All my life, I'd seen her. She was the one who'd get us kids together and rehearse and rehearse us 'til Mother's Day or Easter or whatever day it was; we'd stand up before the whole church and recite those little speeches and rhymes so well that our parents would nearly burst with pride. I'd seen her directing the school choir, teaching children how to plait the May pole, and directing "God's Trombones." She might pinch your ear if you didn't do it right. 'Cause she said she was about "the pursuit of excellence," and you'd better be too. She had her yard planted with every kind of flower there was, and if you'd go over by her house, she'd tell you the name of every bloom and make you tell them back to her.

She was the old folks who sat on porches rocking on warm evenings and telling you the stories of everybody there ever was that was kin to you and all those that ever lived in your town too. Talkin' 'bout cultural literacy, you could sure enough get a solid education from those old folks. You could tell by the intonation of their voices in the telling of the story how to place this or that particular story in your legacy of heroes and heroines. Then again, there she was in the pulpit, particularly the one at that church where people get "happy," that preacher who'd rolled his voice all up and down and do that rhythmic little "a ha!" cough between the lines of his poetic oratory, telling you the stories.

She was often the girl's basketball coach and the boy's baseball or football coach making you exceed what you ever imagined your inept body could do. And that teacher whose room had every positive visual image she could find jumping off the walls at you. She made the quilt on my bed. She was my mama sculpturing the meringue of her lemon pie and telling me in a whisper with her eyes sparkling through squinted lids how you got to do it just so. That was her too that we called "strange," because she fixed up those funny teas and little cloths of leaves and told your mama how to treat you with them. Just like that was her painting pictures about our town and sometimes painting them all over the neighborhood on buildings and things, and him whittling creatures on walking canes, and those other ones who collected odd things and decorated their mantels and porches and yards with them.

Of course, I'd seen her all my life. And in the '60s, too. Oh, did she get sassy then. Wearing wraps on her head and swirls of colorful cloth around her hips. And dashikis. And afros, too. Drumming on street corners. When things got tense, she'd sing a little made-up song that sounded just like an old church song. Or read a poem about how we've got to "rise up" and be self-determining, and how we are from an ancient and proud people. She strutted up and down every street in this land, in Washington, D.C., too, and those narrow roads in Alabama all the way to Montgomery. They called it a cultural movement that was hand-in-hand with the Civil Rights Movement.

The dogs didn't stop her. The seas of blues with their billy clubs and guns—they couldn't stop her. Then they sent the programs with government monies and gave her jobs in Headstart and Community Action. And did she do a job.

She took those programs and made something out of nothing. Seldom did she do what they wanted her to do. For she was keeping the culture and minding the storehouse of traditions and wisdom. So little by little they took back the programs. But that didn't stop her either. Evidently, she is eternal. Always was and always will be. She was "taking care" along the Nile, too, from the beginning.

And she is still everywhere. Today, she can often be found doing child-care while the mamas and daddys are off to factories and mills, offices, and post offices, teaching and bus driving, constructing buildings and tearing them down, policing and soldering, unemployment lines and welfare lines. She is taking care of the future. Sometimes she's on those jobs herself, a doctor, a teacher's aide, running some little shop. Quite often she's in the heat of things.

She is there when the Mississippi catfish workers strike; she is organizing against fisherpeople getting landlocked in South Carolina; she is in the middle of political battles in Louisiana; she is teacher and parent going up against the school board in Alabama. Occasionally, she is a name and a face on television. But mostly, she is the nameless, faceless.

It is quite appropriate that she is doing "the arts," for they have always been among her tools and tactics. You can find her in art centers in the heart of inner-cities and cultural programs on the Main Streets of one-street

Claude Clark, Sr., *Pot of Gold*, 1946. Oil on canvas, 22 × 18 in.
Courtesy of Bomani Gallery, San Francisco, CA.

hamlets. Yet these are uneasy and tenuous places for her. She is confronted by funding hassles, policies, and guidelines, deadlines that work against her community's timetable, and critics who know nothing of what she is about yet want to judge whether she is doing "good art" or not. Her predicament is one of justifying the holistic keeping of the culture and the functional use of art for people's sake in an arena that understands and rewards art for art's sake. She lives under the threat of unfunding and displacement.

But none of that has stopped her yet. She is still everywhere, telling the children who they are and who it was that came before to make a way for them. It is her mission. Well, as for me, as long as she is "taking care," and we are singing those songs, beating the drums, speaking our orations, reading our poems, painting our pictures, making meringues, planting flowers, and strutting our stuff, I will believe that somehow, no matter what they throw at us, we're gon' make it over. Yeah, we're gonna make it.

LISTEN CHILDREN
Lucille Clifton

listen children
keep this in the place
you have for keeping
always
keep it all ways

we have never hated black

listen
we have been ashamed
hopeless   tired   mad
but always
all ways
we loved us

we have always loved each other
children   all ways

pass it on

PART VI

A Home
in That Rock

he African presence on these shores is as old as, and many scholars believe older than, the notion of America itself. From Pedro Alonzo Niño in the Bahamas in 1492 through the dark days of slavery and beyond, we have struggled to maintain a spiritual connection to, first, our ancestral home and later to the rivers, fields, mountains, and trees of this land—this has made us African Americans in the truest sense of the word.

Feel that transcendent connection to the land when Lance Jeffers speaks of his blackness itself defining this land's beauty, or when Eddy L. Harris views the Mississippi River as a means not only of transportation but of linkage to spirit, to ancestors, to understanding himself. Hug a tree with Linda Goss, knowing it provides not only shelter and safekeeping, but a sense of being connected to a homeplace. And whether we find that place in the South or North, on a river, Jill Nelson's island, or James Weldon Johnson's city, we each have a place we consider, honor, and love as home.

But talk of America the nation, what James Baldwin has called "these yet to be United States" and our love takes on an edge, a bitterness, a sadness that renders the love no less real, but fiercer, more clear-eyed, something akin to the lover who loves his or her mate *after* learning of the affair. So when Duke Ellington takes the floor to paraphrase Langston Hughes in "We, Too, 'Sing America,' " he is composing a song of recognition, an eloquent plea for our right to a place at the table of history that many would just as soon deny us. That such contributions are even called into question spark dismay in some of the voices here (what George in his letter from France called "the Down Beat"), a rededicated optimism in others, fierce love and pride in some of those who love America "in spite of," and even anger mixed with profound pain for the evil perpetrated against us.

All of these feelings and more are ours when we think of our place at the table of America's bounty, when we look for, as the spiritual says, a home in that rock.

Photograph on page 223: Hilton Braithwaite, *New England Coastline (clouds, rock & ocean)*, 1992.
Silver gelatin print, 16 × 20 in. Courtesy of the photographer.

MY BLACKNESS IS
THE BEAUTY OF THIS LAND
Lance Jeffers

My blackness is the beauty of this land,
my blackness, tender and strong, wounded and wise,
my blackness:
I, drawling black grandmother, smile muscular and sweet,
unstraightened white hair soon to grow in earth,
work-thickened hand thoughtful and gentle on grandson's head,

my heart is bloody-razored by a million memories' thrall:

      remembering the crook-necked cracker who spat
         on my naked body,
      remembering the splintering of my son's spirit
         because he remembered to be proud
      remembering the tragic eyes in my daughter's
         dark face when she learned her color's meaning,

and my own dark rage a rusty knife with teeth to gnaw my bowels,
my agony ripped loose by anguished shouts in Sunday's humble
      church,
my agony rainbowed to ecstasy when my feet oversoared
      Montgomery's slime,

ah, this hurt, this hate, this ecstasy before I die,
and all my love a strong cathedral!
My blackness is the beauty of this land!

Lay this against my whiteness, this land!
Lay me, young Brutus stamping hard on the cat's tail,
gutting the Indian, gouging the nigger,
booting Little Rock's Minniejean Brown in the buttocks and boast,
      my sharp white teeth derision-bared as I the
        conqueror crush!
Skyscraper-I, white hands burying God's human clouds
      beneath the dust!
Skyscraper-I, slim blond young Empire
      thrusting up my loveless bayonet to rape the sky,
then shrink all my long body with filth and in the gutter lie
as lie I will to perfume this armpit garbage,
While I here standing black beside
wrench tears from which the lies would suck the salt
to make me more American than America . . .
But yet my love and yet my hate shall civilize this land,
this land's salvation.

From Mississippi Solo
Eddy L. Harris

The river. Big hearted like your grandmother. Stern like those stories of your best friend's father. Double edged like a broadsword and sharp as
a razor carving its way through the terrain even as it snakes its way into my
being, creating a deep rift and immediately filling in the void as it goes. A
strange kind of cleft, one that strangely unites instead of dividing. A river
that unifies north and south the same as it connects east and west—rather
than creating an impasse—even though this linking bridge is two thousand
miles long and a great distance across.

The river has changed many times since Itasca, and will change a lot
more before the end. Passing between Minnesota and Wisconsin the river is
a monster. Because of the dams, the river backs up in places and spreads out

Aaron Douglas, *The Negro Speaks of Rivers (for Langston Hughes)*, 1941. Ink on paper, 5¹⁄₂ × 11 in.
Courtesy of Walter O. Evans Collection, Detroit, MI.

more than two miles across. What probably once was a narrow channel in the old days is now a massive lake that has swallowed up acres and acres of land. The Mississippi River proper has been confined to the navigable channel while the waters surrounding it go by various other names: Sturgeon Lake, Lake Pepin—twenty miles long and so wide you can't see to the other side—Robinson Lake, Big Lake, Spring Lake. And in the middle float those scattered islands that were once rises of high ground. Now that the lowlands have been flooded, ridge tops become islands. None of this would have been created without the dams blocking the flow of the river. The dams have fragmented the Mississippi, altering its character in places, slowing it down, widening it, turning the upper river into a long string of lakes, but no matter what they do to it, no matter how many faces the river puts on, the Mississippi remains only one river. Different phases in an old man's life which, because it touches the lives of so many others along the way, actually connects those lives. A great-grandfather, a church elder, an old man sitting day after day on the same bench in a small town. You might never have paid much attention to him. But he has his effect.

The river can't help but connect, like the old man touching lives however subtly. Or like a national purpose. Like a favorite baseball team. Like poverty. Something shared. A common understanding. Different in intensity and meaning perhaps to each who share it, but a common language that holds together like a delicate infrastructure. No nails, no glue, just some sort of mysteriously strong bond. Like baptism.

The river flows through towns as different from one another as Minneapolis and Portage des Sioux. In some places it runs wild, in some places it is wide and standing still. For some the river means industry, for others beauty, or leisure boating, or duck hunting. But it's all the same river, all things to all men.

I've watched this river forever. It is as familiar to me as a relative. But now all of a sudden I see beyond the surface and river becomes friend. The river shows me more of what it truly is. It allows me an understanding that I could never have gotten without the risk of intimacy. As I strip the varnish off my own exterior and expose hidden layers, the river reciprocates and reveals to me what I otherwise would not have known.

That, then, is what I must be after, seeking an understanding of the river and through the mirror of friendship, an understanding of myself, and through the special unity offered by the river, a better way to see.

THE TREE OF LOVE

Linda Goss

Momma used to say, "Listen, Baby Dear, I can't be around with you always, but I want you to remember that no matter where you go or what you do, I want you to always be able to look out and see the trees."

At first I didn't know what she was talking about—some of her homespun folklore, I supposed. But I listened because, after all, this was Momma talking.

"I want you to go out and walk among the trees. Go to the park, the woods, wherever they are. I want you to find one that appeals to you and then I want you to give it a big hug. Now, I know what you're thinking, even though you ain't saying nothing. I raised you so you wouldn't talk back to me or sass me."

"But, Momma," I interrupted.

"Listen, Baby Dear, I know you worry about people seeing you hugging trees and thinking you're crazy or something. If they look at you strange, you go right ahead and hug that tree anyway."

I was beginning to worry about Momma.

"I'm telling you that, no matter how far you climb to the top of the tallest building, you got to be able to come back down and plant your feet on the ground, on the grass, on the dirt. We are a part of nature. Trees are God's gift to us human beings. Sometimes we act foolish and forget how precious life is. A tree is a living thing."

"Momma, I love you," I said, and I kissed her gently on her cheek. Momma was preaching now, so I listened all the more.

"Behold the beauty of a tree. Feel how firm and tough it is. Shake hands with the branches. Kiss the leaves. Don't be embarrassed. Trees have seen it all. They were here before we were. And if they ever disappear from the face of the earth, what hope or belief will humankind have then? The tree won't reject your love. My momma, your grandmother, used to say, 'The tree of love gives shade to all.'

"When I was a young child around nine or so, living down in Alabama, there was a great big old weeping willow in our backyard. The branches were so long and flowing that the children called them 'arms.' My oldest brother, Matthew, called the tree Old Willa.

"Now, that weeping willow had been standing in back of our farm before my great-great-uncle was born, which would have been your great-great-great-uncle. My momma and poppa were married under Old Willa. We would have family gatherings, picnics, and good-time parties near Old Willa. Some folks thought the tree had mystical powers. Miss Sally Mae, a root doctor, would come by every now and then and rub Old Willa's trunk. It was an interesting sight. Miss Sally Mae would talk to Old Willa and rub right in the middle of her trunk as if she were rubbing her stomach.

"Sometimes Poppa would gather me, my sisters and brothers around Old Willa. Poppa was a storyteller, you know. He would tell us about Uncle Love Joy, your great-great-great uncle. One night Uncle Love Joy escaped from the plantation, which was a few miles away from the farm. He could hear the dogs and the slave catchers on the horses gaining up on him. He ran like the devil. He didn't know which direction to run but he could hear something or someone whispering to him 'Come, come.' So he ran in the path of the whispering. He ran and bumped his head right into the weeping willow tree, and he hid behind it. Those dogs took another trail. Uncle Love Joy thanked that tree. Twenty years later he came back with his wife and children and his brothers and sisters. They bought the land with the tree on it and built the farm.

"We'd have some fun times beneath Old Willa—but one day it all came to an end. The city developers came through and said that Old Willa had to be cut down because the tree was standing in the way of progress. Our farm and property were declared condemned by the city. The highways were coming through.

"The workers cut Old Willa down. They poured heaps of salt on her trunk so she wouldn't grow back. My momma was sad after that. You might say she never got over it.

"Poppa gathered the family around what was left of Old Willa. He said a prayer. We held hands and sang softly. Momma began weeping and she cried out, 'Old Willa was a love tree and the Tree of Love gives shade to all. No matter where you go, children, or what you do, you find a tree and give it a big hug. It doesn't matter what kind of tree it is. It can be a

Sycamore,

    Maple,

        Elm,

            Oak,

                Birch . . .

"My momma kept naming different kinds of trees. We were amazed. We didn't know she knew the names of so many trees.

'Pine,

    Cypress,

        Chestnut,

            Walnut . . .'

"She named fruit trees, 'Lemon,

Apple,

Peach,

Plum.'

And then she said,

'Weeping Willow.'

Emilio Cruz, *Tree of Life 5*, 1993. Pastel on paper, 72 × 96 in.
Courtesy of Alitash Kebede Fine Arts, Los Angeles, CA.

She clutched her heart as if she had a pain. She walked over to Poppa and collapsed in his arms.

"After Momma's funeral, Poppa was too sad to stay around the area, so he took me and my seven brothers and sisters up North to Tennessee. We didn't forget Momma but we eventually forgot Old Willa. At least, we never talked about the tree.

"Baby Dear, I tell you the story now because, when I saw you marching down the aisle getting your diploma, you stood tall and proud as a tree. Then I saw an image of Old Willa running through my mind."

I grabbed Momma and hugged her tightly. I felt like I was hugging Old Willa. "Oh, Momma," I cried, "I thank you dearly for telling me this story. I promise you, Momma, that I will hug and kiss as many trees as I can."

The phone rings, interrupting my daydream. The administrative assistant informs me that the board meeting will begin in ten minutes. I thank her and go back to my dream. Every time I see Momma, she tells me about Old Willa. For ten years now, since my college graduation, she always has something new to say about the weeping willow. I sit in a swivel highback/lowback chair working in a gray color-coded office suite in one of the busiest cities in the world, the Big Apple. I haven't seen any apple trees. I do, however, go over to Central Park every now and then. I take my family with me. Sometimes I go alone. I have found an Old Willa in the park. I don't even call her Old Willa. I call her Nuba. I talk to her and she listens; she understands. Momma was right. The Tree of Love gives shade to all.

AT HOME ON AN ISLAND

Jill Nelson

Oak Bluffs, Mass.

I wake up at dawn in book-tour panic. What city am I in? What time is it? Have I slept through a major media market, left a zillion book buyers hanging—finally, after two months on the road, blown it? Lying here, I try to unscramble a tired brain before opening exhausted eyes. The acrid-sweet scent of salt drifts into my nostrils, the seductive back and forth of waves stroking sand curls into my ears, and even before I open my eyes I know I am home at last, on Martha's Vineyard.

Thanks to the presence of the Clintons and their entourage, the island where *Jaws* was filmed is under attack by media sharks. (It's happened before.) Big-city reporters in leisure wear do live broadcasts from one of the six small towns that make up Martha's Vineyard. Hype, anticipation, and paranoia reign. I wonder if the man outside my window, who has tended the flowers in Ocean Park for decades, is himself or a member of the Secret Service in disguise.

But I know who I am. Here I am first myself, my mother's daughter, my daughter's mother, and then everything else. It is as it has been for thirty-eight years: a homecoming. Growing up in New York City, we lived in apartments and moved as often as upward mobility allowed. In the city, home was a temporary shelter until something bigger and better came along. Knowing that we could not dig our roots into the earth, we wrapped them around ourselves and each other and waited until summer came.

My parents first came to the Vineyard in 1956, when I was three. My mother tells the story of how they rented a ramshackle house in the Highlands, the twisting hill community above the harbor, part of the town of Oak

Bluffs where black people first formed a summer community in the early part of the century.

Oak Bluffs is like a fun-house mirror of the black middle class: Here the images expand, multiply, into a world. The children of lawyers, doctors, schoolteachers, engineers, Ph.D.s, businesspeople, and dentists are the rule, not the exception. No one ever chants, "I am somebody." That goes without saying. If you weren't, you couldn't hang.

Affirmation comes from many places, one of which is seeing yourself reflected in the world around you, in a sense of commonality, in the very unspecialness of knowing there are thousands of other folks pretty much like you in hollering distance. Nine months of the year I lived in a world where this was not the case. Where being black, bourgeois, going to private school, and having parents who were hardworking professionals was perceived as aberrant. Positive, but aberrant nonetheless.

It is lonely growing up as one of a few dozen black students in a school of hundreds, or the only black people in a building of thousands, living on Manhattan island in a city of seven million people where there is no certain place, no piece of land, where middle-class black people own land, live in houses, put down their roots.

"It rained all week long," my mother will say of our first visit here, laughing. "But we fell in love with the island."

Me, I remember splashing around in the rain with my brothers and sister, free, safe, muddy, and not having to ask permission to go outside or having to ride down in an elevator, an absence of all the fearful things city kids must know about. But these memories may be more elaborations on a tale oft heard than what was. I know what my parents fell in love with. The neat shingled houses with elaborate ornamentation on porches and eaves, the tiny, intricate, gingerbread cottages in the Campgrounds, a world all its own until Illumination Night, when each house is festooned with colored lanterns and lights and it seems the whole island wanders through, awestruck.

The red, gray, and ochre cliffs of Gay Head, which we used to scramble down as children on our way to long days spent on the beach and cookouts with driftwood fires late into the night. The cliffs are now off-limits, protected, as they should be, from human erosion. But the water remains icy sparkling, somehow magical, the mussels pulled from submerged rocks as fat and sweet as ever. Now, in deference to the land, we no longer cook on the beach. Instead we go to the Aquinnah Shop, founded in the early 1940s by Napoleon Madison, a member of the Wampanoag Tribe, the island's original inhabitants. There we eat blackened bluefish burgers, washed down with a slice of superlative strawberry rhubarb pie baked by Luther Madison, Napoleon's son and the chief medicine man of the Wampanoag.

Like a New England dinner of steamers, sugary island-grown corn on the cob, new potatoes, and lobster cooked in one big pot, the famous, infamous, and regular folk blend together in a delicious island stew. The roux that holds us together is our love for the Vineyard, its sense of peace, solitude, and acceptance.

We come to the Vineyard every summer. As children, the four of us would prepare for the long car trip judiciously, hoarding bags of penny candy and comic books. By the time we were, at best, a few hours out of the city, the candy was gone, comics were read, counting-the-license-plate game was played, and the squabbling was in full swing. We fought about whatever: who was hogging the space in the backseat, who ate the last half sandwich, what radio station to listen to, who was the better group, the Temptations or the Marvelettes.

Now I think the bickering was merely a prelude to entering nirvana, interstate purgatory before boarding the ferry to heaven. All summer long we rode bikes, swam in the ocean every day, went fishing, crabbing, had cookouts on the beach, picked wild blueberries, occasionally got poison ivy. We were free against the backdrop, the beauty of the island itself: winding roads, surprising views, a multitude of beaches, each with its own particular smell, taste, surf.

The Vineyard. The Vineyard. The Vineyard. It's like some geospiritual mantra chanted nine months of the year for nearly a lifetime; a lifeline. If I have a home, it is here, off Cape Cod, in the town of Oak Bluffs, in the house my parents bought thirty years ago.

I have lived many lives here. As a child with pigtails, my mother taught me to swim at the beach across the street from our house. "Stroke, down, breathe. Stroke, down, breathe," she chanted. I thought I would never get it, sinking, and then suddenly I was skimming through the water, forever. I rode the Flying Horses carousel until I could snatch eight rings with one finger.

Here I was a plump adolescent who one summer insisted on wearing a beige, waterproof, knee-length trench coat everywhere, including the beach. I had my first kiss here, at a yard party strung with Japanese lanterns, bestowed wetly by a young man whose name is irrelevant but whose appropriate nickname, Chubby Lips, is unforgettable. I went sailing and learned to dive for mussels, to boil perfect lobster, and to scale, gut, and fillet fish. When big changes came—when I had my daughter, had a broken heart, decided to quit my job at *The Washington Post,* finally sold my book—I came here to get sane.

Henry Ossawa Tanner, *Sand Dunes at Sunset, Atlantic City*, ca. 1886.
Oil on canvas, 29¼ × 58¾ in. Collection of Dr. Rae Alexander-Minter, estate of Mrs. Sadie T. M. Alexander on loan to The Philadelphia Museum of Art, Philadelphia, PA.

I lie in bed, smiling, looking at the ancient wallpaper of entwined roses. Here familiarity breeds contentment. I climb out of bed and walk through my mother's silent house, where everything has both a place and meaning. I search for pictures, a vase from Grenada, a sweater always left hanging, my daughter's clogs by the staircase. I find them all. I sit on the wicker porch swing and watch the ocean, wave occasionally as friends, parents of friends, stride by on their morning constitutional. I check the flower and vegetable gardens, note weeding to be done. Finally I go for an early-morning dip, swim in the path the sun makes along the cold, salty water.

That first morning, I walk through the town of Oak Bluffs, searching for and finding the familiar. The houses of the Finleys, Overtons, Thornes, Thomases, Smiths. The tennis and basketball courts; Waban Park, where as children we chased my father's golf balls, four for a penny; the Oak Bluff Public Library on the corner of Circuit Avenue, the main street, where I have borrowed hundreds of books and now people borrow mine. Unfortunately, it is too early to get a peppermint-stick ice cream cone from Cozy's, or succulent clams from the Clam Bar, or whatever's cooking at Lobster in the Bluffs. I settle for doughnuts from the Old Stone Bakery, happily munch my way through Ocean Park, past the gazebo where the island band plays on summer Sundays, toward home.

Entering, the screen door slams behind me and my mother calls from the kitchen, "Star? Is that you?" It is a nickname earned this summer, since my book was published. It is said lovingly, teasingly. It does not connote any change in family status. No one ever says, "Star, can I fetch you something?" or "Star, shall I peel you a grape?" Instead, it's the same old same old. "Star, would you do the dishes? Go to the grocery? Weed the garden?" This is as it should be.

The wonderful thing about the Vineyard is that most everyone believes you're going to do well, though sometimes they're not quite sure in what or when, or maybe it is that they don't care. It's what is expected, what everyone before you did and after you will do. If the black summer community on Martha's Vineyard forms its own world, it is a world absent the assumptions of inferiority rife elsewhere. It is, I think, the absence of burden of carrying around both the negative assumptions of others, and my own. On the Vineyard, as the old spiritual goes, I can lay my burdens down.

Here there is no feeling of unearned, condescending specialness so often bestowed on successful African Americans by others, that "Golly, gosh, you're not like most black people. You're different."

Here, fourth and fifth generations of college graduates, advisers to presidents, writers, politicians, and artists tend neat shingled houses, plant tomatoes, swim early each morning with the rest of the Polar Bears, mow lawns, have cocktail parties, play cards and tennis and talk politics and stuff. Just like everybody else. The phenomenon is that there is no phenomenon. Quiet as it's kept, this is nothing new. I'm just a link in the chain.

On August 14, in the yard of my mother's house, we celebrated her seventy-fifth birthday. We pitched a tent, hung balloons, and, since seven in the morning, made trays of canapés. By twilight the lawn was filled with laughing, talking people, champagne glasses in hand. My mother held forth, a diminutive diva in black and silver. Miles Davis' "So What" floated through the particular air of twilight.

We waited until dark to pass out sparklers, lighting them on cue. My niece, Olivia, and the other children raced around the yard, squealing as white sparks flew, delighting in that remembered time when the adults, slightly high and talking intently, forgot all about them. The faces of friends and family, ages three to eighty-three, glowed and became childish as sparklers sprouted from fingertips, lighting up the night and their peaceful faces. Whirling our torches in the air, we sang "Happy Birthday," cradled by the ocean on one side, the island on the other, roots firmly sunk.

Someone called out "And many more," and I smiled, knowing that there will be. We are here, we have roots. We are not Halley's Comet, visible only every seventy-five years.

MY CITY

James Weldon Johnson

When I come down to sleep death's endless night,
The threshold of the unknown dark to cross,
What to me then will be the keenest loss,
When this bright world blurs on my fading sight?

Sargent Claude Johnson,
Lenox Avenue, ca. 1938.
Lithograph,
12½ × 8⁹⁄₁₆ in.
National Museum
of American Art,
Smithsonian Institution,
Washington, D.C.
Transfer from the
D.C. Public Library.

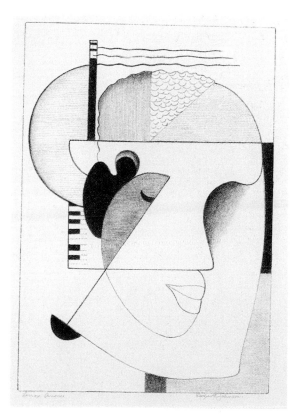

Will it be that no more I shall see the trees
Or smell the flowers or hear the singing birds
Or watch the flashing streams or patient herds?
No, I am sure it will be none of these.

But, ah! Manhattan's sights and sounds, her smells,
Her crowds, her throbbing force, the thrill that comes
From being of her a part, her subtle spells,
Her shining towers, her avenues, her slums—
O God! the stark, unutterable pity,
To be dead, and never again behold my city!

WE, TOO, SING "AMERICA"*
Duke Ellington

irst of all, I should like to extend my sincere appreciation to the Rev. Karl Downs for the opportunity to appear on this very fine program and express myself in a manner not often at my disposal. Music is my business, my profession, my life . . . but, even though it means so much to me, I often feel that I'd like to say something, have my say, on some of the burning issues confronting us, in another language . . . in words of mouth.

There is a good deal of talk in the world today. Some view that as a bad sign. One of the Persian poets, lamenting the great activity of men's tongues, cautioned them to be silent with the reminder that, "In much of your talking, thinking is half murdered." This is true no doubt. Yet, in this day when so many men are silent because they are afraid to speak, indeed, have been forbidden to speak, I view the volubility of the unrestricted with great satisfaction. Here in America, the silence of Europe, silent that is except for the harsh echoes of the dictators' voices, has made us conscious of our privileges of free speech, and like the dumb suddenly given tongue, or the tongue-tied eased of restraint, we babble and bay to beat the band. Singly, as individuals, we don't say much of consequence perhaps, but put together, heard in chorus, the blustering half-truths, the lame and halting logic, the painfully-sincere convictions of Joe and Mary Doaks . . . compose a powerful symphony which, like the small boy's brave whistle in the dark, serves notice on the hobgoblins that we are not asleep, not prey to unchal-

---

* Delivered on Annual Lincoln Day Services, Scott Methodist Church, Los Angeles, February 9, 1941; published as the "Speech of the Week" in the *California Eagle*, February 13, 1941.

lenged attack. And, so it is, with the idea in mind of adding my bit to the meaningful chorus, that I address you briefly this evening.

I have been asked to take as the subject of my remarks the title of a very significant poem, "We, Too, Sing America," written by the distinguished poet and author, Langston Hughes.

In the poem, Mr. Hughes argues the case for democratic recognition of the Negro on the basis of the Negro's contribution to America, a contribution of labor, valor, and culture. One hears that argument repeated frequently in the Race press, from the pulpit and rostrum. America is reminded of the feats of Crispus Attucks, Peter Salem, black armies in the Revolution, the War of 1812, the Civil War, the Spanish-American War, the World War. Further, forgetful America is reminded that we sing without false notes, as borne out by the fact that there are no records of black traitors in the archives of American history. This is all well and good, but I believe it to be only half the story.

We play more than a minority role, in singing "America." Although numerically but 10 per cent of the mammoth chorus that today, with an eye overseas, sings "America" with fervor and thanksgiving, I say our 10 per cent is the very heart of the chorus: the sopranos, so to speak, carrying the melody, the rhythm section of the band, the violins, pointing the way.

I contend that the Negro is the creative voice of America, is creative America, and it was a happy day in America when the first unhappy slave was landed on its shores.

There, in our tortured induction into this "land of liberty," we built its most graceful civilization. Its wealth, its flowering fields and handsome homes; its pretty traditions; its guarded leisure and its music, were all our creations.

We stirred in our shackles and our unrest awakened Justice in the hearts of a courageous few, and we recreated in America the desire for true democracy, freedom for all, the brotherhood of man, principles on which the country had been founded.

We were freed and as before, we fought America's wars, provided her labor, gave her music, kept alive her flickering conscience, prodded her on toward the yet unachieved goal, democracy—until we became more than a part of America! We—this kicking, yelling, touchy, sensitive, scrupulously-demanding minority—are the personification of the ideal begun by the Pilgrims almost 350 years ago.

It is our voice that sang "America" when America grew too lazy, satisfied and confident to sing . . . before the dark threats and fire-lined clouds of destruction frightened it into a thin, panicky quaver.

We are more than a few isolated instances of courage, valor, achievement. We're the injection, the shot in the arm, that has kept America and its forgotten principles alive in the fat and corrupt years intervening between our divine conception and our near tragic present.

LETTER — "GEORGE" TO HIS SISTER

Somewhere in France
March 19, 1945

ear Sis:

Don't be surprised when you receive this letter and find that I am giving serious thought to our race, its problems and its contributions to the welfare of mankind. I shall hope to be able to write a series of letters of this nature.

As you know, Sis, I'm not in a combat unit so I can only write of general conditions behind the "Lines." My story will be the same that many will have to tell someday.

I am in the Service Force. It is a very important branch of service. It's all work. Yes, the hours are sometimes very long. However, I can work with that certain satisfaction that my work behind the "Lines" is the only direct support that the men "Up Front" have. If that convoy with supplies is late because it was not started promptly as ordered the men "Up Front" may meet with capture, unnecessary hardship or even death, because the ammunition or rations were not at the proper place at the proper time. If that Liberty ship isn't unloaded as soon as possible it may miss the convoy and sometimes cost our government the ship and the lives of the men aboard. So you can see why the cry behind the "Lines" is, "Work so that your Combat Buddy may live."

All of us have many reasons for wanting to stay in the States. Yet we know that the war can't be won by our attending dances and enjoying week-end passes. Yes, we too are "Red Blooded Americans" and have as much at stake as anybody. Yes, we have a share in the American Way of Life. We came from all parts of America but we are still Americans. We hope that the

American People won't forget that if we can work and fight for the Democratic Way, that we are entitled to enjoy every privilege it affords when this mess is over.

The going is tough over here. Daily you are thinking of that darling wife, dear mother or sweetheart. You know that feeling that one gets when the mailman passes and doesn't leave any mail. It's funny, Sis, but true. When all around me was covered with snow, we lived in tents. Now that the snow is gone, we are living in houses. Well, what do you think of that? I would call all of this mental torture.

To add to this mental torture we read of those darn strikes and riots over there. We are here to help make the world a decent place for all men to live.

William H. Johnson,
Vieille Maison at Porte,
ca. 1927. Oil on burlap,
24 × 20 in.
National Museum
of American Art,
Smithsonian Institution,
Washington, D.C.
Gift of the
Harmon Foundation.

Even though we are in war we have instances of inter-American conflicts. Yes, Sis, I've met many of the Apostles of Jim Crowisms on foreign soil. Over in England they would try to spread their Doctrine at the Dances, Cafés and Public Houses (Beer Gardens). The way they acted whenever we were around you wouldn't think that we were Americans, too.

Yes, there have been times when the colored and white boys would just fight it out. At this time it seemed like the Negro soldier would have to fight two wars over here. You get pretty low in spirit and just say, "Away with it all." My language would be familiar with the marines. You know me, Sis. I have named the times of such happenings "The Down Beat."

Victory is in sight. We are all confident in the ability of our men "Up Front." I thank God for giving the soldier of color the intestinal fortitude to go on and do a good job in spite of the odds that have been against him. We still have men fighting and dying in the Theaters of War. The colored men stuck to their assigned jobs; if they didn't the men "Up Front" would have known better than anybody else. In closing, Sis, I will write a few words penned by the great Negro poet [Paul Laurence] Dunbar, "Out of the hell and dawn of it all, cometh the good."

Best wishes,
Your Brother
George

From What to the Slaves Is the Fourth of July?
Frederick Douglass

ELLOW CITIZENS

Pardon me, and allow me to ask, why am I called upon to speak here today? What have I or those I represent to do with your national independence? Are the great principles of political freedom and of natural justice, embodied in that Declaration of Independence, extended to us? And am I, therefore, called upon to bring our humble offering to the national altar, and to confess the benefits, and express devout gratitude for the blessings resulting from your independence to us?

Would to God, both for your sakes and ours, that an affirmative answer could be truthfully returned to these questions. Then would my task be light, and my burden easy and delightful. For who is there so cold that a nation's sympathy could not warm him? Who so obdurate and dead to the claims of gratitude, that would not thankfully acknowledge such priceless benefits? Who so stolid and selfish that would not give his voice to swell the hallelujahs of a nation's jubilee, when the chains of servitude had been torn from his limbs? I am not that man . . .

I am not included within the pale of this glorious anniversary! Your high independence only reveals the immeasurable distance between us. The blessings in which you this day rejoice are not enjoyed in common. The rich inheritance of justice, liberty, prosperity, and independence bequeathed by your fathers is shared by you, not by me. The sunlight that brought life and healing to you has brought stripes and death to me. This Fourth of July is *yours,* not *mine. You* may rejoice, I must mourn. To drag a man in fetters into the grand illuminated temple of liberty, and call upon him to join you in joyous anthems, were inhuman mockery and sacrilegious irony. Do you mean, citizens, to mock me, by asking me to speak today? . . .

Fellow citizens, above your national, tumultuous joy, I hear the mournful wail of millions, whose chains, heavy and grievous yesterday, are today rendered more intolerable by the jubilant shouts that reach them. If I do forget, if I do not remember those bleeding children of sorrow this day, "may my right hand forget her cunning, and may my tongue cleave to the roof of my mouth!" To forget them, to pass lightly over their wrongs, and to chime in with the popular theme, would be treason most scandalous and shocking, and would make me a reproach before God and the world. My subject, then, fellow citizens, is "American Slavery." I shall see this day and its popular characteristics from the slave's point of view. Standing here, identified with the American bondman, making his wrongs mine, I do not hesitate to declare, with all my soul, that the character and conduct of this nation never looked blacker to me than on this Fourth of July. Whether we turn to the declarations of the past, or to the professions of the present, the conduct of the nation seems equally hideous and revolting. America is false to the past, false to the present, and solemnly binds herself to be false to the future. Standing with God and the crushed and bleeding slave on this occasion, I will, in the name of humanity, which is outraged, in the name of liberty, which is fettered, in the name of the Constitution and the Bible, which are disregarded and trampled upon, dare to call in question and to denounce, with all the emphasis I can command, everything that serves to perpetuate slavery—the great sin and shame of America! "I will not equivocate; I will not excuse"; I will use the severest language I can command, and yet not one word shall escape me that any man, whose judgment is not blinded by prejudice, or who is not at heart a slave-holder, shall not confess to be right and just.

But I fancy I hear some of my audience say it is just in this circumstance that you and your brother Abolitionists fail to make a favorable impression on the public mind. Would you argue more and denounce less, would you persuade more and rebuke less, your cause would be much more likely to succeed. But, I submit, where all is plain there is nothing to be argued. What point in the anti-slavery creed would you have me argue? On what branch of the subject do the people of this country need light? Must I undertake to prove that the slave is a man? That point is conceded already. Nobody doubts it. The slave-holders themselves acknowledge it in the enactment of laws for their government. They acknowledge it when they punish disobedience on the part of the slave. There are seventy-two crimes in the State of Virginia, which, if committed by a black man (no matter how ignorant he be), subject him to the punishment of death; while only two of these same crimes will subject a white man to like punishment. What is this but the acknowledgment that the slave is a moral, intellectual, and responsible being? The manhood of the slave is conceded. It is admitted in the fact that Southern statute-books are covered with enactments, forbidding, under severe fines and penalties, the teaching of the slave to read and write. When you can point to any such laws in reference to the beasts of the field, then I may consent to argue the manhood of the slave. When the dogs in your streets, when the fowls of the air, when the cattle on your hills, when the fish of the sea, and the reptiles that crawl, shall be unable to distinguish the slave from a brute, then I will argue with you that the slave is a man!

For the present it is enough to affirm the equal manhood of the Negro race. Is it not astonishing that, while we are plowing, planting, and reaping, using all kinds of mechanical tools, erecting houses, constructing bridges, building ships, working in metals of brass, iron, copper, silver, and gold: that while we are reading, writing, and cyphering, acting as clerks, merchants, and secretaries, having among us lawyers, doctors, ministers, poets, authors, editors, orators, and teachers: that while we are engaged in all the enterprises common to other men—digging gold in California, capturing the whale in the Pacific, feeding sheep and cattle on the hillside, living, moving, acting, thinking, planning, living in families as husbands, wives, and children, and above all, confessing and worshipping the Christian God, and looking hopefully for life and immortality beyond the grave—we are called upon to prove that we are men?

Would you have me argue that man is entitled to liberty? That he is the rightful owner of his own body? You have already declared it. Must I argue the wrongfulness of slavery? Is that a question for republicans? Is it to be settled by the rules of logic and argumentation, as a matter beset with great difficulty, involving a doubtful application of the principle of justice, hard to understand? How should I look today in the presence of Americans, dividing and subdividing a discourse, to show that men have a natural right to freedom, speaking of it relatively and positively, negatively and affirmatively? To do so would be to make myself ridiculous, and to offer an insult to your understanding. There is not a man beneath the canopy of heaven who does not know that slavery is wrong *for him.*

What! Am I to argue that it is wrong to make men brutes, to rob them of their liberty, to work them without wages, to keep them ignorant of their relations to their fellow men, to beat them with sticks, to flay their flesh with the last, to load their limbs with irons, to hunt them with dogs, to sell them at auction, to sunder their families, to knock out their teeth, to burn their flesh, to starve them into obedience and submission to their masters? Must I argue that a system thus marked with blood and stained with pollution is wrong? No: I will not. I have better employment for my time and strength than such arguments would imply.

What, then, remains to be argued? Is it that slavery is not divine; that God did not establish it; that our doctors of divinity are mistaken? There is blasphemy in the thought. That which is inhuman cannot be divine. Who can reason on such a proposition? They that can, may; I cannot. The time for such argument is past.

At a time like this, scorching irony, not convincing argument, is needed. Oh! had I the ability, and could I reach the nation's ear, I would today pour out a fiery stream of biting ridicule, blasting reproach, withering sarcasm, and stern rebuke. For it is not light that is needed, but fire; it is not the gen-

tle shower, but thunder. We need the storm, the whirlwind, and the earthquake. The feeling of the nation must be quickened; the conscience of the
nation must be roused; the propriety of the nation must be startled; the
hypocrisy of the nation must be exposed; and its crimes against God and
man must be denounced.

What to the American slave is your Fourth of July? I answer, a day that
reveals to him more than all other days of the year, the gross injustice
and cruelty to which he is the constant victim. To him your celebration is
a sham; your boasted liberty an unholy license; your national greatness, swelling vanity; your sounds of rejoicing are empty and heartless; your
denunciation of tyrants, brass-fronted impudence; your shouts of liberty
and equality, hollow mockery; your prayers and hymns, your sermons and
thanksgivings, with all your religious parade and solemnity, are to him
mere bombast, fraud, deception, impiety, and hypocrisy—a thin veil to
cover up crimes which would disgrace a nation of savages. There is not a
nation of the earth guilty of practices more shocking and bloody than are
the people of these United States at this very hour.

Go where you may, search where you will, roam through all the monar-
chies and despotisms of the Old World, travel through South America,
search out every abuse and when you have found the last, lay your facts by
the side of the every-day practices of this nation, and you will say with me
that, for revolting barbarity and shameless hypocrisy, America reigns without a rival.

KIDS AND THE PLEDGE:
NOT A TRUTH BUT A GOAL
Frank Harris III

Some words you just remember—even without trying.

Like our Pledge of Allegiance.

Thirty-some years ago, I remember standing in Whittier Elementary School in Waukegan, Ill., with my right hand over my heart learning the pledge. I remember locking my brown eyes on the stars and stripes. I remember reciting words that have endured through a lifetime.

I pledge allegiance . . .

It is the first rite of American education. And last week my 5-year-old came home reciting these same words that she now was learning in her first week of kindergarten.

. . . to the flag . . .

It is a pledge which I, and countless other African-Americans, over the years have pledged with mixed feelings. After all, a pledge to do something should mean a pledge in return. A pledge for some consideration. For fair play.

. . . of the United States of America . . .

But as a black schoolboy in the 1960s, I lived in a time when such pledges by blacks were in vain. Throughout the country, there were places one couldn't go, things one couldn't do, jobs one couldn't hold. Justice that was often denied. Freedom that was relative. A time when—despite President John Kennedy's statement about asking not what our country can do for us but what we can do for our country—there came a flashpoint when the pledge became so one-sided that it needed to be asked what our country can do for us rather than to us.

. . . and the republic for which it stands . . .

We were and are American citizens. As citizens we pledged our allegiance to the flag. It was something that we did as a matter of ritual.

. . . one nation under God . . .

Then, on a September morning 30 years ago today, four little girls were killed in a church in Birmingham, Ala. Blown to kingdom come by a bomb because blacks were trying to make the words to that pledge ring true all the way around.

. . . indivisible . . .

Still, we remain so divided.

. . . with liberty and justice for all.

Did they, too, once pledge with eyes on the flag and hand over heart?

I help my kindergartener with the words, knowing that the pledge is not a truth but an optimistic goal to be achieved over the obstacles of reality and the reflections of memory.

Some things you just remember—even without trying.

MY DUNGEON SHOOK:

LETTER TO MY NEPHEW

ON THE HUNDREDTH ANNIVERSARY

OF THE EMANCIPATION PROCLAMATION

James Baldwin

ear James:

I have begun this letter five times and torn it up five times. I keep seeing your face, which is also the face of your father and my brother. Like him, you are tough, dark, vulnerable, moody—with a very definite tendency to sound truculent because you want no one to think you are soft. You may be like your grandfather in this, I don't know, but certainly both you and your father resemble him very much physically. Well, he is dead, he never saw you, and he had a terrible life; he was defeated long before he died because, at the bottom of his heart, he really believed what white people said about him. This is one of the reasons that he became so holy. I am sure that your father has told you something about all that. Neither you nor your father exhibit any tendency towards holiness: you really *are* of another era, part of what happened when the Negro left the land and came into what the late E. Franklin Frazier called "the cities of destruction." You can only be destroyed by believing that you really are what the white world calls a *nigger*. I tell you this because I love you, and please don't you ever forget it.

I have known both of you all your lives, have carried your Daddy in my arms and on my shoulders, kissed and spanked him and watched him learn to walk. I don't know if you've known anybody from that far back; if you've loved anybody that long, first as an infant, then as a child, then as a man, you gain a strange perspective on time and human pain and effort. Other people cannot see what I see whenever I look into your father's face, for behind your father's face as it is today are all those other faces which were his. Let him laugh and I see a cellar your father does not remember and a house he does not remember and I hear in his present laughter his laughter as a child. Let him curse and I remember him falling down the cellar steps, and howling, and I remember, with pain, his tears, which my hand or your grandmother's so easily wiped away. But no one's hand can wipe away those tears he sheds invisibly today, which one hears in his laughter and in his speech and in his songs. I know what the world has done to my brother and how narrowly he has survived it. And I know, which is much worse, and this is the crime of which I accuse my country and my countrymen, and for which neither I nor time nor history will ever forgive them, that they have destroyed and are destroying hundreds of thousands of lives and do not know it and do not want to know it. One can be, indeed one must strive to become, tough and philosophical concerning destruction and death, for this is what most of mankind has been best at since we have heard of man. (But remember: *most* of mankind is not *all* of mankind.) But it is not permissible that the authors of devastation should also be innocent. It is the innocence which constitutes the crime.

Now, my dear namesake, these innocent and well-meaning people, your countrymen, have caused you to be born under conditions not very far removed from those described for us by Charles Dickens in the London of more than a hundred years ago. (I hear the chorus of the innocents screaming, "No! This is not true! How *bitter* you are!"—but I am writing this letter to *you,* to try to tell you something about how to handle *them,* for most of them do not yet really know that you exist. I *know* the conditions under which you were born, for I was there. Your countrymen were *not* there, and haven't made it yet. Your grandmother was also there, and no one has ever accused her of being bitter. I suggest that the innocents check with her. She isn't hard to find. Your countrymen don't know that *she* exists, either; though she has been working for them all their lives.)

Well, you were born, here you came, something like fourteen years ago;

and though your father and mother and grandmother, looking about the streets through which they were carrying you, staring at the walls into which they brought you, had every reason to be heavyhearted, yet they were not. For here you were, Big James, named for me—you were a big baby, I was not—here you were: to be loved. To be loved, baby, hard, at once, and forever, to strengthen you against the loveless world. Remember that: I know how black it looks today, for you. It looked bad that day, too, yes, we were trembling. We have not stopped trembling yet, but if we had not loved each other none of us would have survived. And now you must survive because we love you, and for the sake of your children and your children's children.

This innocent country set you down in a ghetto in which, in fact, it intended that you should perish. Let me spell out precisely what I mean by that, for the heart of the matter is here, and the root of my dispute with my country. You were born where you were born and faced the future that you faced because you were black and *for no other reason.* The limits of your ambition were, thus, expected to be set forever. You were born into a society which spelled out with brutal clarity, and in as many ways as possible, that you were a worthless human being. You were not expected to aspire to excellence: you were expected to make peace with mediocrity. Wherever you have turned, James, in your short time on this earth, you have been told where you could go and what you could do (and *how* you could do it) and where you could live and whom you could marry. I know your countrymen do not agree with me about this, and I hear them saying, "You exaggerate." They do not know Harlem, and I do. So do you. Take no one's word for anything, including mine—but trust your experience. Know whence you came. If you know whence you came, there is really no limit to where you can go. The details and symbols of your life have been deliberately constructed to make you believe what white people say about you. Please try to remember that what they believe, as well as what they do and cause you to endure, does not testify to your inferiority but to their inhumanity and fear. Please try to be clear, dear James, through the storm which rages about your youthful head today, about the reality which lies behind the words *acceptance* and *integration*. There is no reason for you to try to become like white people and there is no basis whatever for their impertinent assumption that *they* must accept *you*. The really terrible thing, old buddy, is that *you* must accept *them*. And I mean that very seriously. You must accept them and accept them with love. For these innocent people have no other hope. They are, in effect, still trapped in a history which they do not understand, and until they understand it, they cannot be released from it. They have had to believe for many years, and for innumerable reasons, that black men are inferior to white men. Many of them, indeed, know better, but, as you will discover, people find it very difficult to act on what they know. To act is to be committed, and to be committed is to be in danger. In this case, the danger, in the minds of most white Americans, is the loss of their identity. Try to imagine how you would feel if you woke up one morning to find the sun shining and all the stars aflame. You would be

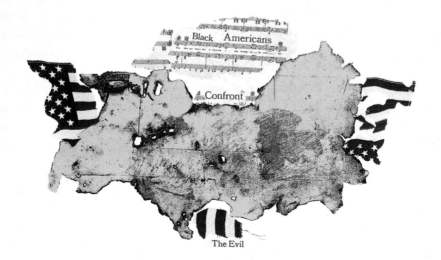

John Rozelle, *12% Solution*, 1992. Serigraph, 12 color, 22½ × 30½ in.
Courtesy of the artist. Private collection. Photo: Stephen Peck.

frightened because it is out of the order of nature. Any upheaval in the universe is terrifying because it so profoundly attacks one's sense of one's own reality. Well, the black man has functioned in the white man's world as a fixed star, as an immovable pillar: and as he moves out of his place, heaven and earth are shaken to their foundations. You, don't be afraid. I said that it was intended that you should perish in the ghetto, perish by never being allowed to go behind the white man's definitions, by never being allowed to spell your proper name. You have, and many of us have, defeated this intention; and, by a terrible law, a terrible paradox, those innocents who believed that your imprisonment made them safe are losing their grasp of reality. But these men are your brothers—your lost, younger brothers. And if the word *integration* means anything, this is what it means: that we, with love, shall force our brothers to see themselves as they are, to cease fleeing from reality and begin to change it. For this is your home, my friend, do not be driven from it; great men have done great things here, and will again, and we can make America what America must become. It will be hard, James, but you come from sturdy, peasant stock, men who picked cotton and dammed rivers and built railroads, and, in the teeth of the most terrifying odds, achieved an unassailable and monumental dignity. You come from a long line of great poets, some of the greatest poets since Homer. One of them said, *The very time I thought I was lost, My dungeon shook and my chains fell off.*

You know, and I know, that the country is celebrating one hundred years of freedom one hundred years too soon. We cannot be free until they are free. God bless you, James, and Godspeed.

Your uncle,
James

AMERICA

Claude McKay

Although she feeds me bread of bitterness,
And sinks into my throat her tiger's tooth,
Stealing my breath of life, I will confess
I love this cultured hell that tests my youth!
Her vigor flows like tides into my blood,
Giving me strength erect against her hate.
Her bigness sweeps my being like a flood.
Yet as a rebel fronts a king in state,
I stand within her walls with not a shred
Of terror, malice, not a word of jeer.
Darkly I gaze into days ahead,
And see her might and granite wonders there,
Beneath the touch of Time's unerring hand,
Like priceless treasures sinking in the sand.

PART VII

I Leave You

Love

ove does not cease because we do. The universe, the loving darkness that protects and supports us, never ends. For those of us who experience the separations of life—the leave-takings, breakups, deaths—we eventually learn one thing: Love is always left behind.

These, then, are the lessons of our living and loving. The people who helped us along the road, whose voices remain with us still, remind us that love is ultimately the only risk sure to be worth taking—it pays us back a hundredfold, pressed down and running over.

Naomi and Harold in Saundra Sharp's "Dearly Beloved" know that nothing can stop the loving. The lessons taught by Nikky Finney's mother detailed in "Making a Scene" will be carried within Nikky long after her mother's daily presence is no longer felt. Our fathers' gruffness and offhanded expressions of love, our mothers' gentleness and perseverance, whatever good and bad we glean from them, all become the stuff from which we fashion our own unique songs of love.

As a people, we also have way-showers, guides who spoke through their words and deeds of a love greater than our daily concerns. Martin, Malcolm, Rosa, Fannie Lou are probably the best known of those we have come to celebrate. But other spiritual and cultural guides, lesser known perhaps but no less worthy, are celebrated here by Maya Angelou, Quincy Troupe, and others, themselves beacons to a clearer vision of loving and accepting ourselves individually and as a people.

Just months before her death, Mary McLeod Bethune bequeathed to us a rich legacy of love and courage she'd spent a lifetime developing. She and the other voices represented here show that the epitaph we write by our own living and loving is finally ours to determine. The gifts bestowed on us by our knowledge of who and whose we are, our family and friends, our loves, our connections to community, land, country, and ancestors, forms the basis for the love we give, the love we take.

Duke Ellington, that master musical genius of the twentieth century, had a way with words equally impressive as his way with melody. And while he spoke from his hospital room decades ago about what we are capable of accomplishing, he could have as easily been speaking of our emotional future, too. We will let his be the final words in this symphony of African-American love:

> We are children of the sun and our race has a definite tradition of beauty and glory and vitality that is as rich and powerful as the sun itself. These traditions are ours to express, and will enrich our careers in proportion to the sincerity and faithfulness with which we interpret them.

> The future of Black love is literally carried in our hands and hearts. We must cherish and use what's been entrusted to us as if our lives depended on it—they do.

DEARLY BELOVED
Saundra Sharp

a very particular cloud hovered over Naomi James' office. It whispered to her. She could hear it, causing her to turn and gaze across the file cabinets to the single wind-brushed cloud that spoke to her.

"I can look at your order again, but . . ." She listened, doodling a small picture of the cloud on her calendar pad. "It's not our policy to do that . . ." The cloud looked in, watching the attractive thirty-year-old woman with deep dimples in her earth-brown cheeks. The voice at the other end of the phone was insistent. Naomi shuffled papers, anxious to get on to the next task.

"Mr. Robinson, let me suggest—"

Midsentence she was struck by a sense of something. Slowly she put the phone down, the muffled voice following her to the window. Naomi stared at the cloud. And it seemed to tease her, to draw a smile from the reluctant corner of a tense mouth. Behind her another phone rang. And then the cloud moved, the wind sweeping it away from her.

She wheeled around, began gathering her things.

"Mrs. James. . . ." Her secretary was at the door. "It's the—"

Naomi cut her off. "Yes, I know."

"—the hospital," she finished in whispered anguish to Naomi's back, which was already at the end of the hall.

"Hello?" Robinson shouted from the desk. "Hello?"

Naomi let herself into the house, grateful for the cool darkness of the foyer. Perhaps she could stay here forever. Perhaps she could cocoon herself into this cool dark spot and never know the coming pain, the onset of wreaking emptiness. She didn't want to be a blues woman, moaning between the notes about an empty bed that rhymed with a hurtin' head. Perhaps if she just stood right here in the cool dark and asked quietly, in her most efficient voice, someone/something would beam her up. Beam her up to a place where there was no coming pain. Pain in all its colors with all its surprise appearances. The door behind her opened and she knew her wish was lost.

Fern Logan, *Yaddo Tower*, 1985. Silver print, 14 × 11 in. Courtesy of the photographer.

"You're here." Frank reached out for her and they held each other. When she was little her big brother had not let the world pick on her without going through him first. Could he still do that? How long could she hide here?

Not long. Practical people abandoned their power to create imaginary realities. Frank would never agree to let her be beamed anywhere because he couldn't believe in the possibility. With his organized, legal inclinations a protective stay in his arms would have to be drawn up into a litigious appellate affidavit or something. There is no shelter from the residue of death's due. Extended payments, perhaps. But no shelter.

"I told the hospital that the body should go to Connors," Frank stated. Naomi nodded affirmatively, pacing the small foyer in a smaller circle. He watched her.

"Have you called the folks?" Naomi shook her head no. Frank got the phone, carrying it back as he talked. "I think we should press charges. You do want to press charges, don't you?"

Press . . . ? What was he talking about? Why was he talking at all? She needed silence. A cool, clear silence so she could think about . . . so she could . . . this.

"On the other driver," Frank continued. "We can sue for civil dam— Hello? Ella Mae? The hospital called. He's gone."

Frank's voice floated away from her as she ascended the stairs. "I'm here with her. She's right here. Hold on . . . Sis . . . Sis"

In their bedroom the sun danced softly on the place where loving was most comfortable, so Naomi sat on the edge and held on. Rocking. She rocked the void. She rocked the dreams that were secrets only she had been told. She rocked the little girl who would never look just like her and be just like him. She rocked the caverns of vulnerability that one man had chosen to reveal to her soul because he believed she would not let him fall into them. She rocked until the sun had danced away and Night entered, finding that in all of its vastness there was not room enough to hold her, and so it went away, and Dawn came, whispering. Whispering instructions that peace was not ready yet, but in the meantime Naomi should follow the mind among her minds that spoke most directly to her.

Hearing, she let go. So when Morning came to bathe her, she was ready.

"Where's the Crisco?" Harold's mother looked furtively through Naomi's cupboards.

"Is this right? I thought he had been teaching at U.C. for four years." Harold's sister, Betty, self-proclaimed obituary writer.

"Didn't seem like it's been that long," responded Daddy James, Harold's gently charming father. "Ask Naomi."

"Naomi, how long—"

"Where *is* the Crisco?!" Ella Mae interrupted. "Some kind of fat!"

Naomi answered, "We don't have any."

"You don't have any white flour, you don't have any fat—how do you expect me to fry this chicken?"

Frank interceded. "You know Naomi and Hal are vegetarians. I bet this house has never seen a chicken, much less a fried one."

"Well, this is no time to be a vegetarian!" Ella Mae protested. "She needs a good solid meal. Frank, run to the store and get me some fat. Some Crisco. Some somethin'."

"Don't bring no pork in here, Frank," Naomi warned. Daddy James cut her a look that said "Keep the peace, girl." Naomi responded with a sly smile.

At the stove, Ella Mae succumbed to memory. "Harold loved my fried chicken. That boy loved my fried chicken." Filled up, she broke down and left the room weeping.

Through gritted teeth Naomi whispered, "I can't have people crying all over the place. I can't stand it."

"She's grieving, girl," Daddy James explained. "You gotta let her grieve."

"Please make her stop crying, Daddy James. It gives me—I just can't stand it." Torn between who needed his support most, Daddy James went to comfort his wife.

Betty, reading partly to herself as she corrected the obituary, stated ". . . he died on Wednesday, March—"

Naomi abruptly interrupted. "He died two weeks ago. He died at the accident."

"Naomi," Frank responded, "he was in a coma for two weeks but he wasn't dead. I believe he could still hear us, even though there were almost no signs of life."

"But that's what death is, isn't it? The absence of life?"

Full of her own opinion about this, Betty continued, ". . . on the *fourteenth,* as a result of injuries sustained from a traffic accident. He is survived by—"

Frank jabbed his finger onto the scribbled page. *"Attorney* Frank . . ." he emphasized.

"Do we need more than one car for the funeral?"

Naomi responded calmly, "I'm not going to the funeral."

Frank grabbed his head. "Oh, Lord! We're not going through this again," he insisted.

Daddy James was encouraging. "You have to be strong . . . it's just one more day you have to get through."

"Really, I don't go to funerals."

Betty, whose mouth had fallen fully open at the first announcement, wailed into the other room, "Mommy, Naomi says she's not going to Harold's funeral!" And Ella Mae wailed back. Naomi was, they each decided, clearly stressed and just needed to lie down.

"How can you not go to your husband's funeral?" Frank demanded to know. After all, what would people think? It was enough when she had, as a child, refused to go to their father's funeral. "He died while we were eating breakfast. She ran out of the house and damn near turned out the neighborhood."

Naomi attempted to come to her own defense. "Harold knows I don't go to funerals."

"Some folks just real scared of death," Daddy James offered as group consolation. "You get used to it after you've put away enough people."

"Daddy, folks don't get used to death!" Betty retorted.

"Well, you learn to deal with it." He turned to Naomi. "Did somebody scare you when you were young? I mean, did they show you a dead body when you weren't ready for it? Scare you with it?"

"Oh, please!" Betty exclaimed in exasperation.

"Well, kids being kids, you know."

Ella Mae returned, ready to deal. "Well, you must attend, Naomi, and that's that. We have to be adult about these things."

A bursting silence embraced the group as they awaited Naomi's capitulation. She spoke without emotion. "I love Harold James. More than anything in this world.

"It just seems like somebody you love and you lived with ought to be able to talk to you. When I see somebody dead I just want to put breath back in their body, so they can understand me, so they can talk to me. I can't stand it when they don't talk to me. I swear, if I have to go back to that funeral home they'll have to bury both of us."

She read their faces and remembered Dawn's promise. "Hal knows I don't go to funerals. I really don't think he's expecting me." She then asked, with extreme graciousness, "Would you excuse me?" and left the room.

Frank's eyes questioned the group. What else could be done? An absolutely outdone Ella Mae mimicked Naomi. " 'I don't think he's expecting me.' . . . I never in all my days heard of such a thing!"

"Take it easy, babe," Daddy James cautioned. "You're gonna get your blood pressure up."

"My blood pressure's already up. Couldn't have it at a church, has to be a cold, impersonal funeral home. Didn't want to bury him proper, wanted to burn him. Wanted to burn up my child. Doesn't eat chicken. Well, I put my foot down about that cremation business. My foot is down but my blood pressure is definitely up!" Eyeing her husband, she continued, "*Somebody ought to talk to her. Talk some good grace into her head!*"

Dozens of uncomfortable university students huddled near the driveway of the funeral home. The limo pulled in and friends rushed forward, pouring sympathy and comfort through the blue-tinted glass. Naomi's secretary peered into the car and was met with the tightened jaws of Frank. As the family unfolded silently the sounds of the metropolis, arguments, screeching brakes, ringing phones wafted upward to mingle with life on another plane. Children's laughter rose through the ethers, tickled the wings of birds and made them smile. From the funeral home the grace notes of "It is well, it is well with my soul . . ." floated up past the tips of elm trees into the clouds.

"Dearly beloved," called out the minister's voice, "our God has called us together this morning . . ." His resonance criss-crossed with the static-ridden "Price check on three, price check on three" from the supermarket, where Naomi strolled leisurely, pushing a grocery cart. She perused items, read labels, nibbled on the ruby-red grapes in her basket.

"And when you come to me in summer . . ." Back in her kitchen, Naomi half hummed, half sang fragments of the haunting song that had wandered into her consciousness as she prepared breakfast. She set the table for two. She poured two glasses of juice. It was the flat tap of the toast hitting the second plate that became an unseen slap against her face, wrenching her into the reality of breakfast for one. Her entire body was being consumed with anguish yet the rage of her weeping was a silent scream. She was going down into an unfathomable abyss and would have hit bottom, except that she heard the front door open.

"Naomi! You home?" Harold called.

Naomi froze.

Harold entered the room, loosening his tie. Thirty-five, easy, he was looking real good this morning. But Naomi couldn't see that yet. Her eyes were still locked on the toast, and to shift them could save her life or cause her to lose it.

"I'm sure glad you're fixing breakfast. I'm hungry," Harold announced as he slid into his seat at the table. He reached for his morning paper, which was not in its usual place next to his meal. He rose to retrieve it from the living room. Returning, he tapped her lightly on the shoulder with the paper and remarked, teasingly, "How quickly we forget."

Something . . . perhaps it was the tap on the shoulder . . . something gave her . . . or it was the familiar warm tease in his voice . . . gave her permission to breathe again. Maybe.

Harold moved easily into their breakfast ritual, sharing the newspaper items.

"Looks like we're gonna lose that primary. I told those people what to do. I told them they had to make an alliance with Fogarty or we'd get wiped out." He skipped to another section, studied it. "I don't know why I always read the stock reports, like I had some."

Slowly Naomi searched for a way to take hold of this . . . this . . . ? That is, she was willing to test it. After all, it was morning, and Dawn had promised . . . Now. Now a slight smile of light grew in her eyes and slipped down onto her lips and she got up and poured coffee for her husband. Harold moved on to the sports pages.

"A new coach at U.C.? They fired Wilkens?" He was outraged. "Naw! Wilkens was my main man." He buried his head into the details of this terrible act and then, without looking up, stated, "You're awful quiet this morning."

"Didn't you . . ." How should she put this? Was there even a question to be asked? "Didn't you . . . um . . . have an appointment—" She scratched the tip of her nose, an old habit that no longer required an itch. "—to do something . . . this morning?"

"Yeah." He looked up. "But one of the brothers decided the bereaved were too distraught to come to the casket, so he started rolling it to them.

Rolling me up and down the aisles. I decided it was time to get the hell out of there for a while."

Naomi couldn't help laughing. "Naw, they didn't!"

"Yeah! You should have seen it. People were ducking out of the way . . ."

"Noooo," she howled, "they didn't!"

"See, that's why I hate funerals. People get ridiculous."

They bent over with laughter, riding its wave into a soft, necessary silence.

"So. How you doin'?" he asked, as he took her hand and kissed it.

"I'm dealing with it."

"Yeah. Me too."

Naomi ate now, as she always did, with an enthusiastic appreciation for the food.

"I hear the car is totaled."

"To say the least."

"Damn, it would happen right after I finished paying for it. You know where all the papers are?"

"Uh-hummm."

"What happened to the other driver?"

"Nothing, 'cause the police said he wasn't drunk and he wasn't negligent. But Frank wants to press civil charges. I don't know. We have to go to the police station tomorrow. Don't forget to take your vitamins."

These last words, coming out of her mouth with such perfect insignificance, spooked her.

"Thanks," Harold responded. "I'm going to need them, since I notice I'm not getting cremated."

"Sweetheart, your mother threw a natural fit. I told them it's what you wanted, but Ella Mae didn't believe me. I think your father did, but he wasn't too hot on the idea.

"Well, I am my momma's number-one baby boy, you know. Her golden toy, her pride and joy."

Naomi responded with mock disgust. "I don't know what she thinks is so hot about what she created."

"You must have thought something, 'cause you married it."

"I was young and crazy, out of my head."

"No," he chided, "you just have better taste than you have ever given yourself credit for."

"You oughtta stop." She began clearing the table.

"Naomi, I . . . this happened so fast. I'm not sure if everything is in order. Please, please make sure my research gets published. Roy can handle it."

Naomi nodded her consent. Of course there were things to be discussed. But she hoped that he hadn't come to divulge some secrets of passion, or worse, to give her his permission to remarry. No soap operas this morning, please.

"Just stay on him," Harold continued. "They should have some money for you from the school. I'm due that. It should cover everything for right now. . . . We never took out that life insurance we talked about."

"I'll be okay," she assured him. "I've got my job. And there's family. And if worse comes to worse I'll just sell your stuff."

Alarmed, he questioned, "What stuff??"

"Oh, I don't know. That flaming red almost-a-jock-strap you bought when we went to Jamaica ought to be worth something."

"You still have that?"

"Your political science students should find it very interesting. Maybe the next time the department is having a fund-raiser we can raffle it off."

"Woman, don't be messing with me after I'm gone!"

"Whew!" She laughed. "I will always remember that night."

"Yeah," he said softly, as he took her in his arms. "We do have some good times to remember. We are very blessed, Naomi. We know what love feels like and how it lives."

"Then why are you leaving?"

It was a question she had not meant to ask. She had practiced not asking it ever since the accident. So in the silence of no answer they held each other until their breathing was in sync the way they had done so many times after making love. But Dawn had not promised forever.

"I think I better get back," Harold said at last, "before they leave for the cemetery without me."

She fixed his tie for him. He used it to wipe the single tear that wiggled down the outside of her nose.

"You know that I can't come again."

"I know."

He left her, or she let him go. It's always hard to tell.

"Thanks for breakfast," as he crossed to the doorway.

"Thank *you,*" she mouthed back to him.

He was gone, then he stuck his head back through the kitchen door. "You gonna be all right?"

She laughed softly. "Yeah." Then she gifted him her most radiant smile. He blew her a kiss and left.

At the sink, Naomi looked out the window at a blue sky with clouds on the move. She turned on the water and, humming, began to wash the breakfast dishes.

CRUMBS THROUGH THE FOREST:
A SOUTH-CENTRAL FAIRY TALE
Paula L. Woods

In 1982, my father and I were having a conversation about love, him listening to my problems and me giving him advice about a lady friend of his. For me to have a conversation with the man who, throughout my adolescence, exerted such rigid control over my dating ran counter to every impulse I ever had of not letting him know my business. But since my mother's death when I was nineteen, Ike and I had developed something akin to a truce in matters personal and, tentatively at first but with increasing candor, had begun to talk as equals and friends about our relationships and attitudes about the loves in our lives.

The fact that we even had these conversations was amazing to me then and, now that I've begun to piece the story of my parents' lives and relationships, is even more remarkable now. For the vision I had come to have of my parents was as titan forces, monoliths doing battle over the nature and shaping of my mind and sexuality. My father ever the oppressor (no, you can't wear nail polish, can't cut your hair, who's that little nigger on the phone?), my mother the surreptitious champion for the cause of sexual freedom, the confidante with whom I could share my first disappointing sexual encounter and who accompanied me to the family doctor for my first packet of birth control pills (girl, don't *ever* let your father see these!). My parents were playing out roles they had perfected over the years with each other in playful encounters and bitter arguments in our house in Compton, less openly in my father's business in Watts, roles they had understudied as children watching their own parents and othermothers and fathers enact in southern, midwestern, and western towns. My father's role was that of a proud yet dangerous lion, true to his astrology, while my mother alternated between damsel in distress and a secular Danielle, constantly trying to soothe the roaring beast with soft words and logic or, when all else failed, feminine subterfuge. They were roles I, too, would play in our family and in my love life, but which ill-suited my personality. Just as I found on that day in 1982, nine years after my mother's death had altered the dynamics of interaction between Ike and me, that the role of lion-hearted disciplinarian was one that did not allow my father the free range of emotional expression he wanted with me or her in matters of love.

My father was born in 1909 and grew up in an age not known for personal freedom, not in social interaction with whites, not in straight-up talk between parents and children, and certainly not in sexual candor between men and women. But Isaac Woods' horizons had always been broader than Batesville, Arkansas, where he was born and spent the first sixteen years of his life as an adventurer, a black boy of relative means who, at six, fell from a church belfry trying to catch pigeons, who played and whooped with abandon in a town where racial boundaries were strictly drawn and never openly challenged, until a thorough ass-whipping my father gave a white kid who called him a nigger resulted in a hurried escape from a lynching party made up of my grandfather's erstwhile customers and active KKK members. They left at dusk, my grandfather's Model-T crammed to the roof with their every portable possession, his thriving blacksmith/auto repair business and comfortable home left to the care of a brother and sister whom he helped out of Arkansas as soon as he got established out west.

The forced change of venue to Watts, California, opened a whole new world to my father, one full of sunshine, sandy (albeit segregated) beaches, numerous and prosperous Negro businesses, and white folks who, by and large, kept their distance. Smart, funny, and gregarious, Ike quickly made friends, running buddies like a young Charles Mingus, who lived across the street from my grandfather's gas station at 108th Street and Compton Avenue, and a variety of other young cats who, like my father, prowled the streets, hunting and being hunted by the young women of the community, who were attracted to the cars, pinstriped suits, and slicked-back hair Ike and the others sported.

My father, it appears from photos I have of the time and accounts of his friends and future mother-in-law, was one of the best-looking of the bunch, a real killer. Not even his mysterious disappearance from '33 to '38 dampened women's enthusiasm for him, and the luster of an Army Air Corps uniform and return whole and unharmed from WW II only added to his allure. The pictures of him during the war are some of my favorites. He's thirty-five, sitting with his mother and cousin Charlene at a party, the black-and-white photo not obscuring the fact that his thinning hair is light, his skin unusually fair for a Negro. But unlike many of the fair Negroes of the time, who could, as my maternal grandmother remembers, "join the Blue Vein societies," Ike was a race man through and through, much less taken with his color than those around him, trying as hard to run from his fairness as he did from participating fully in my grandfather's business and prosperity. Parties like this particular one in December 1944 were one of his means of escape.

This was the party at which he met my mother, who for some reason does not appear in the photos. She was, in many ways, the opposite of my father. Florence Hildebrand was dark-skinned, with flared nostrils and large, doelike eyes. Where my father was gregarious, my mother exuded a quiet good-heartedness that went far beyond what was hoped for, but rarely achieved, in a preacher's kid. Friendly to the women of the Grant A.M.E. congregation and the Watts community, she became the daughter they all wished they had had and, barring adoption, who they began to think of as the perfect mate for their civilian or enlisted sons.

My mother was oblivious to all of this, or laughed it off when the mothers made their overtures. She had just turned twenty-nine when she met my father, over the hill for the times, and although she was not desperate in the least to find a husband, my grandmother and the ever-increasing list of her fans with marriageable sons certainly were. Grandmother would later tell me about the men my mother turned away, "respectable colored boys," in Portland, Oregon, where my grandfather, an A.M.E. minister, had been assigned, or other cities where they had lived. There was a case of two brothers in Portland, Bobby and Billy, who were both in the service at the beginning of the war. In an almost identical scenario to one that would develop in Los Angeles, Florence first met the "B-boys' " mother at church. The mother promptly fell in love with her, and, with two sons coming home on furlough, there was little time to lose. Florence was first hustled before Bobby, the younger and more outgoing of the two. They seemed to hit it off famously, although my grandmother was sorely displeased by the young man's "fast ways," which for the time meant he enjoyed going to nightclubs, which my mother evidently liked, and which my grandmother evidently did not. Billy, the older brother, was more studious, more business-oriented, and while my grandmother gave him the nod, Florence said nothing doing. So, with Bobby, her favorite, not approved of by the only mother she had ever known, a woman who rescued her from the snow when her natural father threw her out at age seventeen, and Billy not being at all the man she wanted, the whole triangle ground to an anguished halt. The mothers were devastated, but Florence started a recital tour of Negro churches in the West, Billy finished his tour of duty, went to L.A. after the war, married and proceeded to amass large amounts of real estate, much to my grandmother's chagrin.

My maternal and paternal grandmothers met when my Grandfather Allen was assigned to Grant A.M.E. Church on 105th Street and Central Avenue. The parsonage was across the street from my grandfather's gas station/garage and the two women, who shared a familiarity with the church and love of church life, became fast friends. They often met at one another's homes and, amid tea and pound cake, bemoaned the fate of their offspring, one seemingly disinterested in marrying and the other having too good a time to give it serious consideration. Florence and Ike, they concluded, would make a wonderful couple. And my grandmothers, both very strong women who had nurtured the lives and careers of husbands and children, decreed that it would be so.

Despite the mothers' supervision, Ike and Florence's courtship was not without its hitches. Certainly my father's free-spirited ways were attractive to my mother, but she was also dating another man during the war, a man more in the mold of the calmer Billy of Portland, whose mother was also making her bid. My grandmother, burned by speaking up too forcefully in the "B-boys" affair, did not discourage her seeing the other suitor. And Jim was evidently a lovely man with whom my mother enjoyed the movies and singing in the church choir. My father, however, upon his return from the service, was having none of it and promptly joined the choir, where he could keep an eye on my mother and where other women would try to catch his, leaving notes on his car and trying to change their voices from soprano to alto so they could stand closer to him in the tenor section. My mother, already firmly entrenched with the altos, ignored it all.

Things came to a head one night when my mother decided to go to a movie with Jim and, after finishing her day's work at the office of a Watts physician, went home and changed clothes, taking a bus downtown to meet Jim at a theater. She should have hitched a ride with my father because Ike followed the bus all the way downtown, moved to action after watching her movements from his sentry position at the rear of the gas station office across the street. Ike, not certain of his position with my mother, had taken to watching her in secret, nursing an evening beer, wounded pride, and the growing suspicion he was somehow being done wrong. That night, as he watched Florence shed her white medical assistant's cocoon for a flowing spring dress, he had a chance to find out for sure.

I don't know what Florence and her date saw at the movies, but it couldn't have been any more dramatic than the scene that ensued when my father (who had returned to the gas station and a few more beers after seeing Jim meet her in front of the theater) accosted her at the front door of the parsonage as soon as he saw the cab drop my mother off.

It takes my grandmother to tell the story, of how he stood *in the living room! of the parsonage! cussing and carrying on!* while my mother stood calmly listening to my father's sputtering rage. My grandmother finally intervened, gently but firmly pushing my father out the door, telling him he could not speak that way in her house and to call on Florence tomorrow when he had better control of himself.

He took control of himself, and the situation, when he returned the next day with an engagement ring.

And what was my mother's response to all of this? Because she died when I was nineteen, my mother and I never had a chance to discuss their courtship or marriage as equals, after I had grown and had begun to examine the facets and meaning of my own interaction with men. While we shared an extraordinary friendship for a mother and daughter, I was clearly still the girlchild and therefore I had been fed the fairy-tale version of the story, embellished by my mother and grandmother through the years: how my mother, not a small woman, had lost thirty, no fifty, no sixty pounds in the months before the wedding (courtesy, according to myth, of an attempted poisoning by my father's jealous ex-wife at a summer party); how the doctors could not name the illness, but agreed that she might not live; how my father vowed to marry her even if she lived only another day; how she was so sick she had to be literally held up in my father's arms to be married by my grandfather in the parsonage; how she had immediately returned to bed and the reception became more of a wake than a celebration in the midst of such deathly illness; how my father carried her bodily from the parsonage to her brand-new home, where their happiness was enhanced only by my arrival seven years later.

My mother's life, as I knew it then, was a series of melodramatic episodes. As it was told and retold, it imparted to me a legacy I would understand only through the mirror of my own adult life: tragedy upon tragedy relieved only by the unswerving love for a man, despite his anger, his drinking, his not respecting her as an equal. My mother was the plucky but tragic heroine, my father the ogre. And while the legend and lore sat heavy between my father and me at the yellow Formica table, my father gave me a gift, just crumbs initially, of another perspective, sprinkled through the forest of this Black fairy tale that ultimately led me to a different understanding of my parents' lives and the choices of my own.

That day in 1982, my father was describing his current lady friend's alarming habit of accusing him of stealing from her. A rental property owner in South Central Los Angeles as my father had been before his retirement, she had asked him to collect her rents, something that my father approached in his typical brusque fashion that got results, despite his seventy-two years. But when she accused him of stealing some of the rent money and later added insult to injury by confronting him about cans of Campbell's cream of mushroom soup missing from her pantry, my father's willingness to stay in his lady's corner angrily dissipated.

"What gets into women?" he wanted to know. "Couldn't she understand I collected rent money for her because I wanted to help her? That I've got my own money? And, as for soup, hmph, I've got more cans of that stuff from your mother than I know what to do with!" Making a mental note to remove potentially botulism-producing seven-year-old soup cans from the cupboard, I shook my head. There was no solace I could offer, nothing to be said in the face of such strange behavior. Could it be Alzheimer's, approaching senility? My father, several years this woman's senior, looked at me with milky brown eyes and then at his gnarled hands, and I knew the answer before the words left my lips. No, he didn't think it was that. She just didn't understand that his doing for her was part of a commitment he made to her in the relationship.

"Your mother understood. Florence was always there for me, even when I didn't deserve it. I couldn't have done better for those twenty-five years." Something about the conversation triggered an idea in his mind and he rose from the kitchen table, location of most of our heart-to-heart talks, and began to rummage about in his bedroom, looking for something he wanted me to read. After several minutes he returned with a yellowed envelope addressed to Mrs. Cora M. Burgan, his maternal grandmother.

Betye Saar, *Letters from Home / Wish You Were Here*, 1976. Collage, 19½ × 15 in.
Courtesy of the artist. Photo: Stephen Peck.

"See, this is what I mean about commitment," he said. The letter, dated October 6, 1915, was from my great-grandfather, Isaac Burgan, and read:

Birthday (Reflections)

WEDNESDAY,
OCTOBER 6, 7:38 P.M.

DEAR CORA—

I write to remind you of the fact that 67 years ago, not far from this Blessed Hour, the Good Lord was pleased to bring into this world a BOY and his GOOD MOTHER called him Isaac. I am very, very thankful to say that through all these long years the same GOOD LORD has been very good to me. Many people that I have met have been very kind and considerate, and some have shown much interest in my welfare. For every kindness and consideration, I am very thankful.

Twenty-six of these long years, C O R A has held me by the hand and done ALL she could to help, to comfort, cheer and encourage me. For ALL you have done I Thank You Ten Thousand TIMES. I wish very much that I could give you Ten Thousand Kisses tonight. Tell your dear mother that I am also thankful that I have been thrown into relationship with her, and that too has been a blessing to my life. God Bless you, DEAR CORA, and your good mother. I now feel sure that He will let us all see the brightness of his Sunlight Upon our Pathway, as we have never seen it before. So I am singing the song I herein send you.

Many thanks for the Birthday Card. It caused me to write this letter. I will send you the music to this song as soon as I can get it.

Isaac

The lyrics were enclosed and reflected my great-grandfather's religious conviction as an A.M.E. minister and in his devotion to his wife, who had been an equally important force in his life:

Heavenly Sunlight

1.   Walking in sunlight, all of my journey;
       Over the mountain, thro' the deep vale;
       Jesus has said I'll never foresake thee,
       Promise divine that never can fail.

       CHORUS

       Heavenly sunlight, heavenly sunlight;
       Flooding my soul with glory divine;
       Hallelujah, I am rejoicing,
       Singing His praises, Jesus is mine.

2.   Shadows around me, shadows above me;
       Never conceal my Saviour and Guide;
       He is my light, in him is no darkness,
       Ever I'm walking close by his side.

       CHORUS

3.   In the bright sunlight, ever rejoicing,
       Pressing my way to mansions above;
       Singing his praises, Gladly I'm walking,
       Walking in sunlight, sunlight of love.

       CHORUS

I sat holding the letter, and looking at the two old photographs of Cora and Isaac Burgan and wondering at the edge of a new emotional territory I was about to enter with my father. "But if you loved my mother so much, why did you argue the way you did?"

He began to work unseen tools in his hands, a habit born of nervousness and arthritis pain. "Married folks never agree about everything. Especially about raising kids. Your mother wanted you to behave but didn't want to be the bad guy, the one to enforce the rules. So she saved all of it up for me when I got home."

"You did your job pretty well, Daddy."

He looked at me sheepishly and screwed his face into a half smile. "Yeah, I was usually tired enough after a twelve-hour day, sometimes it didn't take much for me to light into you. But I never liked being cast in the role of heavy. But your mother kind of left me holding that bag. I would have much rather come home and played with you or read the paper or listened to a ball game."

We sat for a while, remembering the old arguments and tears and lies. Despite all of that, I also felt some new path had been revealed to me that I had never considered. Of course, I took my father's revelation with a grain of salt. I knew, for example, that his vigilance over my behavior around boys had a lot to do with being a rogue himself and his fear I would suffer the ultimate disgrace—unwed motherhood. He had been unable to prevent it in the case of my older sister, who lived with his first wife, but he wasn't about to let that happen to me. While my mother's position as confidante allowed me to talk freely of my growing desires and her to get me birth control pills before any harm was done, my father's overprotectiveness and temper forced me to practice creative lying to get out of the house or explain a late night and to paint him as the ogre of my personal fairy tale. But to consider that my father had other thoughts, other desires, other ways he wanted to be with me and could not was something I was wholly unprepared to hear.

Great-grandfather Burgan died not long after the letter was written, just as my father did less than a year after that kitchen table talk. But what fills me with wonder is seeing into the heart of a man who, on his own birthday, took the time to thank his wife for being in his life. And that my father, an adversary in my early explorations in love was, in his gruff, offhanded way, passing on to me a legacy that clearly meant so much to him and opening a new path for me to understand him, my parents' relationship, and my own growing into womanhood.

MAKING A SCENE
Nikky Finney

I was a little girl who sometimes thought her mother was mean. A sharp-tongued, never-mincing-her-words woman. Once her point made she never backed down. Whatever said, that was that, laid down law.

We were anything but close then. Early on as mother and daughter we were opposites. She was so particularly beautiful and grand. In the tiny southern town where we lived, she physically leaped out at everyone. A walking rose that easily "divaed" up the sidewalks and dusty sweet roads. Even as she chewed you up, one could not help but notice her beauty. A simple farm girl who slipped out of satin, only to wear overalls just as elegantly. Wherever we went, I thought all eyes planted on her. As her only daughter, I was particularly plain and quiet in the bright shadow of her fancyness. I preferred books and tomboyish things. I would watch her movements from the sideline. A place she knew nothing about. Mother Finney's movements were always front and center.

Once she had been a little brown girl growing up in the arms of the segregated South, among a nest of Black farming folk who grew or made or smoked everything they needed to live. From two brothers she learned to fight and never seemed to bruise easily. She kept these gifts of self-sufficiency close to her. As woman and adult, if she was bringing you her money or her business and thought she was waiting too long, being ignored, or treated unfairly, she would wear a hole in the floor until someone turned and acknowledged her. If you were rude or disrespectful, it was her momentary job, while in the checkout line, at the department store, or the fish market, to write down the names, positions, the when and where of the incident, then call immediately for "The One in Charge." A girl during the depression who later became woman during civil rights years. The times taught her to document, record, and insist.

Whatever the intended timed route before leaving the house didn't matter after that. The library, the beach, laundry, church, nothing was as important now. Waiting for "The One in Charge" was the only thing we had to do for the rest of that day. And with his slow Oh-no-not-Mrs.-Finney-again eyes he would slowly appear and Mama would introduce herself quite formally. (As if he didn't already know who she was.) And then as if it were intrinsic to the entire moment she would turn and pull me in front of her. I was introduced as only daughter, then nudged to say hello in true southern polite accord. The entire incident was then relayed in graphic Frances Acquanetta Davenport Finney, coronerlike detail. Dozens upon dozens of people would gather and I would curl back under something, embarrassed as everyone stopped whatever they were doing to turn and see "Miss Finney" speaking loud and clear, her back a perfect plane. This breathtaking wordy Black woman would stand there in their store, on a lazy sultry South Carolina Saturday, and interrupt their easy routines by pointing out and particularizing some unknown white person's inadequacies as a public employee.

But always before turning and twirling ourselves away, she would pull me back in front of whomever she had just laid out, like the newest piece of tile in the floor, so that I might see their shocked contorted face before we left. It was imperative that she give me the last visually framed snapshot of all that had just gone before. Each time she held me there, I wanted to shrink out of sight. I didn't like going to the store with Mama. At some point on our way I knew someone would step over her line. I knew she would make a scene. I also knew as her only daughter, it was tradition, I would have to be in it.

What I didn't know as a child but what I know now is sometimes a scene was needed. Racism was a drum pounding our heads and hearts in the southland, it had to be challenged. True, sometimes a scene wasn't called for. I felt sorry for the clerk who had not been paying close enough attention and had unfortunately waited on the young blond woman before waiting on us, even though we had been there first, or the gas station attendant who filled the *other* car with high test before getting to our block-long Buick.

Back then I didn't know what Mama was doing. I didn't realize what she was giving me. I couldn't understand what she was saying to everybody else within the sound of her perfectly raised voice. She was holding court. She was announcing to everyone there, "You will respect and treat me fairly or you will be called out before your peers." She was teaching them and me that in her eyes, racism was habitual. She was insisting that they work on breaking the simple but inexcusable habit of it, in order that oversights didn't continue to be made. She refused to be invisible or insignificant and she refused to allow her children to be.

My mother never let anything pass. She couldn't. She didn't have that option. She couldn't stop to care that somebody might be having a bad day or perhaps, on that Saturday, the store was unusually crowded. She couldn't hesitate to hear that someone had made a simple human mistake. In my mother's heart and head there wasn't time to figure all that out. There was time enough only to make a point. She relinquished being in that group of sweet southern mothers who were their children's buddies. There was no time to buddy. There was only time enough to make a scene, so that one more brown face could make it through. America was at war with itself, and our community was but one small battlefield. Her rule was simple: Never allow anybody's rudeness to go unchecked. I remember at times trying to convince her that maybe it wasn't always because we were Black that we had been overlooked or treated unfairly. She would listen to my theories and answer back, "I may not always be right, girl, but I'm never wrong." And that was that.

It has taken me all of my life to understand, to realize what she was doing. It was not meanness. Mama was the squeaking wheel calling for the grease. My mother was winterizing me for the harsh seasons she saw coming ahead. She was shoveling the walk for me. She was saying "Daughter, I have

Wilmer Jennings, *Portrait of Ernestine E. Brazeal*, ca. 1928. Oil on canvas.
Courtesy of Ernestine W. Brazeal from the collection of the B. R. Brazeals.

brought you here, set you down, and given you shoes. The path is not completely clear, but it will not be as hard to walk as it once was. Now find your own way through the world."

She was my first teacher. She did not always play even-steven but she always had a lesson plan. She did things I couldn't do. My spirit was plainer, quieter. I believed in fair play. She and Papa had taught me that. My mother lived out on the limb so that maybe I wouldn't have to. My mother played to win. And in order to win she had to keep us alive, inside and out.

I didn't know what her spirit was then. I didn't know mothers had individual spirits. They were just mothers. We were opposites yet so very much alike. She taught me to search for a way to stomp my foot, oh yes, clear the table if necessary whatever you do, you must mark the moment clearly. She blueprinted for me exactly how to make a scene. "Let them whisper or say whatever they wish, but the next time they will think twice before treating you insignificantly. Never let them take you for granted or deny your right to the same privileges that all human beings should have." This first woman in my life taught me that we always have choices in life and when we enter the door as a consumer we have even more.

I remember the times we drove home from one of her scenes. I wouldn't talk to her, confused and mad, I believed she had been wrong and unfair. She would cut through the hard silence that sat between us by saying what she always said, by repeating her single uneloquent explanation for everything: "I may not always be right, but I'm never wrong." And that was that. She was unyielding. She never backed up, never apologized, even when she was wrong. Some of that was southern country girl ego, but most of it was lesson.

Oh, the things you learn, the things you must never forget. The things you must pass on. Mother Finney was not mean. She was the tall brown majorette at Drayton Street High, Newberry, South Carolina. She was a sorority and fraternity queen who sang "house opera" and "kitchen jazz." She was a young and terrified mother of three brown-skinned babies. She was the wife of a young passionate civil rights attorney of the sixties, who left for work every morning determined to change the world through the courts, while she was determined to make the very same changes in the marketplace.

With pens now drawn, I find that I am a scene maker too. I have held on to that mother-daughter ground that she tilled and worked and passed around the table just as regularly as the fried chicken and rice she made for so many Sunday dinners. With pens now drawn, I jug and shovel down into the same earth that my mother first set her toes into and richly blackened for me, and therein fill my barrel. Through my writing I insist, as my mother insisted, as I'm sure the mothers before her insisted. Granted we insist differently.

The poems and stories this Black woman writes are the ones she insists on writing. Not the ones to the popular left or the promising right or the ones the pew pays or wishes to hear but the ones timbale and quiet enough, the ones steel-drummed in love and banging song out inside my chest. This daughter of a scene maker will keep on making a scene, as long as it takes to rewrite the entire encyclopedia, the whole story, yes, all three acts, that are not and have never been our lives as Black women.

In the tradition of one beautiful, firebreathing, intuitive dragon, I too have come, to make a scene.

LETTER — JOSEPH BEAM
TO HIS MOTHER AND FATHER

1 March 1986

*D*ear Mom and Dad:

In a couple of hours I'll be interviewing Bayard Rustin, who, as you may remember, was the deputy of the 1963 March on Washington. Rustin is an openly gay Black civil rights activist; he recently turned 75 and is Executive Director of the A. Philip Randolph Institute in New York City. On August 28, 1963, I was a child of only eight and a half years but sensed deeply the importance of that historic march, which Mother did attend. It was said that I was too young to go. But I am no longer too young to actively pursue the kind of freedom that that march represents and is still denied quite generally to Black people in this country. It is not an accident that I am at this juncture in my life. Even though I am openly gay, I am my parents' son: a combination of my mother's earlier strives for freedom and my father's stern gentleness —I am your product.

The work that I am doing, my Black gay activist work, *will* at some time afford me an actual living, perhaps not a great one, but a living nonetheless. Just recently I have been invited to speak at the University of Penna. in April and to address an international convention in July, and expect to receive any day an invitation to speak at Cornell University in Ithaca also in April. These are paid speaking engagements, all prior to the publication of the anthology. Imagine what will happen when the book actually comes out. What I'm also just beginning to realize is that what I'm doing is much larger than just you or I. When I went to St. Louis in November I encountered a Black woman from London who had read my work and often copied it to share with friends. I was dumbstruck. I had no idea that what I wrote traveled that far.

Sometimes I wonder what it must be like to have a son like me. What kinds of changes do I put you through. Would it be so much simpler if I was another way? Sometimes I wonder how I can explain that which I want to do. How I want to see the world change or why I am so tired and troubled all the time. Or, how once you've really seen how things are that must be spoken to or one deteriorates from that hatred internalized. Black people are dying because we have internalized so much hatred. Fathers cannot look at sons because all they reflect is that hatred, that societal despisal *[sic.].* My writing is all that allows me to maintain some sense of sanity, allows me to not internalize the racial and sexual discrimination I face, allows me to be strong. Strength is the legacy that you have given me that in some way I must pass on. I will probably not bring any children into this world so perhaps I can leave some books behind that say my life moved Black people a millimeter closer to liberation and that I didn't devote my existence to the acquisition of goods. . . .

Love,

Joseph

In Memoriam

For James Baldwin (1924–1987)

Quincy Troupe

it's like a gray, dreary day, wet with tears & mourning
when someone you love ups & goes away
leaving behind a hole in your laughter, an empty space
following you around, like an echo you always hear & never see
high up in the mountains
the spirit gone & left, circling, there, its diminishing sound
a song looking for a place inside this gray day of tears
to lay down its earthly load
to drop down its weary voice among the many blue ones missing
there, who are elbowing their clacking bones, rattling, like false
      teeth
loose in a jelly jar, up against each other, their voices
dead as lead, & silence yawning
with the indifference final breaths achieve
& the open mouths are black holes framing endless space
words fall through, like stars sprinkled through the breath
of your holy sentences, jimmy
up there now with the glorious voice of bessie
the glory hallelujah, shouting gospel
you loved so deeply, wrote it out in your blood
running like dazzling rivers of volcanic lava, blood
so dazzling, your words blooming van gogh sunflowers

you planted, as sacred breaths inside our minds & hearts
the image of the real deal going down funky & hard
& so we celebrate you, holy witness, celebrate
your skybreaking smile, infectious laughter
hear your glory hallelujah warnings everywhere we look
see clearly, the all-american, scrubbed down, button down
greed, rampant, in these "yet to be united states"
& so we take heed, beg for your forgiveness, that you might
forgive us our smallness, for not rising up with you
for being less than our awesome, pitiful needs
forgive us now in your silence, jimmy
forgive us all who knew & were silent & fearful
& forgive us all, O wordsaint, who never even listened
forgive us for all the torture, for all the pain

AILEY, BALDWIN, FLOYD, KILLENS, AND MAYFIELD

Maya Angelou

When great trees fall,
rocks on distant hills shudder,
lions hunker down
in tall grasses,
and even elephants
lumber after safety.

When great trees fall
in forests,
small things recoil into silence,
their senses
eroded beyond fear.

When great souls die,
the air around us becomes
light, rare, sterile.
We breathe, briefly.
Our eyes, briefly,
see with
a hurtful clarity.
Our memory, suddenly sharpened,
examines,
gnaws on kind words
unsaid,

Suzanne Jackson, *Quietly Carmine*, 1982. Acrylic on canvas, 5 × 8 in.
Courtesy of the artist. Private collection.

promised walks
never taken.

Great souls die and
our reality, bound to
them, takes leave of us.
Our souls,
dependent upon their
nurture,
now shrink, wizened.
Our minds, formed
and informed by their
radiance,
fall away.
We are not so much maddened
as reduced to the unutterable ignorance
of dark, cold
caves.

And when great souls die,
after a period peace blooms,
slowly and always
irregularly. Spaces fill
with a kind of
sooting electric vibration.
Our senses, restored, never
to be the same, whisper to us.
They existed. They existed.
We can be. Be and be
better. For they existed.

NOBEL LAUREATE SPEECH

Toni Morrison

at the Nobel Banquet,

December 10, 1993

*Y*our Majesties, Your Highnesses, Ladies and Gentlemen:

I entered this hall pleasantly haunted by those who have entered it before me. That company of laureates is both daunting and welcoming, for among its lists are names of persons whose work has made whole worlds available to me. The sweep and specificity of their art have sometimes broken my heart with the courage and clarity of its vision. The astonishing brilliance with which they practiced their craft has challenged and nurtured my own. My debt to them rivals the profound one I owe to the Swedish Academy for having selected me to join that distinguished alumnae.

Early in October an artist friend left a message which I kept on the answering service for weeks and played back every once in a while just to hear the trembling pleasure in her voice and the faith in her words. "My dear sister," she said, "the prize that is yours is also ours and could not have been placed in better hands." The spirit of her message with its earned optimism and sublime trust marks this day for me.

I will leave this hall, however, with a new and much more delightful haunting than the one I felt upon entering: that is the company of laureates yet to come. Those who, even as I speak, are mining, sifting and polishing languages for illuminations none of us has dreamed of. But whether or not any one of them secures a place in this pantheon, the gathering of these writers is unmistakable and mounting. Their voices bespeak civilizations gone and yet to be; the precipice from which their imaginations gaze will rivet us; they do not blink nor turn away.

It is, therefore, mindful of the gifts of my predecessors, the blessing of my sisters, in joyful anticipation of writers to come that I accept the honor the Swedish Academy has done me, and ask you to share what is for me a moment of grace.

Fern Logan, *Inner Light*, 1974. Silver print, 11 × 14 in.
Courtesy of the photographer.

My Last Will and Testament

Mary McLeod Bethune

Sometimes as I sit communing in my study I feel that death is not far off. I am aware that it will overtake me before the greatest of my dreams—full equality for the Negro in our time—is realized. Yet, I face that reality without tears or regrets. I am resigned to death as all humans must be at the proper time. Death neither alarms nor frightens one who has had a long career of fruitful toil. The knowledge that my work has been helpful to many fills me with joy and great satisfaction.

Since my retirement from an active role in educational work and from the affairs of the National Council of Negro Women, I have been living quietly and working at my desk at my home here in Florida. The years have directed a change of pace for me. I am now 78 years old and my activities are no longer so strenuous as they once were. I feel that I must conserve my strength to finish the work at hand.

Already I have begun working on my autobiography which will record my life-journey in detail, together with the innumerable side trips which have carried me abroad, into every corner of our country, into homes both lowly and luxurious, and even into the White House to confer with Presidents. I have also deeded my home and its contents to the Mary McLeod Bethune Foundation, organized in March, 1953, for research, interracial activity and the sponsorship of wider educational opportunities. . . .

Sometimes I ask myself if I have any other legacy to leave. Truly, my worldly possessions are few. Yet, my experiences have been rich. From them, I have distilled principles and policies in which I believe firmly, for they represent the meaning of my life's work. They are the product of much sweat and sorrow. Perhaps in them there is something of value. So, as my life draws to a close, I will pass them on to Negroes everywhere in the hope that an old woman's philosophy may give them inspiration. Here, then, is my legacy.

I leave you love. Love builds. It is positive and helpful. It is more beneficial than hate. Injuries quickly forgotten quickly pass away. Personally and racially, our enemies must be forgiven. Our aim must be to create a world of fellowship and justice where no man's skin, color or religion, is held against him. "Love thy neighbor" is a precept which could transform the world if it were universally practiced. It connotes brotherhood and, to me, brotherhood of man is the noblest concept in all human relations. Loving your neighbor means being interracial, interreligious and international.

I leave you hope. The Negro's growth will be great in the years to come. Yesterday, our ancestors endured the degradation of slavery, yet they retained their dignity. Today, we direct our economic and political strength toward winning a more abundant and secure life. Tomorrow, a new Negro, unhindered by race taboos and shackles, will benefit from more than 330 years of ceaseless striving and struggle. Theirs will be a better world. This I believe with all my heart.

I leave you the challenge of developing confidence in one another. As long as Negroes are hemmed into racial blocs by prejudice and pressure, it will be necessary for them to band together for economic betterment. Negro banks, insurance companies and other businesses are examples of successful, racial economic enterprises. These institutions were made possible by vision and mutual aid. Confidence was vital in getting them started and keeping them going. Negroes have got to demonstrate still more confidence in each other in business. This kind of confidence will aid the economic rise of the race by bringing together the pennies and dollars of our people and ploughing them into useful channels. Economic separatism cannot be tolerated in this enlightened age, and it is not practicable. We must spread out as far and as fast as we can, but we must also help each other as we go.

Wini McQueen, *Family Tree*, 1987. Embroidery, pieced fabric, Xerox transfer on fabric,
cotton, linen, satin, and stencil printing on tie-dyed fabric, 100 × 86 in.
Courtesy of the artist, Museum of Arts & Sciences, Macon, GA.

I leave you a thirst for education. Knowledge is the prime need of the hour. More and more, Negroes are taking full advantage of hard-won opportunities for learning, and the educational level of the Negro population is at its highest point in history. We are making greater use of the privileges inherent in living in a democracy. If we continue in this trend, we will be able to rear increasing numbers of strong, purposeful men and women, equipped with vision, mental clarity, health and education.

I leave you a respect for the uses of power. We live in a world which respects power above all things. Power, intelligently directed, can lead to more freedom. Unwisely directed, it can be a dreadful, destructive force. During my lifetime I have seen the power of the Negro grow enormously: It has always been my first concern that this power should be placed on the side of human justice.

Now that the barriers are crumbling everywhere, the Negro in America must be ever vigilant less his forces be marshalled behind wrong causes and undemocratic movements. He must not lend his support to any group that seeks to subvert democracy. That is why we must select leaders who are wise, courageous, and of great moral stature and ability. We have great leaders among us today: Ralph Bunche, Channing Tobias, Mordecai Johnson, Walter White, and Mary Church Terrell. (The latter two are now deceased.) We have had other great men and women in the past: Frederick Douglass, Booker T. Washington, Harriet Tubman, Sojourner Truth. We must produce more qualified people like them, who will work not for themselves, but for others.

I leave you faith. Faith is the first factor in a life devoted to service. Without faith, nothing is possible. With it, nothing is impossible. Faith in God is the greatest power, but great, too, is faith in oneself. In 50 years the faith of the American Negro in himself has grown immensely and is still increasing. The measure of our progress as a race is in precise relation to the depth of the faith in our people held by our leaders. Frederick Douglass, genius though he was, was spurred by a deep conviction that his people would heed his counsel and follow him to freedom. Our greatest Negro figures have been imbued with faith. Our forefathers struggled for liberty in conditions far more onerous than those we now face, but they never lost the faith. Their perseverance paid rich dividends. We must never forget their sufferings and their sacrifices, for they were the foundations of the progress of our people.

I leave you racial dignity. I want Negroes to maintain their human dignity at all costs. We, as Negroes, must recognize that we are the custodians as well as the heirs of a great civilization. We have given something to the world as a race and for this we are proud and fully conscious of our place in the total picture of mankind's development. We must learn also to share and mix with all men. We must make an effort to be less race conscious and more conscious of individual and human values. I have never been sensitive about my complexion. My color has never destroyed my self respect nor has it ever caused me to conduct myself in such a manner as to merit the disrespect of any person. I have not let my color handicap me. Despite many crushing burdens and handicaps, I have risen from the cotton fields of South Carolina to found a college, administer it during its years of growth, become a public servant in the government of our country and a leader of women. I would not exchange my color for all the wealth in the world, for had I been born white I might not have been able to do all that I have done or yet hope to do.

I leave you a desire to live harmoniously with your fellow men. The problem of color is world-wide. It is found in Africa and Asia, Europe and South America. I appeal to American Negroes—North, South, East and West— to recognize their common problems and unite to solve them.

I pray that we will learn to live harmoniously with the white race. So often, our difficulties have made us hyper-sensitive and truculent. I want to see my people conduct themselves naturally in all relationships—fully conscious of their manly responsibilities and deeply aware of their heritage. I want them to learn to understand whites and influence them for good, for it is advisable and sensible for us to do so. We are a minority of 15 million living side by side with a white majority. We must learn to deal with these people positively and on an individual basis.

I leave you finally a responsibility to our young people. The world around us really belongs to youth for youth will take over its future management. Our children must never lose their zeal for building a better world. They must not be discouraged from aspiring toward greatness, for they are to be the leaders of tomorrow. Nor must they forget that the masses of our people are still underprivileged, ill-housed, impoverished and victimized by discrimination. We have a powerful potential in our youth, and we must have the courage to change old ideas and practices so that we may direct their power toward good ends.

Faith, courage, brotherhood, dignity, ambition, responsibility—these are needed today as never before. We must cultivate them and use them as tools for our task of completing the establishment of equality for the Negro. We must sharpen these tools in the struggle that faces us and find new ways of using them. The Freedom Gates are half a-jar. We must pry them fully open.

If I have a legacy to leave my people, it is my philosophy of living and serving. As I face tomorrow, I am content, for I think I have spent my life well. I pray now that my philosophy may be helpful to those who share my vision of a world of Peace, Progress, Brotherhood and Love.

Opal Palmer Adisa has taught at San Francisco State University and the University of California, Berkeley. Her poetry and stories have appeared in numerous journals in the United States, Canada, and Jamaica as well as the anthologies *Erotique Noire: Black Erotica* and *Adam of Ifé*. Her books include *Tamarind and Mango Women, traveling women,* and *Bake-Face and Other Guava Stories*.

Ahmasi became interested in poetry when he worked as the first cultural coordinator at the Langston Hughes Community Library and Cultural Center in New York City. His work has appeared in the Transition Press, *Essence, Encore, Black Enterprise,* the *Black Collegian,* and most recently in the anthology *Erotique Noire: Black Erotica*.

Elizabeth Alexander's first book of poems, *The Venus Hottentot,* was published in 1990, and her essays, short stories, and poetry have been widely published and anthologized. She teaches in the English Department at the University of Chicago.

Maya Angelou is a prolific poet and writer. In addition to her five volumes of poetry, she is the author of the autobiographical *I Know Why the Caged Bird Sings, Gather Together in My Name,* and *The Heart of a Woman*. She delivered her poem *On the Pulse of Morning* at the 1993 inauguration of President William Jefferson Clinton. Angelou, a native of St. Louis, Missouri, is presently the Reynolds Professor at Wake Forest University, Winston-Salem, North Carolina.

James Baldwin (1924–1987) was born in Harlem and became an expatriate who lived in France. He was author of six novels, including *Go Tell It on the Mountain, Another Country,* and *Giovanni's Room;* two plays, *Blues for Mr. Charlie* and *Amen Corner;* a collection of short stories; and several collections of essays, including *The Fire Next Time*.

"Grandma and Grandpa" are Etta Moten Barnett and Claude A. Barnett (1889–1967). Etta Moten Barnett, known professionally as Etta Moten, is a well-known actress, singer, and radio personality whose movies included *Golddiggers of 1933* and *Swing Low Sweet Chariot*. Claude A. Barnett was best known as founder, in 1919, of the Associated Negro Press, the first nationwide news service for African-American newspapers.

JOSEPH BEAM (1954–1988) was a cultural critic, writer, and editor of the groundbreaking *In the Life: A Black Gay Anthology.* He was also a board member of the National Coalition of Black Lesbians and Gays and founding editor of *Black/Out* magazine.

ROMARE BEARDEN (1914–1988) was one of the most influential artists of the twentieth century. A student in New York and Paris, Bearden was known for his evocative depiction of African-American rural and urban life, particularly in Mecklenburg County, North Carolina, his birthplace, as well as Pittsburgh and Harlem, where he lived during his long career. An artist, teacher, art historian, member of the American Academy of Arts and Letters, and recipient of the National Medal of Arts, Bearden's work has appeared in major exhibitions and has graced the covers of *Fortune, Time, Black Enterprise,* the *New York Times Magazine,* and numerous books.

MARY MCLEOD BETHUNE (1875–1955) was born in Mayesville, South Carolina. One of the most notable educators, civil rights leaders, and presidential advisers of the early twentieth century, Bethune founded Daytona Normal and Industrial School (now Bethune-Cookman College) in Daytona Beach, Florida, in 1904 and, in 1935, the National Council of Negro Women, an umbrella organization for African-American women's groups.

HILTON BRAITHWAITE is an Assistant Professor of Photography at Howard University. His work has been included in several solo and group exhibitions throughout the United States and collected by the Metropolitan Museum of Art, Museum of Modern Art, International Museum of Photography/George Eastman House, and the Studio Museum of Harlem.

GWENDOLYN BROOKS was born in Topeka, Kansas, and is one of the most honored living poets in the United States. A Pulitzer Prize winner in 1950 for the poetry volume *Annie Allen,* she was the first African-American woman to be named Consultant-in-Poetry to the Library of Congress. She has written over twenty books, including poetry *(A Street in Bronzeville, The Bean Eaters, In the Mecca, Riot, Blacks, Beckonings),* the novel *Maud Martha,* several children's books, and the autobiographical *Report from Part One.*

CHARLES BURWELL was born in Henderson, North Carolina, and received his art training at Temple University's Tyler School of Art and Yale University, where he received an M.F.A. A former artist-in-residence at the Studio Museum in Harlem, Burwell's work is collected by private individuals, corporations, and major museums, including the Pennsylvania Academy of Fine Arts in Philadelphia.

LONEY BUTLER and SOPHRONIA COLLINS were sweethearts and correspondents in the late nineteenth century, during and after the time Sophronia attended Rust College. They never married.

BEBE MOORE CAMPBELL is the author of *Successful Women, Angry Men: Backlash in the Two-Career Marriage,* the autobiographical *Sweet Summer: Growing Up With and Without My Dad,* and the novels *Your Blues Ain't Like Mine,* which won an NAACP Image Award for fiction, and *Brothers and Sisters.* A contributing editor of *Essence* magazine, with her articles also appearing in *Ms., Working Mother, Ebony,* the *New York Times,* the *Washington Post, Seventeen, Parents,* and *Glamour,* she is a regular commentator for "Morning Edition" on National Public Radio.

CHARLES W. CHESNUTT (1858–1932), born in Cleveland, Ohio, at one time worked simultaneously as a stenographer, lawyer, author, and lecturer. He is best known for his works *The Wife of His Youth and Other Stories of the Color Line, The Marrow of Tradition,* and *The Conjure Woman and Other Tales.*

ALICE CHILDRESS was born in Charleston, South Carolina, and is a playwright (the Obie award–winning *Trouble in Mind*) and author of such novels as *Like One of the Family: Conversations from a Domestic's Life* and *A Hero Ain't Nothing but a Sandwich.*

CLAUDE CLARK, SR., was born in Rockingham, Georgia, and was a student at the Philadelphia Museum of Art, the Barnes Foundation, and the University of California, Berkeley. In addition to his floral paintings, Clark is noted for his studies of urban life and the strong social realism of his work. His work has appeared widely in solo and group exhibitions, including the New York World's Fair of 1939 and the Sorbonne.

LUCILLE CLIFTON was born in Depew, New York, and has published several poetry volumes for adults and children. Her work includes *Good Times, Good News About the Earth, Ordinary Woman, Two-Headed Woman, Good Woman: Poems and a Memoir, Quilting,* and *Book of Light.*

WANDA COLEMAN is a poet, essayist, and short-story writer. She is a contributing editor for the *Los Angeles Times Magazine;* a co-host of "The Poetry Connexion," an interview program with Austin Straus; and author of six books, most recently *Hand Dance,* a collection of poems and short stories.

J. CALIFORNIA COOPER is the author of a novel, *Family;* four short-story collections, *A Piece of Mine, Some Soul to Keep, The Matter Is Life,* and *Homemade Love;* and a recipient of the 1989 American Book Award. She is also a playwright whose work has been widely performed and anthologized. A recipient of numerous writing awards, Cooper lives in a small town in Texas and is the mother of one daughter.

EMILIO CRUZ was born in New York City, and studied at the Art Students League as well as with Bob Thompson and other painters. Noted for his figurative and abstract paintings, Cruz's work has been represented in solo and group shows for almost forty years. His paintings are collected by the Hirshhorn Museum and Sculpture Garden, the National Gallery of Art, the National Museum of American Art, the Brooklyn Museum, and the Museum of Modern Art, among others.

TOI DERRICOTTE was born in Detroit, Michigan. She has published three poetry collections, *Natural Birth, The Empress of the Death House,* and *Captivity,* and is the recipient of many honors and awards. Derricotte is currently Associate Professor of English at the University of Pittsburgh and lives in Potomac, Maryland, with her husband and son.

AARON DOUGLAS (1899–1979) was born in Topeka, Kansas. He was a world-renowned painter and muralist most active during the Harlem Renaissance. Douglas's work embraced the African ancestral arts and expressed a pride in the African-American image that was highly controversial for its time. His correspondence with ALTA SAWYER began in 1924, prior to their marriage and while she was briefly married to another man.

FREDERICK DOUGLASS (1817–1895) was born into slavery in Tuckahoe, Maryland. After escaping from slavery in 1838 disguised as a sailor, he published an account of his life, *The Narrative of the Life of Frederick Douglass,* in 1845. Douglas was a well-known abolitionist orator, founder of the abolitionist newspaper *North Star,* marshal and recorder of deeds for the District of Columbia, consul-general to the Republic of Haiti, and chargé d'affaires for the Dominican Republic. His speech "What to the Slaves Is the Fourth of July?" was delivered in 1852.

CHARLES R. DREW (1904–1950) was born in Washington, D.C. A notable student athlete, Drew received his medical degree from McGill University in Montreal. Best known for his pioneering work in creating the blood plasma method of blood preservation, Drew met his future wife, (MINNIE) LENORE ROBBINS, in 1939, before his later medical achievements. They were married the same year.

W. E. B. DU BOIS (1868–1963) was born in Great Barrington, Massachusetts. One of America's most outstanding and prolific men of letters, Du Bois was one of the founders of the NAACP and founder and editor of *The Crisis.* He was the author of several works of fiction and nonfiction, including *The Souls of Black Folks, The Quest of the Silver Fleece,* and *Dark Princess.*

HENRY DUMAS (1934–1968), born in Sweet Home, Arkansas, was a poet, novelist, and short-story writer. Shot and killed by a policeman on a Harlem subway platform in 1968, among Dumas's posthumously published works are *Ark of Bones and Other Stories, Rope of Wind, Jonoah and the Green Stone,* and *Knees of a Natural Man: The Selected Poems of Henry Dumas.*

PAUL LAURENCE DUNBAR (1872–1906) was born in Dayton, Ohio. The most popular African-American poet of the nineteenth century, among Dunbar's best-known works are *Oak and Ivy, Majors and Minors, Lyrics of Lowly Life,* and the novel *The Sport of Gods.*

ROBERT SCOTT DUNCANSON (1821–1872), considered to be the most accomplished African-American painter in the mid-nineteenth century, was born in Seneca County, New York. Studying in the United States and Europe, Duncanson was also owner of a photography studio in Cincinnati, Ohio, before devoting his attention to painting full-time. Best known for such landscapes as *Pompeii, Loch Long, Blue Hole, Flood Waters,* and *Little Miami River,* Duncanson was heralded in the 1860s as "the best landscape painter in the West." *Roses, Still Life* was painted several years prior to his first trip to Europe.

EDWARD KENNEDY "DUKE" ELLINGTON (1899–1974), one of the most significant contributors to twentieth century music and a renowned jazz composer and musician, was born in Washington, D.C. Among his most notable works were *Black and Tan Fantasy, It Don't Mean a Thing, Mood Indigo, Sophisticated Lady, Don't Get Around Much Anymore, I Got It Bad,* and *Satin Doll.*

WALTER W. ELLISON (1899–1977) was born in Eatonton, Georgia, and studied at the Art Institute of Chicago. Ellison's works were exhibited in the American Negro Exposition in Chicago of 1940, the opening exhibition of the South Side Community Art Center in 1941, and the famed Atlanta University show of 1942. Many of his works, including *Train Station,* are in the collection of the Art Institute of Chicago.

JAMES A. EMANUEL is a teacher, scholar, critic, editor, and poet who has lived in Paris, France, for the past ten years. His work has appeared in a variety of anthologies, including *New Negro Poets: USA* and *The Poetry of Black America.* He is represented with an entry in *Contemporary Authors Autobiography Series* and his most recent collection of poetry is *Whole Grain: Collected Poems, 1958–1989.*

MARI EVANS was born in Toledo, Ohio, and resides in Indianapolis, Indiana. Her work has received many awards and appeared in numerous periodicals and anthologies. She is the author of the poetry collections *I Am a Black Woman, Nightstar,* and *A Dark and Splendid Mass;* works for children, including *J.D.* and *I Look at Me;* and *Black Women Writers (1950–1980): A Critical Evaluation,* which she edited.

NIKKY FINNEY was born in Conway, South Carolina, and is a graduate of Talladega College. She is an Assistant Professor of Creative Writing at the University of Kentucky in Lexington and is the author of *On Wings Made of Gauze.* Her work has appeared in numerous journals and magazines, including *Callaloo, Kaleidoscope, Catalyst, Sage,* and *Essence.*

RUTH FORMAN is a poet and filmmaker whose first volume of poetry, *We Are the Young Musicians,* won the prestigious Barnard New Women Poets Prize. She is a student in the Master's program at UCLA's Center for Afro-American Studies.

AURELIA and JOHN HOPE FRANKLIN were married in 1940 and wrote the essay "For Better, For Worse" to commemorate their forty-fifth wedding anniversary. JOHN HOPE FRANKLIN, born in Rentiesville, Oklahoma, is one of the United States's foremost living historians. His books include *The Free Negro in North Carolina, 1790–1860, The Negro in the Twentieth Century America, Color and Race,* and, with August Meier, *Black Leaders of the Twentieth Century.* His most popular book, *From Slavery to Freedom,* has sold over two million copies and is currently in its sixth printing.

NIKKI GIOVANNI was born in Knoxville, Tennessee. She is a writer and poet whose poetry collections include *Black Feeling Black Talk, Black Judgement, My House, The Women and the Men, Cotton Candy on a Rainy Day,* and *Those Who Ride the Night Wind.* She is also the author of the essay collections *Sacred Cows . . . And Other Edibles* and *Racism 101,* as well as editor of the recent anthology *Grand/Mothers.*

MARITA GOLDEN, a native of Washington, D.C., is the author of the autobiographical *Migrations of the Heart,* as well as the novels *Long Distance Life, A Woman's Place,* and *And Do Remember Me.* She is also editor of the anthology *Wild Women Don't Wear No Blues* and author of the forthcoming *Saving Our Sons.* Golden is a founding member of the African-American Writers' Guild in Washington, D.C., and is on the faculty of the MFA Graduate Program in Creative Writing at George Mason University in Fairfax, Virginia.

LINDA GOSS was born in Alcoa, Tennessee, and is a leading African-American storyteller. She is co-editor of *Talk That Talk* and co-author, with Clay Goss, of *Baby Leopard,*

It's Kwanzaa Time, and *Watching Uncle Shocum Eat.* She is also author of the popular fable *The Frog Who Wanted to Be a Singer.*

EDWIN A. HARLESTON (1882–1931) was born in Charleston, South Carolina. A student at the art school of the Boston Museum of Fine Arts and the Art Institute of Chicago, Harleston received an Amy Spingarn Award in 1925 for a portrait of his wife and the Alain Locke Prize for portrait painting at the Harmon Foundation exhibit of 1931. His *Portrait of Aaron Douglas* was painted while he assisted the latter artist with the murals for the Fisk University Library in 1930.

EDDY L. HARRIS graduated from Stanford University and studied in London. A screenwriter and journalist, he is the author of *Mississippi Solo, Native Stranger,* and *South of Haunted Dreams.*

FRANK HARRIS III is a columnist for the *New London Day* and *New Haven Register.* His essays have appeared in over forty publications, including *USA Today* and *Essence* magazine.

PETER J. HARRIS is a graduate of Howard University and has taught writing workshops in Maryland, Washington, D.C., and California. His fiction has been anthologized in *Breaking Ice,* and he is the author of *Hand Me My Griot Clothes: The Autobiography of Junior Baby* and *Wherever Dreams Live,* a book of original Kwanzaa folktales.

ESSEX HEMPHILL was born in Chicago, Illinois. He is a poet, essayist, performance artist, and gay cultural activist noted for such works as *Earthsong, Conditions, Ceremonies,* and the anthology *Brother to Brother: New Writings by Black Gay Men,* which he edited. His works have also been featured in the critically acclaimed Black gay films *Looking for Langston* and *Tongues Untied.*

BELL HOOKS was born in rural Kentucky and has become a well-known teacher, author, and speaker on the issues of personal empowerment and the politics of race, gender, and class. Among her seven published books are *Breaking Bread* (a collection of dialogues with Cornel West), *Black Looks: Race and Representation, Yearning: Race, Gender, and Cultural Politics, Thinking Black,* and *Sisters of the Yam: Black Women and Self-Recovery.* Her essays have appeared in *Essence, Emerge,* and *Ms.* magazines.

WENDELL HOOPER was born in South Central Los Angeles and is a writer, actor, and performance artist.

LANGSTON HUGHES (1902–1967) was born in Joplin, Missouri. A major writer of the Harlem Renaissance who was best known for his poetry (including *The Weary Blues* and

Not Without Laughter) and short stories, Hughes was also a columnist, playwright, juvenile author, editor of eight anthologies, and author of the autobiographical *The Big Sea.*

SUZANNE JACKSON was born in St. Louis, Missouri, and earned a degree in painting from San Francisco State College. Her work has been exhibited in and collected by numerous galleries and museums including the Carnegie Institute, Studio Museum of Harlem, and the Joseph Hirshhorn Museum and Sculpture Garden, and Smithsonian Institution, among others. She currently lives in Oakland, California, where she continues to paint and is a theatrical costume designer.

LANCE JEFFERS was born in Fremont, Nebraska, and was educated at Columbia University. He is the author of the poetry collections *My Blackness Is the Beauty of This Land* and *I Know the Power of My Black Hand,* and his work has been published in several journals, including *Black Scholar, CLA Journal,* and *Negro Digest.*

WILMER JENNINGS (1910–1991) was born in Atlanta, Georgia. He graduated from Morehouse College in 1931 and was a student of Hale Woodruff for several years. Jennings worked in the Public Works of Art Project and the Works Progress Administration (WPA) before attending the Rhode Island School of Design. Although best known as a painter and printmaker, Jennings was also a designer of stage sets and jewelry. His painting *Portrait of Ernestine E. Brazeal* is believed to have been painted while a student at Morehouse.

JAMES WELDON JOHNSON (1871–1938) was born in Jacksonville, Florida. Johnson was an attorney, writer, poet, songwriter, editor, diplomat, professor, and executive secretary of the NAACP. He is best known for his lyrics to *Lift Every Voice and Sing,* popularly known as the "Negro national anthem."

SARGENT CLAUDE JOHNSON (1887–1967) was born in Boston, Massachusetts, and lived with an aunt, the sculptor May Howard Jackson, after being orphaned as a child. A student at the California School of Fine Arts, he exhibited widely with the Harmon Foundation and executed numerous works for the Works Progress Administration during the mid-1930s, most notably statues for the Golden Gate International Exposition in San Francisco and a mosaic mural for the Maritime Museum in San Francisco.

WILLIAM H. JOHNSON (1901–1970) was one of the most notable and tragic African-American painters of the early twentieth century. Born in Florence, South Carolina, Johnson traveled to New York; Provincetown, Massachusetts; and later Europe to study painting. He painted in a variety of media and styles, including Impressionism,

Cubism, Fauvism, German Expressionism, and a consciously naïve manner. A recipient of the Harmon Foundation's Gold Medal, Johnson was represented in major group and solo exhibitions before a mental breakdown in 1947 and death from acute pancreatitis in 1970.

HENRY BOZEMAN JONES (1889–1963) was born in Philadelphia, and studied at the Pennsylvania Academy of Fine Arts. Jones taught physical education and pursued painting and graphic design part-time. A writer and illustrator of children's books, Jones' work was exhibited widely in Harmon Foundation exhibits as well as in exhibits at the New Jersey State Museum and at private galleries.

IRA B. JONES was born in St. Louis, Missouri, and is publisher of *Eyeball*, a St. Louis-based literary magazine. A co-founder of the St. Louis Black Man's Think Tank, his work has been published in numerous anthologies and publications including *Drum Voices Review, Take Five Magazine, Young Tongues,* and *In the Tradition: An Anthology of Young Black Writers.*

LOIS MAILOU JONES was born in Boston, Massachusetts, and received her art education from the High School of Practical Arts, the Museum of Fine Arts, and the Design Arts School in Boston. In her long and productive career as a painter, illustrator, costume and stage designer, and textile designer, Jones has served on the faculty of the Howard University Art Department from 1930 to 1977, has exhibited in sixty solo and over two hundred group exhibitions, and has traveled extensively to Europe, Haiti, and Africa, where she taught art and researched Haitian and African art.

ELIZABETH KECKLEY (c. 1818–1907) was born into slavery in Dinwiddie, Virginia. A seamstress and dressmaker, Keckley purchased her freedom and that of her son in 1855 and, in 1861, became dressmaker and confidante to Mary Todd Lincoln, wife of Abraham Lincoln. Her memoir of her life and her years with the Lincolns, *Behind the Scenes or Thirty Years a Slave, and Four Years in the White House,* was published in 1868.

PINKIE GORDON LANE is the author of four volumes of poetry, including *Girl at the Window.* She is a past Poet Laureate of the state of Louisiana and has served as artist-in-residence at the University of Northern Iowa and a Du Pont scholar at Bridgewater College, Virginia.

FELIX H. LIDDELL was born in Chicago, Illinois, and is a graduate of Loyola University of Chicago and Lake Forest Graduate School of Management. A co-founder of Woods/Liddell Group, a strategic planning and marketing consulting firm, he is also co-author of *I, Too, Sing America: The African-American Book of Days.*

FERN LOGAN was born in Jamaica, Queens, New York. A graduate of Pratt Institute, Logan has exhibited widely in the United States and is represented in *Black Photographers from 1940–1988* and *Viewfinders: Black Women Photographers.* Among her best-known works are the Artist Portrait Series of African-American artists, including Romare Bearden, Roy deCarava, Jacob Lawrence, and Gordon Parks. Logan currently is a Professor of Photography at Elmhurst College in Illinois.

JUAN LOGAN was born in Nashville, Tennessee. A graduate of Howard University and Clark College in Atlanta, Georgia, Logan has had numerous solo and group exhibitions over the past twenty-five years. His work has been collected by the National Museum of African Art, Mint Museum, corporations, and private individuals.

AUDRE LORDE (1934–1992) was a noted international activist, poet, and essayist. She was the author of fifteen volumes of poetry and prose, including *Undersong: Chosen Poems Old and New, Our Dead Behind Us,* the highly acclaimed *Sister Outsider,* and the autobiography *Zami: A New Spelling of My Name.* Her first book of prose, *The Cancer Journals,* won the American Library Association Gay Caucus Book Award and she was awarded an American Book Award in 1989 for her essay collection *A Burst of Light.* Among her honors were the Manhattan Borough President's Award for Excellence in the Arts (1988) and a 1991 designation as New York State poet.

NAOMI LONG MADGETT is the author of eight books of poetry, including *Remembrances of Spring: Collected Early Poems.* She has also edited two anthologies and written two textbooks. She was the editor of Lotus Press in Detroit, Michigan, and is senior editor of the newly established Lotus Poetry Series of Michigan State University Press. She won an American Book Award in May 1993 for her work as a publisher and editor.

HAKI R. MADHUBUTI is editor of Third World Press and director of the Institute of Positive Education in Chicago. A co-founder of the Organization of Black American Culture Writer's Workshop, Madhubuti has published numerous books of poetry and nonfiction, including *Think Black; Don't Cry, Scream; Kwanzaa: A Progressive and Uplifting African-American Holiday; Killing Memory, Seeking Ancestors; Say That the River Turns: The Impact of Gwendolyn Brooks;* and *Black Men: Obsolete, Single, Dangerous? The Afrikan American Family in Transition.*

DEVORAH MAJOR is a poet, essayist, and fiction writer. She co-authored a book of poetry, *traveling women,* with Opal Palmer Adisa, and her work has appeared in the periodicals *Callaloo, Left Curve,* and *Zyzvva,* as well as the anthologies *Adam of Ifé, California Childhood,* and *Pushcart XII.* Her forthcoming book of poetry, *street smarts,* will be published by Curbstone Press.

RICHARD MAYHEW was born in Amityville, New York, and studied art at the Art Students League; Columbia University; and the Academia in Florence, Italy. A revolutionary and well-respected landscape artist, Mayhew was a contemporary of artists like Romare Bearden, Charles Alston, and Hale Woodruff and formed with them and others Spiral, a forum for artistic innovation and exploration of the African-American artist's relationship to the civil rights movement.

CLAUDE MCKAY (1889–1948) was born in Clarendon, Jamaica, and emigrated to the United States in 1912. He was a writer whose poetry volumes included *Harlem Shadows* and whose novels included *Home to Harlem* and *Banjo*.

TERRY MCMILLAN was born in Port Huron, Michigan. She is the author of the novels, *Mama, Disappearing Acts,* and *Waiting to Exhale,* and the winner of an NAACP Image Award. She also edited the critically acclaimed *Breaking Ice: An Anthology of Contemporary African-American Fiction.* McMillan has written articles and reviews for the *Atlanta Constitution,* the *New York Times Book Review,* and the *Philadelphia Inquirer* and been a three-time fellow at Yaddo Artist Colony and the Macdowell Colony.

WINI MCQUEEN is a fabric artist from Macon, Georgia, who turned to quilting over a decade ago. Her quilts are represented in the collections of museums and private individuals and have been featured in numerous quilting exhibits, including *Stitching Memories: African-American Story Quilts.* Her quilt *Family Tree* includes not only McQueen's immediate family members but scenes of workers in Durham, North Carolina, her birthplace; a slave-auction handbill; images of "White Only" and "Colored Only" signs; and references to Africa, including leaves and blossoms of the acacia tree, indigenous to both Africa and the United States.

LENARD D. MOORE was born in Jacksonville, Florida, and is the founder of the Raleigh-based Carolina African American Writers' Collective and co-editor-in-chief of *Shawensis.* His most recent publications are *Forever Home* and *Desert Storm: A Brief History.* He is the recipient of the Haiku Museum of Tokyo Award and a consultant to the North Carolina Humanities Commission Outreach program.

TONI MORRISON was born in Lorain, Ohio. One of the most celebrated writers of the twentieth century and winner of the 1993 Nobel Prize for Literature, her novels include *The Bluest Eye, Sula, Tar Baby, Song of Solomon,* and the Pulitzer Prize–winning *Beloved.*

ARCHIBALD J. MOTLEY, JR. (1891–1981) was born in New Orleans, Louisiana. A graduate of the School of the Art Institute of Chicago, Motley was known for his portraiture and his careful depictions of African-American nightlife and street scenes. His work has been collected by major museums and private collectors, was exhibited in notable solo and group exhibitions, and was the subject of the recent retrospective, *The Art of Archibald J. Motley, Jr.*

JILL NELSON is a journalist and author of *Volunteer Slavery: My Authentic Negro Experience.* Her next book, *Negro Free State,* will be published by Putnam in 1995.

SAUNDRA MURRAY NETTLES is a writer and psychologist. She has published numerous essays and studies on education and gender issues in addition to writing poetry and short stories. She lives with her two daughters in Howard County, Maryland.

ELIJAH PIERCE (1892–1984) was a noted woodcarver, folk artist, barber, minister, and community historian. A keen observer of contemporary life, Pierce's woodcarvings, which include such religious masterpieces as *Book of Wood* and *Crucifixion,* as well as autobiographical, political, and sports carvings, were the subject of the major retrospective *Elijah Pierce, Woodcarver,* which opened at the Columbus Museum of Art in 1992.

STEPHANIE E. POGUE was born in Shelby, North Carolina. Pogue's work is collected by the Whitney Museum of American Art and the Studio Museum of Harlem, among others. She is presently Dean of the School of Art at the University of Maryland–College Park.

JAMES A. PORTER (1905–1971) was the first African-American art historian. The Baltimore, Maryland, native studied at Columbia University and the Art Students League as well as extensively in Europe before establishing Howard University's Gallery of Art and becoming Chairman of the university's Art Department and writing the groundbreaking *Modern Negro Art* (1943). In 1966, Porter was named by President Lyndon B. Johnson "one of America's most outstanding men of the arts."

DEXTER RIVENS was born in 1980 and is a student at J.T. Williams Middle School in Charlotte, North Carolina. His essay "My First Kiss" was submitted as part of his application to the Love of Learning Program at Davidson College, Davidson, North Carolina. Rivens wants to be an engineer or a professional football player.

JOHN ROZELLE is a professor at the Art Institute of Chicago. His work reflects the St. Louis, Missouri, native's self-definition as an "African-American sentinel" or visual historian, guide, and advocate of contemporary African-American culture.

BETYE SAAR was born in Los Angeles, California, where she attended the University of California, Los Angeles. A noted master of collage and assemblage whose work exhibits strong spiritual themes, Saar has participated in over forty group and solo exhibitions in the United States, Canada, Europe, and Asia, including *Secrets; Dialogues; and Revelations,* a joint exhibit with her daughter, Alison.

NTOZAKE SHANGE is a playwright, poet, essayist, and novelist. While she is best known for her play *for colored girls who have considered suicide, when the rainbow is enuf,* she is also author of the novels *Sassafrass, Cypress and Indigo,* and *Betsey Brown* as well as the poetry collections *nappy edges, A Daughter's Geography,* and *The Love Space Demands.*

SAUNDRA SHARP was born in Cleveland, Ohio, and is an actress, screenwriter, poet, and independent filmmaker. Among her works are the poetry volumes *Typing in the Dark, Soft Song,* and *In the Midst of Change; On the Sharp Side,* a spoken-word recording; the films *Life Is a Saxophone* and *Picking Tribes;* and the stage play *The Sistuhs.*

HUGHIE LEE SMITH was born in Eustis, Florida. After studying at the Cleveland Institute of Art, Wayne State University, and elsewhere, Lee-Smith began an artistic career that has garnered him acclaim as a master of social realism, surrealism, and romantic realism. His work has been collected by individuals, corporations, and museums, including the Detroit Institute of Art, New Jersey State Museum, and the Schomburg Center for Research in Black Culture.

HENRY OSSAWA TANNER (1859–1937), the most acclaimed African-American painter of the nineteenth century, was born in Pittsburgh, and studied at the Pennsylvania Academy of Art with American genre painter Thomas Eakins, among others. Tanner eventually migrated to France and studied and painted there until his death, making only occasional visits to the United States, where he was dismayed by the racial prejudice he encountered. His secular paintings like *The Banjo Lesson, The Thankful Poor,* and numerous religious works are prized by such museums as the Louvre, the National Museum of American Art, the Philadelphia Museum of Art, and private collectors.

HOWARD THURMAN (1900–1981) was a distinguished philosopher, theologian, poet, and mystic. Founder of the Church for the Fellowship of All Peoples in San Francisco, the first interracial, interdenominational church in the United States, Thurman was also the author of more than twenty books, including *Meditations of the Heart; The Inward*

Journey; The Centering Moment; The Creative Encounter; The Search for Common Ground; and *With Head and Heart,* his autobiography.

SUE BAILEY THURMAN, who was the first African-American woman to have an audience with Mahatma Gandhi, was the founder-editor of the *Aframerican Woman's Journal,* first official organ of the National Council of Negro Women, and worked with her husband, Howard Thurman, in establishing the Church for the Fellowship of All Peoples. The founder of the Museum of Afro-American History in Boston, Massachusetts, Mrs. Thurman presently lives in San Francisco.

JEAN TOOMER (1894–1967) was born in Washington, D.C., and is best known as the author of the novel *Cane.* Two collections of his previously uncollected work have also been published, *The Wayward and the Seeking* and *The Collected Poems of Jean Toomer.*

QUINCY TROUPE is the author of numerous essays, articles, and feature stories, which have appeared in over one hundred magazines and journals. He has published three volumes of poetry: *Embryo; Snake-Back Solos* (winner of the 1980 American Book Award for Poetry); and *Skulls Along the River;* and he has edited two anthologies: *Watts Poets and Writers* and *Giant Talk: An Anthology of Third World Writing.* Troupe is the author of the award-winning *Miles: The Autobiography,* and is the founding editor of both *Confrontation: A Journal of Third World Literature* and *The American Rag.*

GLORIA WADE-GAYLES is a poet, novelist, literary critic, and Professor of English and Women's Studies at Spelman College, Atlanta, Georgia. A 1991 Fellow at the Du Bois Institute at Harvard University, she is the author of *No Crystal Stair: Visions of Race and Sex in Black Women's Fiction,* the poetry collection *Anointed to Fly,* as well as the autobiographical *Pushed Back to Strength.*

MARILYN WANIEK's book *The Homeplace,* was a finalist for the 1991 National Book Award and winner of the 1992 Annisfield-Wolf Award. Her new book is *Magnificat.* Married and the mother of two, she is a professor of English at the University of Connecticut, Storrs.

LAURA WHEELER WARING (1887–1948) was born in Hartford, Connecticut. She made her first trip to Europe and North Africa in 1914 to study art and also studied at the Pennsylvania Academy of Fine Arts in Philadelphia and the Académie de la Grande Chaumière in Paris before returning to the United States. Her 1927 portrait *Anna Washington Derry* received the Gold Medal of the William E. Harmon

Awards for Distinguished Achievement Among Negroes, one of the earliest efforts to recognize the achievement of African Americans and to promote the work of visual artists.

NAYO BARBARA MALCOLM WATKINS is a poet, essayist, and playwright. Formerly the Executive Director of the African American Dance Ensemble, she is currently an arts consultant in Durham, North Carolina.

"DAD AND MOTHER" are JAMES S. WATSON (1882–1952), the first African-American judge in New York State and his wife, VIOLET. JAMES L. WATSON, born in 1922, was one of four Watson children. The younger Watson had enlisted during World War II, serving with the 92nd Infantry Division, and was wounded in combat in Italy. A lawyer, James L. Watson held elective and judicial office in New York State before being appointed, in 1966, judge of the United States Customs Court (now the United States Court of International Trade).

JOHN EDGAR WIDEMAN was born in Washington, D.C., but grew up in the Homewood section of Pittsburgh, location of several of his fictional works. Among his best known works are *Hurry Home, Philadelphia Fire,* and *The Stories of John Edgar Wideman.* He is a Professor of English at the University of Massachusetts.

CECIL WILLIAMS is minister of Glide Memorial Church in San Francisco, California. He is author of the book *No Hiding Place.*

DEBORAH WILLIS is a photographer and photography historian who currently serves as Collections Coordinator for the Smithsonian Institution's National African American Museum Project in Washington, D.C. Willis is the author of, among other publications, *J.P. Ball, Dageurrean and Studio Photographer, Black Photographers 1940–1988: An Illustrated Bio-Bibliography, The Portraits of James VanDerZee,* and the forthcoming *Picturing Us: African American Identity in Photography.*

PAULA L. WOODS is a native of Los Angeles, California. In addition to her work as a partner in Woods/Liddell Group, a strategic planning and marketing consultant firm, she is co-author of *I, Too, Sing America: The African-American Book of Days.*

MALCOLM X (1925–1965) was born in Omaha, Nebraska. A Muslim minister who was one of the most electrifying leaders of the civil rights movement, he was the author, with the assistance of Alex Haley, of *The Autobiography of Malcolm X.*

ACKNOWLEDGMENTS OF COPYRIGHT

Every effort has been made to contact copyright holders.
If an inadvertent error or omission has occurred, please notify the editors.

PART I

BLACK MUST BE BEAUTIFUL AGAIN

"Black Must Be Beautiful Again" by Bebe Moore Campbell. From *Why L.A. Happened: Implications of the '92 Los Angeles Rebellion,* edited by Haki R. Madhubuti. Copyright © 1993 by Bebe Moore Campbell. Reprinted by permission of the author.

"Negritude" by James A. Emanuel. From *Whole Grain: Collected Poems, 1958–1989.* Copyright © 1991 by James A. Emanuel. Published by Lotus Press. Reprinted by permission of the author.

Excerpt from "Dreaming Ourselves Dark and Deep" from *Sisters of the Yam: Black Women and Self-Recovery* by bell hooks. Copyright © 1993 by Gloria Watkins. Reprinted by permission of South End Press.

Excerpt from *Mysticism and the Experience of Love* by Howard Thurman. Copyright © 1961 by Pendle Hill. Copyright renewed. Reprinted by permission of Sue Bailey Thurman.

"Who and Whose You Are: An Interview with Brenda Tapia" by Felix H. Liddell and Paula L. Woods. Copyright © 1994 by Felix H. Liddell and Paula L. Woods. Printed by permission of the authors.

"Speak the Truth to the People" by Mari Evans. From *I Am a Black Woman* by Mari Evans. Published by William Morrow & Company. Copyright © 1970 by Mari Evans. Reprinted by permission of the author.

"First Man" by Naomi Long Madgett. Copyright © 1992 by Naomi Long Madgett. Reprinted by permission of the author.

"Question: What Is the Greatest Challenge You Face as a Black Man?" by Haki R. Madhubuti. From *Killing Memory, Seeking Ancestors* by Haki R. Madhubuti. Published by

PART II
FAMILIES OF THE HEART

PART III

A Jewel for a Friend

"Pages for a Friend" by Ntozake Shange. From *Ridin' the Moon in Texas: Word Paintings* by Ntozake Shange. Copyright © 1987 by Ntozake Shange. Reprinted by permission of St. Martin's Press, Inc.

Letter from Sue Bailey Thurman to Meta Warwick Fuller, Meta Warwick Fuller Papers, Manuscript, Archives and Rare Books Division, Schomburg Center for Research in Black Culture, The New York Public Library, Astor, Lenox, and Tilden Foundations. Printed by permission of Sue Bailey Thurman.

"A Jewel for a Friend" by J. California Cooper. From *A Piece of Mine* by J. California Cooper. Copyright © 1984 by J. California Cooper. Originally published by Wild Trees Press. Reprinted by permission of Doubleday, a division of Bantam Doubleday Dell Publishing Group, Inc.

"The Drugstore" by Toi Derricotte. Originally published in *Feminist Studies,* Spring 1991. Copyright © 1991 by Toi Derricotte. Reprinted by permission of the author.

"For a Friend Who Considers Suicide" by Gloria Wade-Gayles. From *Anointed to Fly* by Gloria Wade-Gayles. Copyright © 1991 by Gloria Wade-Gayles. Reprinted by permission of Harlem River Press.

"War Stories" by Saundra Murray Nettles. Copyright © 1993 Saundra Murray Nettles. Printed by permission of the author.

"The Letter" by Wendell Hooper. Copyright © 1992 by Wendell Hooper. Printed by permission of the author.

"Ain't Too Proud to Beg" by Peter J. Harris. From the unpublished manuscript *My Man: (Baby Steps) On the Trail of Black Male Loveliness.* Copyright © 1993 by Peter J. Harris. Printed by permission of the author.

"A Poem of Friendship" by Nikki Giovanni. From *cotton candy on a rainy day* by Nikki Giovanni. Copyright © 1978 by Nikki Giovanni. Reprinted by permission of William Morrow and Company.

PART IV

FOR BETTER, FOR WORSE

Letter from Loney Butler to Sophronia Collins. From the Collins Family Papers, Amistad Research Center. Printed by permission of Clarie Collins Harvey.

Letter from Sophronia Collins to Loney Butler. From the Collins Family Papers, Amistad Research Center. Printed by permission of Larry Butler.

"Valentines" by Henry Dumas. From *Knees of a Natural Man* by Henry Dumas. Copyright © 1989 by Loretta Dumas and Eugene B. Redmond. Reprinted by permission of Thunder's Mouth Press.

"My First Kiss" by Dexter Rivens. Copyright © 1993 by Dexter Rivens. Printed by permission of the author and Mrs. Gloria Rivens.

"Lyric: I Am Looking at Music" by Pinkie Gordon Lane. From *Girl at the Window.* Published by Louisiana State University Press. Copyright © 1991 by Pinkie Gordon Lane. Reprinted by permission of the author.

"Water of Your Bath" by Ahmasi. Copyright © 1971 by Ahmasi. Originally published in *Essence* magazine, May 1977. Reprinted by permission of the author.

Excerpt from *And Do Remember Me* by Marita Golden. Copyright © 1992 by Marita Golden. Reprinted by permission of Doubleday, a division of Bantam Doubleday Dell Publishing Group, Inc.

"Be Somebody Fragrant" by Peter J. Harris. Copyright © 1993 by Peter J. Harris. Printed by permission of the author.

Letters from Aaron Douglas to Alta Sawyer. From the Aaron Douglas Papers, Manuscript, Archives and Rare Books Division, Schomburg Center for Research in Black Culture, The New York Public Library, Astor, Lenox, and Tilden Foundations. Printed by permission of Valena Minor Waits.

Excerpt from *The Autobiography of Malcolm X* by Malcolm X, with the assistance of Alex Haley. Copyright © 1964 by Alex Haley and Malcolm X and copyright © 1965 by Alex Haley and Betty Shabazz. Reprinted by permission of Random House, Inc.

PART V

SEE THE HEART

PART VI

A HOME IN THAT ROCK

PART VII

I LEAVE YOU LOVE

10/94